Through Our Long Exile

First published in 2001 by
Darton, Longman and Todd Ltd
1 Spencer Court
140-142 Wandsworth High Street
London SW18 4JJ

Reprinted 2002

ISBN 0 232 52334 7

A catalogue record for this book is available from the British Library.

The cover illustration is by Dan Jones, the best-known community artist in
the East End of London. It depicts the demonstration on the
sixtieth anniversary of the Battle of Cable Street of 1936.

Designed by Sandie Boccacci
Set in 10¾/12½ Adobe Garamond by Intype London Ltd
Printed and bound in Great Britain by
The Cromwell Press, Trowbridge, Wiltshire

Through Our Long Exile

Contextual Theology
and the Urban Experience

KENNETH LEECH

But in the meanwhile, with hearts raised on high,
We for that country must yearn and must sigh,
Seeking Jerusalem, dear native land,
Through our long exile on Babylon's strand.

PETER ABELARD, *Quanta Qualia*

John
with best wishes and prayers
Ken Leech.

DARTON · LONGMAN + TODD

Contents

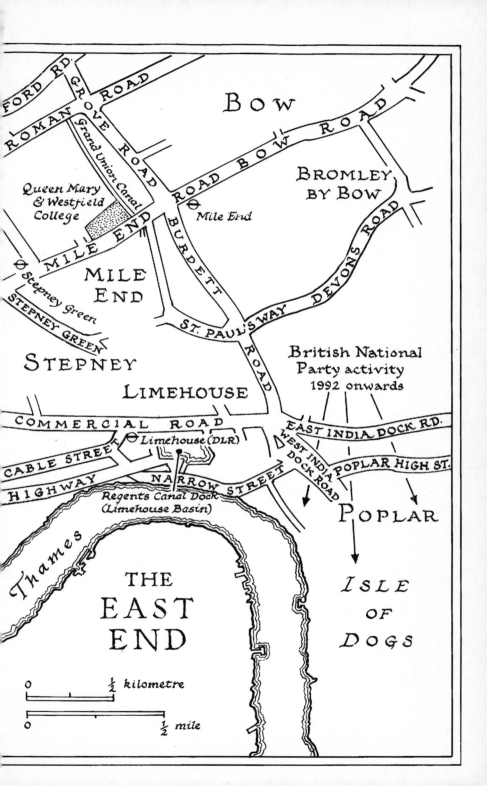

Introduction

This book has a complex history. Its two parts have their origins in two phases of my life and ministry in East London. Yet, even in saying this, I can give a misleading impression, for the two phases are integrally linked, inseparable dimensions of myself. Indeed, this is why it is essential that they form one book, not two. My early training as a historian, as well as my approach to Christian theology as a historically rooted discipline, have made me realise, and inspired in me the need to stress, the central importance of understanding history if we are to pursue pastoral, theological and spiritual work. The historical sections of this book are therefore extremely important. They cannot be 'skipped', and, indeed, without them the rest of the book becomes, if not incomprehensible, at least difficult to comprehend.

Part One began as work for a doctoral thesis in the University of London in 1964. It was a study of patterns of immigration into the two wards which formed the heart of the East End of London, Whitechapel and St George's in the East, between 1841 and 1961. It was never completed, partly because pastoral work forced it more and more onto the back burner, partly because it grew and grew and grew. The study of this fascinating, yet complex, area yielded so much material that the work became unmanageable. It is this historical work which has provided the bulk of the material in Part One, and these two wards which have provided the historical and geographical context for much of my adult life and ministry.

So in Part One I look at the growth of the communities in the East End of London in some historical and sociological detail, examining the religious dimensions of that history within the wider context. I look, in some depth, at the history of this area, including its social, class, racial and religious history, with sections on the history of exodus, exile, and subsequent resettlement of Huguenot, Irish, Jewish and Muslim communities.

The historical material in Part One ends in 1971, a year in which, conveniently, the Population Census of England and Wales coincided with the emergence of Bangladesh as a nation. It was also the year in which British immigration legislation, based on race and colour as determining factors, was consolidated. I have treated 1971 as a significant turning-point in the history of Britain, of East London, of Bangladesh, and of minorities in the UK. Specifically, in terms of the East End, I have seen 1971 as being in a sense the end of one phase of its history and the beginning of another. The history and developments since 1971 are incorporated in the reflections in Part Two.

As the year in which I ended a second curacy, and began a three-year period as a university teacher, with a specific focus on pastoral theology, 1971 was also an important point in my own pastoral ministry. The years from 1964 to 1971 had been years of immense activity, much of it related to drugs, homelessness and the pursuit of racial justice. From 1971 to 1974 I was a tutor in pastoral studies at King's College, London, based most of the time at the fourth-year study centre in St Augustine's College, Canterbury. It was a very intensive period, working each year with about forty students, of whom almost all were to become deacons and priests in the Church of England and many of whom were to move to urban parishes. I estimate that some two-thirds of them are still ministering in urban areas. These years – prior to my return to the East End in 1974 – marked a time of consolidation, transition, and rethinking which helped to prepare the way for the urban theology work with which I am currently involved.

I realised, on my arrival in Canterbury, that it was the first time in my life that I had not lived on a main road. Living in the ruins of St Augustine's Abbey, where the only neighbours were the dead Saxon kings, was something of a culture shock! Yet these years were important, first, as a time to reflect, inwardly in my own prayer and thought, and outwardly with students and others, on the role of theology in relation to pastoral ministry. They were important, secondly, as a time of focus on work-based learning. Each student was attached for one year to a parish or other church-based group (including two prison chaplaincy teams), and to a 'secular' agency. These included schools, a homelessness project, a child guidance clinic, a Citizens' Advice Bureau, two prisons, the probation service, a youth and community work project, and several colleges – a postgraduate medical centre, teacher training college, centre for rural studies, and a university. My work involved supervision and critical scrutiny of work done.

Within a short distance of Canterbury, there are a wide range of communities – working-class communities in Ashford, 'posh' seaside communities in Broadstairs, mixed seaside town groups in Folkestone, Dover, Margate and Ramsgate, mining communities on the outskirts of Canterbury, the Medway towns with their industrial mission work, Canterbury itself, and London which was not too far away. It was in many ways an ideal location for theological reflection. The years in Canterbury were therefore critical years; three years extended into three decades of engagement.

In Part Two, I reflect on the East End of London as it is today, and on theological work within this area. There have been a number of contextually-based theological studies, but most of them have been in 'Third World' countries. There have also been many personal accounts of pieces of work in Britain and elsewhere. This book is, I think, the first time such a combination of analysis and reflection has been done in this kind of detail in the British context, though I remain open to correction on this. I have drawn in this work, not only on my own experience in the East End of London, but also on the work of other community-based theologians in Britain, the USA, and elsewhere. My aim is to reflect on British society, on theology, and on pastoral ministry from the perspective of a community-based theologian located in the East End of London.

I have tried both to present a piece of theological reflection (and encourage others to do the same for their own context) and also to contribute to, and learn from, a process which is still going on. I am more and more conscious of my failings, inadequacies and falterings as a theologian, and of the need to learn from others who have not put their experience on paper, and perhaps never will. We need to develop new ways of integrating theological reflection with the ongoing life of Christian communities and, through that process, with the life of other communities and networks.

There is an element of autobiography running through this book which is important. Yet I am clear that this work is not primarily autobiographical. It is theological reflection from the context of the history of East London. This history is with us still, and, whether I like it or not, I am part of it, having originated elsewhere and having settled here. I am not indigenous. I am not part of any historic community of interest in the East End. My roots are elsewhere. Yet, having uprooted myself many years ago, I am now something of a rootless person, and I find myself in company with many other root-less people, people who have become both rootless and resident in the streets of the East End for reasons other than choice. My theo-logical work has been shaped and affected by events, social and personal, which have occurred in these streets. It is impossible for me to write theology without constantly referring back to this context.

There is therefore throughout this book a dialectical relationship between personal reflection and 'objective' analysis, historical, social and theological. I have always rejected the 'depersonalising' of theology, that approach which sees the human subject as irrelevant to the theological work. As in any disciplined work, person and project are intertwined. And, as Rowan Williams has reminded us, 'no one learns their Christianity without a local accent'.[1]

The view from my window encapsulates it all. I live at the heart of the area described in *The Bitter Cry of Outcast London,* published in 1883, and directly across the road from the site of the first Jack the Ripper murder in 1888. The pamphlet and the murders together were of critical importance in alerting the middle class and the wider population of Britain to the extreme conditions which were manifested in, but not restricted to, the East End of London. From my window in Whitechapel Road, I can see the spot where the Salvation Army was founded in 1865. Living on the site of the original medieval 'White chapel', where in 1978 Altab Ali was murdered, I can look east towards the Bell Foundry where the Liberty Bell was made, to Fulbourne Street where in 1903 Lenin and Trotsky met to plan the Fifth Congress, and to the Blind Beggar pub where the Kray twins shot George Cornell. To the south is Cable Street, scene of the famous battle of 4 October 1936; to the north is Shoreditch where the original workhouse from *Oliver Twist* has only recently been demolished; and to the east are districts such as Mile End which elected a communist, Phil Piratin, as MP in 1945, Millwall, which elected a fascist, Derek Beackon, to the local council in 1993, and Lansbury Ward which produced the lowest vote ever recorded for a Conservative – twenty-four votes.

I have taken the East End of London as a basis, because I know it and love it, know it better than I know any other place, but also because it is a microcosm of urban society in a number of ways.

First, it was one of the first urban areas to develop, parts of it as early as the sixteenth century. Second, most of the 'social problems' of 'inner cities' (I put both these expressions in inverted commas for the present since each carries with it a weight of loaded meanings, assumptions, stereotypes, and so on) are evident in the East End. Here we find poverty, ill health, bad housing, hostility to minorities, and the emergence of marginalised groups. Yet alongside all this we find resilience, joy, neighbourliness, wisdom, and a wealth of insight into human life and human community. Third, the marginalisation of the Christian churches, in their historic form, was evident here long before it was evident elsewhere, and was documented in the Booth Survey and in other writings. Fourth, most recently, we have seen the impact of global capitalism on deprived communities more dramatically than in other areas. For these, if for no other reasons, I hope that, by looking in depth at this small area, I can be helpful to other people in other areas.

My work is based at the church of 'St Botolph without Aldgate' – a church 'outside the gate'. I will discuss the location, ministry and work at St Botolph's in forthcoming chapters, but it is important at the outset to emphasise the location. St Botolph's Church stands at the point where the City of London, the financial district, collides with the East End, and specifically, collides with the most over-crowded ward in Britain. This is a point of extreme polarisation. St Botolph's has been a church 'outside the gate' for centuries. It is both its official title ('without Aldgate') and a symbol of its ministry. Of this, more later.[2]

There is another aspect of my work which needs to be mentioned here. For over twenty-five years I have spent between three and six weeks each year in American cities. This began when I was a parish priest in Bethnal Green in the 1970s. In 1978 I spoke at the Catholic Renewal Conference in Loughborough on the renewal of the Anglo-Catholic social conscience. In the bar, later that evening, an American priest said to me, 'You should come and say that in Chicago.' There followed a curious conversation, at the end of which I was no wiser than at the beginning as to who he was, or why he wanted me to go. However, he seemed an interesting person who clearly did some-thing in Chicago. Several months later the phone rang at midnight.

'Hi, Dick Young. When are you coming?' said the voice. After pointing out that I could not come the following Tuesday, as he proposed, we negotiated what turned out to be an attempt to see what two inner city areas, the East End of London and the South Side of Chicago, could learn from, and give to, one another. That kind of relationship, though now involving many other places, is still a primary focus of my time in the USA.

The early years with Dick Young were very interesting. Chicago is one of the most racially segregated cities in the world. The South Side of Chicago is divided by various main roads, one of which is 47th Street. North of 47th Street, at the junction with Ellis Avenue, is a vast ghetto occupied by a large black proletariat. South of 47th Street and north of 63rd Street is the University of Chicago, a district known as Hyde Park. Beyond 63rd Street, one moves back into a ghetto area of great deprivation. Between 47th Street and the University area is a neighbourhood known as Oakland-Kenwood, which is a mixed, multi-racial neighbourhood, including white and black, some academics, young families, and members of the black bourgeoisie as well as poor black and white people. Some of the cafés and restaurants are significant meeting places for diverse, and otherwise divided, groups. One of these, where I spent a good deal of time, was Valois's Cafeteria in 53rd Street, which became widely known as a result of Mitchell Duneier's book *Slim's Table*.[3] Breakfast at Valois's with local people helped me to correct some of the stereotypes of polarisation and racial separatism which recur in the writing and discourse about Chicago.

In the early years in Chicago, I encountered churches which, while they were physically present on the South Side, and elsewhere, hardly touched the people of the neighbourhood, and indeed didn't seem interested in doing so. They were – and often still are – gathered churches of people drawn by a particular style of form of worship or by a particular pastor or preacher, or for historical reasons, but their involvement with the local residents or local issues is minimal or non-existent. This 'gathered' type of church, in which 'parish' effectively means 'congregation', and in which the local community is simply the backcloth to the work of the church, seems particularly common among Anglicans. I also encountered storefront churches, often Pentecostal or Baptist churches, which were integral to black organisation in their neighbourhood. Two churches stand out in my memories of the late 1970s. One was the African Orthodox Church which has its only Chicago base on the South Side. This small church, a breakaway from Anglicanism over racism in the 1920s, really did seem to be ministering with the very poor and oppressed people of that area. Indeed, in the late 1970s, its membership was more representative of the neighbourhood than the local Anglican parish a few hundred yards away.

More dramatic, colourful and triumphant was the huge Apostolic Church of God in 63rd Street, part of the Pentecostal Assemblies of the World. With a congregation of several thousand, the church has played a key role in community life for many years, and its pastor, Bishop Arthur Brazier, is something of a legend in Chicago. Here I found contextual theology being done, theology being rediscovered as the people's work, within a framework of gospel singing and vigorous social involvement.

It was in Chicago in the late 1970s also that I first encountered the work of Claude Marie Barbour, founder of the Shalom Ministries. This remarkable woman, a French Protestant minister teaching in a Roman Catholic seminary, has made an impact throughout the world through her stress on listening to, and learning with, marginalised communities.[4]

Since 1988 my work in the USA has been co-ordinated by Sam Portaro, the Anglican chaplain at the University of Chicago. His enormous range of contacts all over the country has meant that my experience of urban (and to a lesser extent rural) church life has extended way beyond Chicago to include Washington, DC, New York, Oklahoma, Arkansas, Northern Michigan, Idaho, Los Angeles and San Diego, and many other parts of the USA, and beyond the USA to include Toronto, Vancouver and Nova Scotia. Much of what I have learned in these places is also reflected in these pages.

Throughout this book, as in almost all my writing, there is a dynamic engagement with the questions of space and place. I see space as a scientifically measurable location, while place involves the encounter between space and human interpretation of its significance. The idea of a place involves emotional bonds, identity, and so on. Place is the result of human beings working with and giving character to space. But space itself is never a neutral background to action. Space in East London is seen throughout its history as the site of social struggles, and it is in the course of such struggles that it becomes place, contested territory, home. Like the bread of the eucharistic offertory, place is something 'which earth has given and human hands have made.' For me, whether I am in Nova Scotia or in Whitechapel Road in East London, the local context, the place, even the physical space, is of critical importance to theological work. If the combination of air travel and computer technology has brought about 'the death of distance', it has also brought home to us on a global scale how central is place to human life and human flourishing.[5]

In this book I describe how Aldgate and its environs have been places of refuge, settlement and transition for many communities of people. It seemed appropriate therefore to use the symbol of exile as a governing symbol, and so I have entitled it *Through Our Long Exile*. Many recent writers have drawn on ideas of exile, displacement and diaspora. Edward Said, following Edward Shils, sees exile as the normal state of the intellectual, while Rosi Braidotti has written of 'nomadic subjectivities' and Gloria Anzaldua of 'living on the borders'. Black writers such as Paul Gilroy make much use of the theme of diaspora.[6]

The symbol of exile is deeply rooted in the history of peoples, not least in the Jewish and Christian traditions. It is possible to see the entire Hebrew scriptural record as a response to the Babylonian exile. The oppressive symbol of Babylon stresses the importance of maintaining spiritual integrity in exile, which is the central theme of the Book of Daniel. The crisis of displacement which constituted the exile of the ancient Jewish community was a definitive moment in its self-understanding as a people. In Daniel Libeskind's new Jewish Museum in Berlin, one of the three long corridors is called 'the way of exile'. The other two are 'the way of destruction' and 'the way of continuity', and the meaning of these ways is seen in the connections and disconnections between the three. As I show in later chapters, the exile of the eastern European Jews in the late nineteenth century led to a similar experience, albeit on a smaller scale, in East London.

Within the Christian tradition, too, there is both the sense of being 'exiles of the dispersion' (1 Pet. 1:1), and also of being strangers and aliens no longer (Eph. 2:19) because our home is elsewhere. The early writer of the Letter to Diognetus reflects on the strange life of the Christians, who live as aliens, believing that 'every foreign country is their fatherland, and every fatherland is foreign.'[7] (This is perhaps the truth in Richard Sennett's claim that Christianity has been 'at odds with place'.[8]) Walter Brueggemann, who stresses that 'the core of faith . . . is situated in the matrix of exile', goes further and claims that the God of the Bible is 'a continually unsettled character'.[9]

Today the world economic order produces the conditions of exile – refugees, displaced persons, homeless persons, people who belong nowhere – on a vast scale. In part my account is an account of an inhospitable culture. The East End of London presents the conditions of exile and displacement in microcosm – from the displaced poor of the sixteenth century to the homeless people of our own day, from the Huguenots and the Irish to the Jews and the Bengalis, from the labourers from the north of England and from Scotland to the refugees from Yugoslavia and Somalia. In writing this book, the symbol of exile has never been far from my mind. By the waters of Babylon, and by Whitechapel Station, I have sometimes sat down and wept. But it has been a journey also filled with joy, hope and wonder. For many thousands of people, the East End has been a point of arrival, a point of entry, a new home, a place of warmth, hospitality and safety.

It has been said that any true theology is a 'theology of travellers',[10] and, if this is so, then this book is a travel book, through history and geography, through communities, and through the sharing of experiences of exile and displacement, of loss and disconnection, but also of the rebuilding of community in the midst of conflict, of hope in the climate of despair, and of truth emerging out of chaos and turbulence. The experience of East London has made me see that we need to develop more transitional, dynamic, moving models of the church, in which ideas such as pilgrim people, sojourners, or, in Alan Ecclestone's words, 'a people of tents rather than temples', are of central importance.[11]

Many people, over many years, have helped with the historical and sociological material, and with the work of theological reflection. If I leave people out, I am sorry. In the historical work, I was greatly helped by conversations, some of them continuing for many years, with the late Sir John Boreham, former Head of the Central Statistical Office, Professor Nicholas Deakin, first at the Survey of Race Relations and later at the Greater London Council's Research and Intelligence Unit, the late Professor Ruth Glass of the Centre for Urban Studies at University College, London, A. Sivanandan of the Institute of Race Relations, and various local history librarians in the London Borough of Tower Hamlets and its precursor boroughs – particularly Bernard Lewis, Arthur Hellicar, Mr Meadows (an extremely meticulous and polite man who never revealed his first name!), and Chris Lloyd. Each of them also opened up important areas of research. I am grateful for correspondence with Professor Michael Banton on his early research in Cable Street; Commander P.K. Kemp of the Naval Historical Branch at The Admiralty on Kru seamen in East London; John Wilder of the Psychiatric Rehabilitation Association on mental illness in East London; the late Fr Joseph Williamson and the late Councillor Edith Ramsey for material on housing and prostitution.

The following people have also been helpful at various points: the late Dr Sam Aaronovitch, Kinsi Abdulleh, Caroline Adams, Tassaduq Ahmed, Hamza Alavi, Kaushika Amin, Sindee Bass and the children of Class 5 at Kobi Nazrul Primary School, Whitechapel, Janet Batsleer, Mary Beasley, Professor David Brandon, Derek Cox, Fr Andrew Davey, Professor Geoff Dench, Arthur Downes, Professor David Downes, Terry Drummond, Liz Ellis, Professor W.J. Fishman, Professor Elaine Graham, Fr Nic Holtam, the people of Holy Comforter Parish, Atlanta, Kay Jordan, Solly Kaye, Steve Latham, Sue Mayo, Ruth Miskin, the late Phil Piratin, the late Fr David Randall, Fr Brian Ralph, Hilary Russell, Shiraj Salekin, Greg Smith, Fr William Taylor, Rio Vella, Stephen Watts, Fr John Webber, Julie Wood and William Young.

Most of all, I thank two groups of people without whom this work could not have been done. First, the trustees of the Christendom Trust who helped us to set up the urban theology work in East London and were our major funders for ten years. Second, the community around St Botolph's Church, Aldgate, who have provided me with a base from which to pursue this work, and, within this community, my Support Group, Management Committee and Advisory Panel, from whom I have gained so much. Increasingly for me, writing a book has become part of a process of personal ascesis, self-scrutiny, self-critique, and of critical reflection on the context within which I work. Context is not a neutral backcloth to personal action, but a dynamic active milieu which both shapes, and is to some extent shaped by, me. Thus the reader will find here a good deal which has emerged from these processes as they have occurred at St Botolph's. We have not 'got it right'. We are weak and fragile, a struggling Christian community, marked by imperfection, timidity and all the consequences of human weakness. But we are 'on the way', strangers and pilgrims, seeking the road of Christian discipleship. And so I particularly thank my colleagues and former colleagues here: Rosie Deedes, James Francis, Malcolm Johnson, Elaine Jones, Nerissa Jones, Brian Lee, Colin Midlane, John Peirce, Ros Trafford-Roberts and Pat Wright for their solidarity and prayerful support over the period out of which, specifically, this book has emerged.

KENNETH LEECH

15 January 2001,
Feast of St Paul the First Hermit
Anniversary of the birth of Martin Luther King Jr, 1929
Anniversary of the murder of Rosa Luxemburg, 1919
A day committed to solitude,
solidarity and the struggle for socialism

Part 1

East of Aldgate: the formation of a community

I

The East End: an emerging community

The greater part of what is now known as the East End of London was flat or marshy ground where cattle and sheep found excellent pasture.

EAST LONDON MAGAZINE, 1892[1]

The land of King Henry III, the forest of Middlesex, and the warren of Staines, were disafforested; since the which time the suburbs about London hath been also mightily increased with buildings; for first, to begin in the East, by the Tower of London, is the hospital of St Katherine, founded by Matilda the queen, wife to King Stephen, as is afore shown in Portsoken Ward. From this precinct of St Katherine to Wapping in the West ... was never a house standing these forty years; but since the gallows being after removed farther off, a continual street, or filthy strait passage, with alleys of small tenements, or cottages, built, inhabited by sailors' victuallers, along by the river of Thames, almost to Radcliff, a good mile from the Tower.

THE SURVEY OF LONDON BY JOHN STOW, 1598[2]

The East End in early times

The districts which were to form the heart of London's East End had been centres of population from an early period, in some cases from Roman times. The eastern wall of the City was built by the Romans in the fourth century, and Roman roads had covered the area which is now Bethnal Green and Mile End. To this day one of them is still called Roman Road, while the 'mile end' indicated the limit beyond which the military jurisdiction of the Roman consul was absolute. However, the Romans used East London as a dwelling place as much for the dead as for the living. One of the earliest cemeteries was at Lolesworth Field, Spitalfields, and many Roman urns and coins were discovered in 1576 when the field was broken up for brick manufacture, a process which gave the name 'Brick Lane' to one of the principal thoroughfares in the area.

The East End is historically defined as those districts which are immediately east of Aldgate, the 'old gate' of the City.[3] Aldgate ('Ealdgate') was first mentioned in the reign of King Edgar in the tenth century, and the road to the east passed beneath it. A church, dedicated to St Botolph, is known to have existed by 1066, and probably by around 950. In 1147 Queen Matilda established the monastic Hospital of St Katherine close to the Tower, and there are many references to the monks, not least to their dissolute behaviour. Indeed, there is evidence that Queen Matilda wrote letters of complaint to the Bishop of London on this matter, but never received a reply!

For hundreds of years Aldgate has formed a critical boundary, a point of polarisation and of division. In 1484 Richard III forbade aliens to work within the City, a decision which led to the development of 'alien' communities in Whitechapel and elsewhere. The history of exclusion goes back further than many have recognised.[4] This geographical point has also manifested itself as a point of conflict for religious traditions, for beyond the City boundaries were communities of 'nonconformists' and religious dissidents. Thus on 3 April 1575 at Aldgate, a number of Anabaptists were sentenced to deportation, and two others were burned at the stake in July. At the dawn of the twenty-first century, Aldgate is the point where, with some confusion, the 'golden mile' of the City gives way to the most overcrowded ward in the United Kingdom. It is the point where concentrated wealth collides with extremes of poverty.

The first permanent settlement in the East End was developed under Saxon leadership at 'Stibba's haven' or 'Stibenhede', from which was derived the name Stepney. According to the Domesday Book, 183 peasants lived in Stibenhede. The other local name Wapping, originally 'Waeppa's People', also dates from Saxon times. When the Tower of London was built, Stepney became one of the 'tower hamlets'. (Today Tower Hamlets is the name of the local government unit which serves the East End.) The area was badly affected by plague in 1349, and Stepney lost about a third of its population at this time. From 1550 to 1720 the medieval manor was in the hands of the Wentworth family, and today Wentworth Street, the site of a daily street market, stands at the boundary between the City of London and the East End.

Lines of demarcation between the City and what is now the East End became sharper when the boundaries of the City were established in the twelfth century. In 1197 William Brune founded St Mary's Priory in Spitalfields, and in 1235 it was refounded as the 'new hospital', whence 'Spitalfields', the hospital standing among fields. In 1247 the Priory of St Mary of Bethlehem was founded in nearby Bishopsgate. It was being referred to as a 'hospice' as early as 1329 and contained ten mentally ill residents. The name 'Bedlam' was attached to it in the fourteenth century, and it moved south of the river in 1815.[5]

In addition to the medieval parish of Stepney, another church, the 'white chapel' of St Mary Matfelon, was built in the area during the latter half of the fourteenth century. Whitechapel became a separate parish in 1338, and the church was built in 1374.[6]

Throughout the Middle Ages, the main East End districts were rural, though some primitive forms of industry existed, including the production of milk for the London market from Goodman's Fields, and the growing of 'teasles' for cloth manufacture at Tassel Close in Spitalfields. It was not, however, until the coming of the Tudors that genuine industrial growth began. Under Henry VIII a gun factory was set up at Houndsditch. The Red Lion Brewery was established in the sixteenth century, followed in 1669 by the Black Eagle Brewery, which in 1694 passed into the control of Joseph Truman. Truman's beer was to dominate the East End pubs for hundreds of years. The Whitechapel Bell Foundry was opened in 1570, and moved to its present site in Whitechapel Road in 1738. (The Liberty Bell was made here.) Sugar refining, which became a central activity of the German immigrants in the nineteenth century, had begun to develop in the sixteenth century, and there was at least one sugar house in Ratcliff as early as 1597. Shadwell, virtually uninhabited in the sixteenth century, grew in population during the following hundred years. In 1684 the justices, referring to that district, commented that 'the people for the most part consist of weavers and other manufacturers, and of seamen and such who relate to shipping, and are generally very factious and poore'.[7]

The area at the western extremity of what is now Cable Street, known as Goodman's Fields, had originally been the site of the Abbey of St Clare, founded in 1294. After the dissolution of the monasteries, the monastic farm was carried on by various people including Robert Goodman and, later, Sir Walter Leman. The inter-related families of Prescot, Alie, Leman and Mansell gave their names to streets in the area. By the 1860s the last relics of any 'field' had disappeared, though 'Goodman's Stile' survives as the name of one stretch of Alie Street. Between 1715 and 1729 the church of St George in the East, close to what is now Cable Street, was built by Nicholas Hawksmoor. Before its construction many Roman remains were discovered, and more were found in 1787. By this period the area around St George's, as well as Whitechapel further north, had become heavily populated.

The growth of population

The early estimates of population vary in reliability. The Domesday Survey of 1086 gave a figure of 800 for the Stepney area as a whole. From Poll Tax receipts of 1377, several years before the Peasants' Rising, it appears that the 'East London' parishes contained a population of around 1,500. By 1580 the population of East London as a whole was estimated to be about 14,000 of whom a third (4,500) were in Whitechapel, and a half in Stepney. Shadwell was almost uninhabited throughout the century, much of it consisting of ditches. Between 1580 and 1630 the population of the whole area rose from 14,000 to 48,000, and that of Whitechapel alone from under 5,000 to 20,000.

Spitalfields was mainly built up during the reign of William and Mary, and was becoming heavily populated by 1703. Dorothy George estimated that Spitalfields in 1710 contained 21,420 persons, while a writer in 1748 referred to 'the numberless ranges of buildings called Spitalfields', though he appeared to be using the term to cover a very wide area, including parts of Hoxton and Bethnal Green. It was, the writer claimed, 'an area built and inhabited by an infinite number of people'.[8]

Maps from the eighteenth century indicate the extent of the building. Norton Folgate was built up in the early years of the century as were parts of Brick Lane – a well paved street by 1738 – as well as

Princelet Street, Folgate Street, Elder Street, and others. Bethnal Green, however, appears as a rustic hamlet in a map of 1703. When the parish there was created in 1743, the population was 15,000, living in 1,800 houses. John Wesley, after a visit to Bethnal Green in 1777, was horrified by the degree of poverty he found there – 'such poverty as few can conceive without seeing it', while in 1861 Hollingshead's *Ragged London* described Bethnal Green as 'flat . . . ancient, dirty and degraded'.[9]

It has often been said that London was never planned. However, the central area was subject to intensive planning in the period from 1580 to 1630 when over twelve royal proclamations and two acts of parliament tried to restrict and regulate new building. Elizabeth I had attempted to control the growth of building in the East End in particular. A Proclamation of 1580 had forbidden new building, and this was reinforced by Charles I in 1625, but the attempts failed, and Lady Wentworth had little difficulty in 1673 in obtaining a licence from the Crown to build on the north side of Mile End Road.[10]

Urban growth and urban decay

The origins of the housing deprivation for which the East End became notorious lie in these early years. In fact the districts which became slums in the middle and late years of the eighteenth century had been built up in the years following Elizabeth I's 'immature town planning attempts',[11] that is, the years after 1580. The statute of 1593 did allow mariners, sailors and shipwrights to build near the Thames, but the housing was weak and the population poor. It was the growth of this poor population which was a central feature of the late sixteenth century, and which created the East End of London as a distinct urban unit.

Stow, writing in 1598, described the spread of houses along Petticoat Lane from St Mary Spittle to Shoreditch, along Whitechapel High Street, and also along the riverside from Tower Hill to Ratcliff. He described the growth of the 'filthy strait passage' in the riverside district, going on to point out that growth had occurred also in the northern areas around Aldgate and Whitechapel. This latter growth was of some concern to him, for, he complained, it was 'no small blemish to so famous a city to have so unsavoury and unseemly an entrance or passage thereunto'.[12] By 1680 the East London population had grown to 80,000 and by 1730 to 120,000.

During these years too there had been a growth of small lodging houses. A council letter of 1598 complained of 'small tenements' inhabited by 'base people' and 'lewd persons that doe kepe evell rule and harbour theefes, rogues and vagabonds'.[13] Two hundred years later the state of the area was still an issue. In 1782 a foreign visitor referred to this district as 'one of the most execrable holes in all this great city', and to 'this miserable narrow dirty street'.[14]

However, the late eighteenth and early nineteenth centuries saw the clearance of a large number of slum areas. The Minories, which joined Aldgate to the Tower of London, for example, had been completely transformed by 1775, and further improvements followed new paving legislation. Francis Place, writing in September 1824, gave an account of what he called 'considerable improvement'. He mentioned Wapping as an example of great change, but noted that 'Rosemary Lane and its continuation' – what we now know as Cable Street – was 'the least improved'.[15]

Meanwhile industries which were forbidden in the City were moving east. Brewing, clothing, sugar refining, rope making, and sailcloth weaving all had their place in the riverside districts. Spital-fields was mainly industrial by the late seventeenth century.

It was in the early eighteenth century that Whitechapel and St George's in the East began to acquire the reputation which they have never lost of being districts of vagrancy and vice. In 1737 the Court of Common Council received a complaint from the Master and Wardens of the Company of Merchant Taylors and several citizens of Portsoken Ward. They complained that 'great numbers of idle, vagrant, loose and disorderly persons' had assembled in Rosemary Lane for 'a sort of market or fair'. A few years later, in 1753, there was an account of 'disorderly and common Bawdy houses in the Parish of St Mary Whitechapel'.[16] Alie Street and Goodman's Fields were specifically mentioned, while in 1765 Church Lane, White-chapel – today known as Whitechurch Lane – was also referred to in the same connection. It is clear that by the middle years of the eighteenth century, vagrants and prostitutes had established them-selves within the districts of Whitechapel and St George's. These two districts have attracted both groups fairly consistently until the present day.

Immigrants in early East End history

While it has been said that 'the story of London begins with foreigners',[17] there are few references to immigrants in the East End until the imposition of the alien subsidy under Henry VI in 1439. This subsidy was repeated every year from 1442. It seems clear that many aliens lived in the riverside districts and were involved in such trades as brewing and brickmaking. Richard III in 1484 forbade aliens to work within the City and there was, as a result, an increased movement into the East End. In 1517 there were anti-alien riots in the Spitalfields district. According to the Lord Mayor's survey in 1551, there were around 40,000 aliens in the London area, described as 'for the most part heretics, fled from other countries'. A return of 1571 reported that there were 169 foreigners in Whitechapel, 284 in East Smithfield, and 210 in the Precinct of St Katherine. A more detailed breakdown for the Liberty of St Katherine's gave the following figures: Dutch 328, French 69, Danes 8, Poles 5, Spaniards 2, Italians 1, Scots 12. The Hospital of St Katherine, the religious foundation which had survived the dissolution of the monasteries, harboured many foreigners. Stow described it as 'now of late years inclosed about or pestered with small tenements and homely cottages having inhabitants, English and strangers, more in number than in some city in England'.[18] To Ben Jonson, St Katherine's was the place 'where they use to keep the better sort of mad folks'. But he wrote elsewhere of going

To Shoreditch, Whitechapel, and so to St Katherine's,
To drink with the Dutch there and take forth their patterns.[19]

Of 1620 entries in the burial registers of the Parish of Stepney from 1606 to 1610, 84 were identified as 'strangers' (though only nine of them came from distant countries), while in addition there were thirteen other aliens. Of these, eight were from Scotland, one from Ireland, one from Guernsey, and four from France. The marriage registers for the same period showed a total of 259 persons, of whom sixteen came from distant countries, and one, described as a Negro, came from the East Indies, a ratio of six per cent of the total. In 1700, in the City itself, less than fifty per cent were actually born there. However, migration from other parts of Britain has always been more significant than immigration from elsewhere.

From the late seventeenth century onwards, there were considerable numbers of Jewish immigrants in the East End. But the immigrant community which provoked most comment from the eighteenth century onwards was the Irish. By the end of the eighteenth century the numbers of Irish paupers was causing concern. Appendix Four of the Mendicity Report of 1814–15 showed that, in 1796–7, of some 5,097 persons receiving relief in London, 1,770 (including 1,091 children) belonged to parishes in Ireland. Anxiety about the poverty within the Irish community increased in 1828 with the publication of *The Report on Irish and Scots Vagrants*.

In the East End, a number of disturbances involving Irish immigrants occurred in the eighteenth century. In 1736 local residents in Spitalfields took part in riots against Irish weavers and builders' labourers. Two Irish pubs were almost destroyed and the windows of lodging houses were smashed. There were further disturbances in the same area in the 1760s and at the time of the Gordon Riots in 1780. The secretary of the Protestant Association lived in Goulston Street in Whitechapel, and much of the anti-Roman feeling was stirred up in this district. On 5 June 1780 the Roman Catholic chapel in Nightingale Street, St George's in the East, was attacked, and this was followed by the destruction of Virginia Chapel in Wapping.

Two days later, rioters seized the stores in the Artillery Ground. The Jews in Houndsditch and Duke's Place wrote on their shutters, 'This house is a good Protestant'. The whole of the Whitechapel area was seen as a danger zone, and reinforcements of militia were sent into Wellclose Square. On 30 July rioters attacked Irish dwellings and almshouses in Goodman's Fields and Rosemary Lane. Austin Allen of the Gentleman and Porter in Leman Street had his premises broken up as did some other local residents, while John Walden, publican of the Bell and Butcher in Cable Street, had two windows smashed.

Much of the documentation on the Irish immigrants was hostile. According to the *Report on Education* of 1816, the Irish in the Shadwell area were 'dissolute and depraved', while Francis Place, writing in the same year, claimed that 'the poorest and most dissolute people in Spitalfields are several grades above the mere Irish'. It was not, however, only the Irish who were the recipients of such abuse.

'Little can be done by taking away the licences of houses in Shadwell,' a magistrate observed in 1817, 'for this reason that the population consists entirely of foreign sailors, Lascars, Chinese, Greeks, and other filthy dirty people of that description'. Yet it was the poor Irish who were constantly singled out for criticism as containing the most degenerate and unhealthy elements in the population. 'The Irish in London,' it was argued, 'were a police problem, a sanitary problem, a poor law problem, and an industrial problem'.[20]

In the eighteenth century the black population in the East End was probably quite small, though press cuttings suggest that the numbers were increasing towards the end of the century. Most of those referred to were employed as servants. Advertisements which have survived from this period refer to servants who had run away, and districts such as Alie Street (1707) and Wellclose Square (1742) were mentioned. A record from 1765 refers to the death by drowning of a foreigner in Mile End Road, and notes that 'a black' dived in and brought his body to shore, while it was said of Dr Mayo, a Stepney clergyman from 1733 to 1791, 'no clergyman in England ever baptised so many black men and mulattoes'.[21]

Other press cuttings from the eighteenth century refer to the presence of Italian and Portuguese seamen in the western part of Stepney, and of Chinese and Lascars (Indian seamen) in the eastern part. These reports are frequently combined with descriptions of violence. Thus in 1785 a newspaper reported that 'a desperate affray' had occurred in Stepney between some Chinese Tartars and a body of Lascars, while in 1808 there was a 'dreadful affray' between American and Portuguese sailors in Whitechapel. There are a number of graphic accounts of similar incidents, but little concrete information about the size of these communities.[22]

One immigrant group, however, about which there is considerable documentation is that of the continental Huguenots.[23] As early as the reign of Edward III, a number of Flemish artisans had settled in London, but it was not until the reign of Edward VI that the influx reached sizeable dimensions. In 1571 the City of London contained 1,763 foreign members of Dutch, French and Italian churches. However, the Huguenots who fled before and after the Revocation of the Edict of Nantes in 1685, and who settled in London, represented a refugee community of such proportions that no less than thirty-five French churches were needed in London and the suburbs to cater for their needs. By the middle of the eighteenth century there were eleven French churches to the east of Bishopsgate in such places as Crispin Street, Artillery Street, Petticoat Lane, Wheler Street and elsewhere.

The earlier group of weavers who had arrived during the reign of Elizabeth I lived in the Hog Lane district, but in later years a move towards Spitalfields took place, a move which brought both industry and culture into that district. There were three waves of Huguenot migration – 1681–2, 1686–8, and 1698–1700. The Mathematical Society was founded in Spitalfields in 1717, and in 1743 a sundial, erected on a wall in Fournier Street, symbolised the dawning of the 'age of enlightenment' for the East End. A Huguenot chapel was set up in Hanbury Street in 1719, and in 1744 L'Eglise Neuve was established on the corner of Brick Lane and Fournier Street. (It became a Methodist chapel in 1819, a synagogue in the late nineteenth century, and is now a mosque.)

With the arrival of the Huguenots, Spitalfields began to inherit much of the silk trade for which Lyons had previously been famous. A study of the collections of eighteenth-century designs for Spital-fields' silks in the Victoria and Albert Museum made it possible both to date and to locate with some precision the main structure of the Huguenot community in the East End. Spital Square had become the centre for wealthy master weavers, and the 1746 *Guide to London* called it 'the great centre of the weaving trade in all its branches'. The more prosperous of the weavers lived in Spitalfields and Bishopsgate Without, and a few in the City itself. The poorer weavers lived mainly in adjacent parishes, particularly in Bethnal Green. It seems likely that the total number of Huguenots who settled in the area was around 15,000.

Toward the end of the seventeenth century the Huguenot community in Spitalfields met with considerable hostility. Riots against them occurred in 1763, 1765, 1766, and 1769. Two were hanged outside the Salmon and Ball pub at Bethnal Green. In the nineteenth century the silk trade collapsed. The Spitalfields Acts of 1773, 1792 and 1801, and the commercial treaty with France in 1860, may be seen as marking the beginning and the climax of the Huguenot silk weaving industry's decline.

There is an ironic twist to the final phase. In 1870, when Pope Pius IX defined the dogma of papal infallibility, it was necessary for him to wear a new vestment woven in one piece. Search was made all over Europe, without success, for a weaver with sufficient skill. Eventually one was found in Spitalfields, a descendant of the Huguenot community which had fled there from Roman Catholic persecution! But by this date the Huguenot community no longer existed as a recognisable group. Other immigrants had moved into the district and the future history of Spitalfields was to lie with them. By the end of the nineteenth century the Huguenot community only survived in the loosest sense, although to this day a number of the streets in the area retain their French names, such as Fournier and Fleur de Lys, and family names of Huguenot origin still survive in the Bethnal Green area.

Changing patterns of population and migration

From the beginning of the nineteenth century London was on the move. Steamboats sailed up the Thames in the 1820s, while in 1829 the first horse-bus provided a cheaper and more frequent service than the stage coaches had done. In the 1830s came the first of the railways, and for some years after 1849 several railway companies tried to encourage suburban settlement by providing major concessions in fares. The demolition of houses to create the railways led to the concentration and congestion of working-class housing near the railways.[24] The expansion of London began in earnest in the 1860s, with the opening of the first section of the underground system in 1863, and there developed a pattern of outward movement from the centre of London. In many ways it was this outward movement which was the most characteristic feature of population change in the nineteenth century.

So in the 1860s, as new railways, warehouses and offices appeared, along with Smithfield and other markets, the residential population of the City fell, and that of the emerging suburbs increased. Although the very poor could not use the new transport, the changes did affect the East End fairly quickly, particularly after the appearance of the horse-drawn omnibus in 1832. One route ran from Chelsea to Mile End. East London was also served by railway stations at Cannon Street Road, Shadwell, Stepney, Limehouse, and elsewhere. By the 1840s Stratford was linked to the East End by continuous building. Previously the outward expansion of suburbia had not penetrated very much in an eastern direction, but the period from 1840 to 1890 saw the growth of West Ham, Cann Hall, North Woolwich, and the southern parts of East Ham and West Barking. It was in the 1890s that the really significant growth in suburban Essex began.

The growth of the waterfront, with the completion of the Royal Victoria Docks (1855) and the Royal Albert Docks (1880), was another factor in the outward expansion of East London, as was the regulation of offensive trades after 1844 which encouraged the spread of chemical and soap-making industries to West Ham. So the latter part of the century saw the creation of a large built-up area embracing Leyton, Walthamstow, Little Ilford, and East and West Ham with a population in 1871 of 29,065. By 1901 the population of this area, with the addition of Wanstead, had grown to 289,261. This process of migration from the inner East End to the outlying districts is of central importance in understanding the subsequent social and economic history of the area. The belief that there was, during the latter half of the nineteenth century in particular, an unprecedented growth of population in the inner districts, a growth directly traceable to external immigration, is not supported by the data. Rather there was an exchange of population as large numbers of East Enders began to disperse in the direction of the outer suburbs. This phenomenon, which much later came to be known as 'counter-urbanisation', was already established in the second half of the nineteenth century. Charles Booth, writing of West Ham in 1892, pointed out that the most rapid growth had taken place in districts such as this. There was also, he said, 'a continual stream of population from the centre to the circumference', for example, from Whitechapel to Poplar.[25]

But the movement outward from the inner East End was not only in an easterly direction. The adjacent district of Shoreditch was losing its rural character by the beginning of the century, though Hackney and Stoke Newington were still largely rural. Hackney in 1801 contained only 2,137 houses and a population of 12,730, while Stoke Newington contained 208 houses and a population of 1,462. In Shoreditch, on the other hand, the population increased from 34,766 in 1801 to 43,930 in 1811, 68,564 in 1831, and 129,364 in 1861. Shoreditch attracted both migrants from the City and immigrants from overseas, including Irish and some early Jewish refugees. A study of nine Shoreditch streets in 1841, 1851 and 1861 showed the extent to which multi-occupation had spread in these years.[26]

There was, however, a determined refusal by many of the elderly poor of Shoreditch to leave the area when slum property in the notorious 'Nichol' (or 'Jago') district was demolished. The peak period for immigration into Shoreditch was the 1860s when a significant number of Irish moved across the Boundary district into Hoxton. After this there was calm, and later a slow decline of population.

The two wards of Whitechapel and St George's in the East showed consistent population increases from the beginning of the nineteenth century, reaching their peak in 1851 and 1861 respectively, and from then subsiding. In 1851 Whitechapel had a density per acre of 214.41. In 1861 St George's had a figure of 229.54. But overcrowding of households continued to increase until the end of the century. The highest ratios for overcrowding were in the Spitalfields Sub-District of Whitechapel (11.28 in 1881) and in the St John's Sub-District of St George's (10.28 in 1881).

The censuses prior to 1841 were entirely numerical and gave no information either about individuals or their places of origin. However, using the data from 1801–31, it is possible to build up a general picture of the population and of the distribution of housing and employment in the area. Only after 1841 is it possible to attempt an account of the structure of the immigrant communities in the area from the Census Enumerators' Books. However, the 1841 Census classified those born outside England and Wales under three headings only: Scottish-born, Irish-born, and foreign-born. There is no reliable way of estimating the size and distribution of the different groups of foreign-born residents. In addition, not only has some of the material been lost, but also a certain amount of it is difficult to decipher. However, on the basis of the material for 1841, 1851 and 1861, a reasonably accurate picture can be drawn of the immigrant communities in this part of the East End.

The 1841 data show an overwhelmingly local-born population in both districts with the Irish forming the only really large immigrant community. In 1841 there were no indications of anything approaching a 'ghetto' except in one small area of St George's. By 1851 the general pattern of distribution had not altered much. The highest ratio of Irish-born residents in any Enumeration District

(ED) in St George's in 1851 was 39.5 per cent. In 1861 the Irish-born accounted for around 9.65 per cent of the population in Whitechapel, and around 8.18 per cent in St George's. There were other smaller immigrant groups of whom the German and Dutch constituted the most important, the latter reaching significant dimensions only in Whitechapel. The German residents in this period were almost all employed in the sugar industry and were predominantly resident in the St Mary's Registration District of St George's. In no ED did they account for more than 8.01 per cent of the population. St George's contained more sugar refiners than any parish in Tower Hamlets, and in 1833 the Vestry petitioned for the removal of 'all restrictions and prohibitions affecting the admission and refining of foreign sugars'. The partial collapse of the sugar industry was one of the key factors in the social history of St George's in these years. Many German refiners had arrived in the eighteenth century, and by 1857 it was observed that 'the sugar refiners employ for the most part Hamburgers'.[27]

In 1848 a cholera epidemic swept through the East End with devastating effects in St George's and Whitechapel. But the population and the incidence of overcrowding increased, and these trends continued and accelerated between 1851 and 1861. In 1863 the Medical Officer of Health was expressing concern at the likelihood of a continued population increase (though a decline had begun while he was writing) and of further overcrowding. In 1864 he expressed concern that 'lodgings for foreigners and others belonging to the casual or floating population' were increasing in the area.

The mortality rate fluctuated throughout the 1860s. In 1864 the Medical Officer claimed that 'the health of the inhabitants has improved to an unusual degree'. But 1864 was 'an unusually unhealthy year' and saw an increase in the death rate which was 'the more serious because . . . not balanced by any appreciable increase of population'. There were increases in deaths from measles, whooping cough, and respiratory conditions. The situation improved again in 1865. While deaths from diseases of the lungs remained at much the same level as before, deaths from other causes declined. But cholera again raged throughout the East End in the following year, resulting in 387 deaths in St George's, of which 160 occurred in St John's Registration District and in the Workhouse'.[28]

The year 1867 also saw improvements, and the mortality rate fell to its lowest point in ten years. Deaths from cholera in that year numbered only five in St George's. In the following year, however, there was a slight increase, which continued into 1870. Throughout the 1860s the population was declining, a decline which was particularly marked in the southern part of St John's Registration District where the population fell from 8,387 in 1861 to 7,682 in 1871. The main factors in this decline were the demolition of property to make way for the building of the East London Railway, the new infirmary, St Peter's Church and London Docks, and the clearing of some houses in Plough Alley which had become unfit for habitation. But, while in 1871 there were 262 fewer inhabited houses, the density of population had increased, and the average number of persons per house had risen in the inter-censal period from 7.93 to 8.10. This trend continued into the 1880s, and the 1881 figure was 8.16. The same pattern is traceable in Whitechapel where, between 1851 and 1881, the population fell from 79,759 to 71,363, a figure lower than that of 1841. But there in the same period the average number of persons per house rose from 9.05 to 9.48.

The movement of population away from the East End into the new suburbs was very marked. The population declined in Whitechapel after 1851 and in St George's after 1861. Such migration as did occur was a replacement of population rather than direct increase. With the exception of the Irish, the immigrant communities were small. Only with the mass Jewish exodus from Eastern Europe did immigrant settlements in the East End assume major proportions. There were a number of small communities, such as the Germans in St George's, and Dutch, Russian and Polish immigrants in Whitechapel after 1851. These communities came into an area marked both by the dispersal of the indigenous population and also by severe overcrowding and social distress, problems which would increase as the century moved on.

Access to the rough sheets of the 1881 Census and to the annual schedules of the School Board Sub-Districts from 1878 onwards, combined with data on foreign immigration, enabled Booth and his colleagues to produce a valuable account of the role of migration in the East End in the 1870s and 1880s. Their conclusion was that 'there has been of late little, if any, influx into East London, in the sense of an excessive growth directly traceable to immigration . . . The interest of the migration from the country to East London

therefore lies in the interchange rather than the addition of population, for direct addition there is none'.[29] Indeed the 1881 data
indicated an opposite trend. Calculation of the East London population in 1881, based on excess of births over deaths, produced a
figure of 886,128, but the actual population was 879,200, showing
a deficiency of 6,928. Migration outwards was continuing and was
particularly evident in Whitechapel and St George's.

On the other hand, it is clear that there was a continual movement
into the East End from other parts of the country. Study of places
of birth of the East End population shows the extent to which the
agricultural counties in particular fed the area. This process was part
of a general pattern of rural depopulation and increasing urbanisation. Between 1841 and 1881 the percentage of the population of
England and Wales which was urban-based increased from 48.3 to
70. On Booth's calculations, around 33,322 residents of East London
in 1881 had been born in the twelve agricultural counties, while
24,898 had been born in the twelve manufacturing counties.
However, throughout the period Bethnal Green remained the
'absolute "low water mark" of immigration for the whole of
London'.[30] Here under 200 per 1,000 of the population were born
outside East London. In parts of Whitechapel, by contrast, the figure
was over 400 per 1,000. (This is a crucial factor in understanding
the subsequent role of Bethnal Green in the rise of racist and fascist
movements in the East End.)

The immediately adjoining counties poured migrants into the
East End. Thus over 28,000 natives of Essex were living in East
London in 1881, almost a third of all the Essex-born residents in
the London area. The movement of population between the East
End and Essex therefore was not a one-way stream though the
outward migration dominated the scene as the century drew towards
its close.

The period from 1891 to 1901 was marked by a general increase
in population throughout the area. This was an exception to the
general pattern of decline, and was due both to slum clearance and
the building of new dwellings, and to the immigration of Jewish
people from Eastern Europe. Many new parishes had come into
existence during the second half of the century, and, out of twenty
parishes, only seven showed a decline in population during this

period. But it was also during this period that external immigration increased considerably.

Immigrant communities in the nineteenth century

In 1892 Booth observed that 'London is the great centre in England of the foreign resident population, and Whitechapel is the great centre of the foreign population of London'.[31] In 1881 the entire area of the Tower Hamlets contained 21,469 foreign and colonial residents, of whom 17,576 were foreign-born. In Whitechapel and St George's there were three main groups: Germans, Poles and Dutch. The Germans remained a substantial community in both wards. 'Germany,' claimed Booth, 'is by far the largest contributor to the foreign population of London . . . There is no district in East London without a large contingent of German inhabitants'. As late as 1912 a part of St George's in the East was known as 'Little Germany',[32] while Whitechapel contained the only German Roman Catholic church in Britain.[33]

The Poles, by 1881, were becoming more heavily concentrated in Whitechapel. Of the 6,000 or so Poles in Tower Hamlets, 4,468 were in the Whitechapel Ward. The Dutch, a long established group, were still present in the Spitalfields area where they were mainly occupied in cigar making. There were 1,850 Dutch residents of Whitechapel in 1881. But the largest contributors to the foreign-born population of Whitechapel in the late 1880s and 1890s were the Jewish immigrants from Eastern Europe. They remained heavily concentrated in Whitechapel and did not spread out into St George's or further east into Stepney. Indeed, the further one moved from Whitechapel, the smaller and more scattered did the foreign communities become.

A significant proportion of the foreign-born residents in the East End during the nineteenth century were seamen. Booth claimed in 1896 that one-third of the men in the merchant service were either Lascars or foreigners.[34] In 1857 the Strangers' Home for Asiatics, Africans and South Sea Islanders was opened at Limehouse, and between 1857 and 1868 it received, at its own expense, 2,870 Asiatics, Africans and South Sea Islanders, while 785 seamen from India, China, Malacca, Arabia, East and West Africa, and the South Pacific were sheltered free of charge.[35]

There were a large number of other lodging houses, much smaller, further west in St George's. In Cable Street in 1884, according to a local historian writing in the early part of the twentieth century, many of the houses were 'common lodging houses occupied by English, Scotch, Irish, Welsh, Americans, Germans, Norwegians, Flemish, Chinese, West Indians and others'.[36]

Joseph Salter, in his small book *The Asiatic in England*, published in 1873, claimed that 'nearly forty sons of India have perished in our London streets with cold and hunger within a limited time.' Salter identified the area around High Street, Shadwell, and specifically Blue Gate Fields as 'the Oriental quarter'. One of the missioners at the Home had observed that No. 12 was 'full of native sons of India' and that Nos. 6, 7, 8 and 9 were 'all occupied by natives of the East'.[37] In another small work, Salter pointed to the existence of opium smoking centres in this area, again noting the High Street, Shadwell area as a main focal point. He also mentioned George Yard and Wentworth Street in Whitechapel as centres for Asiatics.[38]

Observers in Whitechapel and St George's in the 1860s had also noted the numbers of foreign lodging houses in the Cable Street area. 'Ship Alley,' wrote Mayhew in 1861, 'is full of foreign lodging houses.' He had met German and Irish sailors' consorts around the Ratcliff Highway, as well as 'a sprinkling of coloured men and a few thorough negroes scattered about here and there', including some 'negro beggars' in Whitechapel.[39] Press reports from the early nineteenth century refer to inter-racial strife in the dockland area.

However, for much of the time prior to Booth's survey, one is dependent on scrappy bits of anecdotal material, and there is little reliable evidence, for example, about the size and character of the black community in the East End. Thus it has been thought that there were groups of West African seamen (Kroomen) living in the dockland area in the nineteenth century. Naval records, however, contain no clear data on members of the Kroo tribe who were serving in ships in home ports. A regulation contained in an Admiralty Circular of 24 April 1819 refers to the number of 'negroes' on His Majesty's ships on the coast of Africa, and certain restrictions on numbers were specified in Queen's Regulations and Admiralty Instructions in 1844, with further regulations in 1862, 1879, and 1887. It is possible that some Kroomen came to England after being 'paid off' and that some of them may have settled in the East End.[40]

The notion of Limehouse and Shadwell as 'Oriental quarters', however, contains as much legend as fact. Until well into the twentieth century, Limehouse, containing its famous 'Chinatown' (Pennyfields), was synonymous with mystery and fear for many, including people from elsewhere in the East End. For a long period it was assumed that there existed a large number of Asiatic and black, as well as Chinese, people in the area. But these communities were quite small compared with the much larger Irish and Eastern European communities further west. In 1917 Thomas Burke sought refuge from the growing Jewish ghetto in Whitechapel in the Oriental quarter of Limehouse. For, he wrote:

> The Russian and Jewish quarters are growing stale and commercial, and the London Docks are a region whose chief features are Cockney warehouse clerks. This corner of Limehouse alone remains definitely its Oriental self, no part of London.[41]

Immigration has played a key role in the making of London, and it has often been said that the entire history of East London could be written in terms of successive waves of immigrants, while, it is similarly claimed, that 'London has been continually remade for its entire span of existence and it has always been made by people coming in'.[42] These are at best half-truths. In the nineteenth century the bulk of the population of the East End had been born, if not locally, certainly within the county of Middlesex. Only towards the end of the century did this begin to change.

2

Between slum and ghetto: social conditions in the nineteenth century

When the foreigner asks, 'Which is the worst district in London?', the answer will probably be 'Whitechapel.'

SAMUEL BARNETT, 1894[1]

'Oh my lady!' she cried, the tears coming afresh, 'you can never understand what it is to be poor and live in the East End of London. My lady, you say it is horrible – it's worse, it's worse.'

JOHN A. STEWART, 1899[2]

The 'discovery' of the East End

The 'discovery' of the East End by writers and social investigators led to what Arthur Morrison called 'graphically written descriptions of Whitechapel by people who have never seen the place'.[3] Morrison, whose *Tales of Mean Streets* (1894) is often seen as the founding document of the 'Cockney school' of urban novels, was writing in 1889, the year after the 'discovery' assumed national proportions in the wake of the Jack the Ripper murders. The continuing fascination with those murders is extraordinary, depressing, clearly exciting, almost to the point of derangement of feeling and of desire. Even the term 'East End' itself seems to have been an invention of the late nineteenth century, appearing in the magazine of that name in 1888. The magazine saw the term as itself 'a cruel stigma'.[4] Writing almost a century later, Stedman Jones said that the image of the East End in the 1880s was one of 'a nursery of destitute poverty and thriftless demoralised pauperism in a community cast adrift from the salutary presence and leadership of men of wealth and culture, and . . . a political threat to the riches and civilisation of London and the Empire'.[5]

The East End was often seen as the 'mysterious East', a zone of fascination waiting to be 'discovered'. Booth, in 1889, described the East End as 'hidden from view' and claimed that his aim was to lift the curtain which veiled it.[6] In fact, since the 1850s 'few parts of the world have been as endlessly studied and re-imagined as the East End'.[7] However, at the same time as the 'hidden', 'other', and 'mysterious' labels were being used, there was another image being created, that of the East End as the archetypal slum. The concept of 'slum', now widely accepted as a neutral description of types of housing, was in fact a 'myth', created and fostered by the print media as 'an all embracing concept of an outcast society'.[8] We need then to see how the language of 'slum' carried with it a whole cultural constellation of assumptions, innuendos, and so on, if we are to make sense of the way in which the East End has been portrayed in the past, and the power of the mythology today. In the same way, we need to recognise the part 'narratives of sexual danger' played in shaping wider attitudes to women and sexuality in the late nineteenth century.[9]

It is beyond dispute that the East End in the nineteenth century was an area of acute social distress. The wards of Whitechapel and St George's in particular suffered severe social problems, problems which in many cases had been present for years before the area was 'discovered' by philanthropists, social investigators and novelists in the latter years of the century. The authors invoked both horror and pity, focusing sometimes on the squalor of the area as a warning of the dangers to health and safety, at other times on the terrible condition of the people. However, the novelists preceded the social investigators. While most of the novels of Charles Dickens were not rooted in the East End, but rather in Clerkenwell and King's Cross, he did spend much of his time in Limehouse, and the Grapes pub in Narrow Street is particularly associated with him. East End locations occur throughout the novels. Bill Sikes's household was in Bethnal Green, the workhouse described in *Oliver Twist* was in Hoxton, and David Copperfield made his arrival in London at Aldgate. Shortly before his death in 1870, Dickens was researching the opium dens in Limehouse for the unfinished novel *Edwin Drood.* All of Dickens' work antedated Booth.

It was fear, more than pity or compassion (though these were present also), which dominated the concern about the 'East End problem'. That fear, which was to reach near hysterical level after 1888, had been expressed earlier, for example, in 1852 by Thomas Beamish in his account of London's 'rookeries', which he described as 'beds of pestilence', sources of fever and of crime. 'A future generation of thieves is there hatched from the viper's egg who shall one day astonish London by their monstrous birth'.[10] It was the fear of contagion, of the spread of the violence and vice which squalor and despair had produced, into the respectable areas of the city, which was the motivation for the demands for reform, however much they were dressed up in the garments of charity and compassion.

There were sharp contrasts in property and social position in the early nineteenth century. The back streets of Bishopsgate and Houndsditch were described by an observer in the 1840s as 'a dirty and neglected district', though nearby were fashionable houses around Finsbury Square. In St George's in the 1820s, Goodman's Fields contained affluent streets, and Leman Street was mainly occupied by wealthy Jews, though nearby was the slum quarter of Rosemary Lane. By 1880 all the old sea captains had left Wellclose Square, and the building of Rowton House in Fieldgate Street in 1892 set the seal on the process by which the area became 'the home of the strangers, the shiftless and the derelict'.[11] By the time Jack London published *The People of the Abyss* in 1903, the area was marked by the presence of large numbers of rootless persons.

Booth in 1892 concluded that St George's was the poorest area in East London with 48.2 per cent living below the poverty line, compared with 39.2 per cent in Whitechapel. In Whitechapel, however, there was a much higher ratio of what Booth called 'the poorest class of all'. The social conditions in Whitechapel were described throughout the nineteenth century. The East London Magistrates, in evidence to the Committee on the State of the Police of the Metropolis in 1816, referred to the 'promiscuous depravity' of children in Whitechapel pubs. These were used, according to one magistrate, 'by persons of the worst description'. In 1816 there were 114 pubs in Whitechapel, and 96 in St George's, as well as many 'low lodging houses'.[12] Mayhew in 1861 listed many centres of disreputable lodging houses including Thrawl Street, Flower and Dean Street, Wentworth Street, Rosemary Lane, and Whitechapel High Street.

It is sometimes claimed that prostitution in the East End only developed after the Second World War. In fact, Mayhew devoted most of Volume Four of his study of 'street people' to prostitution. Hollingshead, in the same year, described Angel Alley as a centre of prostitution. The number of known prostitutes in Whitechapel increased from 474 in 1850 to 1,803 in 1857, falling slightly in 1858 to 811, while in Stepney there was an increase from 827 in 1850 to 965 in 1857, and then to 1,015 in 1858. The area remained a centre for prostitute activity until the end of the century. Booth observed that 'the part played by prostitution socially and economically . . . is greater than would be generally supposed'.[13]

The streets where the Ripper murders occurred in 1888, and those where the victims lived, were well known as areas of prostitution. Thrawl Street consisted of prostitutes' lodging houses which backed directly on to other houses. Although by the end of the century, much of Thrawl Street, along with Flower and Dean Street and Wentworth Street, had become Jewish, and had been converted into a complex of working-class dwellings, conditions in 1888 were appalling. Nearby, Dorset Street was similar, perhaps the most notorious street after Flower and Dean Street. Booth referred to 'the hells of Dorset Street', while Samuel Barnett wrote about it in *The Times* in 1898. In 1904 it was renamed Duval Street. At the time of the 1888 murders, a representative of the Central News Agency wrote of the streets in this district as 'very unwholesome and dirty thoroughfares' which 'appear unutterably forlorn and dismal in the darkness of night'. Yet of all these streets it was Flower and Dean Street which boasted the most terrible reputation.

Flower and Dean Street was built in the seventeenth century by the property developers Flower and Dean. In the 1870s it was 'generally regarded as the most menacing working class area in London', while, writing of it in 1883, James Greenwood called it 'the foulest and most dangerous street in the whole metropolis'.[14] After the passing of the Artisans and Labourers Dwellings Improvement Act (the Cross Act) in 1875, there was in fact some demolition. But around two-thirds of the street survived, including most of the common lodging houses. According to *The Bitter Cry of Outcast London* (1883), the act had made matters worse since the newly erected dwellings were beyond the means of the poor who therefore crowded more closely in those dwellings that were left.

The prostitutes of Flower and Dean Street were known locally as 'Fourpenny Bits' and 'Woodbine Kates'. The Rector of Bishopsgate, William Rogers, writing just after the murders, urged the registration and licensing of prostitution. Many of the immigrant Jews who had moved into Rothschild Buildings were afraid of the prostitute district 'cos it's terrible round that way'.[15] In 1871 there were thirty-one common lodging houses there with a population of 902 persons: the total population of the street being only 1,078.

One local newspaper commented in 1881 that Flower and Dean Street was associated in most people's minds with 'vice, immorality and crime in their most hideous shapes', and that 'there is no street in any other part of this great Metropolis that has for its inhabitants a like number of the dangerous class'. Flower and Dean Street had 'a character of its own'. Many years later, a character in one of Arnold Wesker's plays looked back on Flower and Dean Street as a prison with iron railings. But the torrent of middle-class protest which the murders released was not on the whole concerned with what White has termed 'the real Flower and Dean Street problem'[16] – that of reliance on casual and seasonal employment, low wages, inadequate poor relief, and slum conditions – but rather with the side effects of prostitution and crime which they feared might spread to more 'respectable' districts. They were concerned too with the danger of revolt. The *Daily Telegraph* summed up the feelings of its readership in 1888 when it called for a 'cleanly, orderly and contented proletariat'.[17]

In nearby St George's Ward, Peter Thompson, who had pioneered the work of the Methodist Church in Cable Street, claimed that the publicity about the murders had vindicated what church workers in the area had been saying for years, though their comments had been 'flippantly discounted'.[18]

Alongside the prostitute community in Whitechapel lived the equally long established community of vagrant and derelict people. It was the sight of these rootless and desperate men and women which greeted the Jewish immigrants who arrived in the 1890s, and which impressed on some of them the need for social revolution. Thus the anarchist Rudolf Rocker described his first visit to the East

End in 1893: 'thousands of human beings who could hardly be still considered people who were no longer capable of any kind of work . . . dirty and lousy, never free from hunger, starving, scavenging their food out of dustbins and the refuse heaps that were left behind after the markets closed.'

Rocker went on to describe a scene in Commercial Street which could have come not from the 1890s but from the 1950s, 1960s or 1990s, or indeed from any intervening period:

> There was a church at the corner of Commercial Street, at the Spitalfields end, where at any time of the day you would see a crowd of dirty lousy men and women, looking like scarecrows, in filthy rags, with dull hopeless faces, scratching themselves. That was why it was called Itchy Park.[19]

Itchy Park – Christ Church Gardens – was to remain a centre for vagrant and derelict people until the present day.[20]

The East End in the nineteenth century then was an area in which extreme poverty and severe overcrowding affected large sections of the population. Parts of Whitechapel in particular were also districts of crime, prostitution, vagrancy and dereliction. The very poor area extended north from Whitechapel into Shoreditch and Bethnal Green. In 1848 a report by Dr Gavin to the Health of Towns Association described Bethnal Green as an area where people 'have their health injured, their lives sacrificed, their property squandered, their morals depraved'.[21] By 1903 Bethnal Green was the only borough in north-east London which was not lit by electricity. Whitechapel, on the other hand, began to show improvements from the 1880s. The Jewish Board of Guardians was particularly concerned with sanitation, and its sanitary committee sent regular reports to the Medical Officer of Health.

By the end of 1894, almost all the old Flower and Dean Street area had been demolished, and three-quarters of Thrawl Street transformed. Jerry White commented: 'Within six years then Jack the Ripper had done more to destroy the Flower and Dean Street rookery than fifty years of road building, slum clearance, and unabated pressure from police, Poor Law Guardians, vestries and sanitary officers'.[22]

Slum clearance did not significantly reduce over-occupation or population density. But by 1902 around 16,000 out of 80,000 people in Whitechapel were living in block dwellings. While the problem of the common lodging houses remained, there had been major transformations. In St George's, Francis Place wrote of improvements in the early nineteenth century, but noted that Rosemary Lane and its continuation were the least improved. The Ratcliff Highway murders of 1811 led John Ward, later Earl of Dudley and foreign secretary, to say that such outrages were unavoidable since the area was 'inhabited exclusively by the lowest and most profligate wretches in the nation'.[23]

The middle years of the century saw a deterioration in social conditions. Prostitutes, claimed a writer about St George's in 1855, were 'the staple of the place. All the trade of the parish seems to depend on them'. Peter Thompson wrote: 'The neighbourhood teems with lazy, idle, drunken, lustful men and degraded, brutalised, hell-branded women – some alas! girls just in their teens. The physical, mental and social conditions of tens of thousands is horrible.'[24]

The East End Mission presented a number of petitions to the Council against the renewal of the licences of some of the brothels. In 1858 the Rector of St George's claimed that one stretch of four streets contained 733 houses, of which 27 were pubs, 13 were beer houses, and 154 were brothels. In fact, the Vestry of St George's itself was controlled by publicans and brothel keepers.

In the same period the pauper population of St George's was also growing as the data from poor relief between 1836 and 1856 show. Hollingshead said that an enormous increase in pauperism had taken place.

The East End was badly hit by the cholera outbreak of 1866. There had been earlier outbreaks since 1832, but it was the cholera of 1866 which affected the area most seriously. Father Lowder of St Peter's, London Docks, wrote of the severe poverty and distress, and of the drainage which had not been improved. The refuse from 'a large manure manufactory' produced 'a very mountain of impurity, hundreds of tons of the very refuse of the streets'.[25] While the Medical Officer's reports for the 1870s and 1880s showed considerable improvements, streets such as London Terrace and Ratcliff Highway continued to figure in accounts of overcrowded housing. Indeed the whole of St George's was, according to Booth, 'the most desolate' and 'appears to stagnate with a squalor peculiar to itself'.[26] In 1883,

25 per cent of deaths in St George's occurred in the workhouses, while infant mortality accounted for over 27 per cent of the total.

The desperate poverty imprinted itself on the consciousness of many observers. One of them wrote in 1891: 'The East End of London is a hell of poverty. Like one enormous, black, motionless giant kraken, the poverty of London lies there in lurking silence, and encircles with its mighty tentacles the life and wealth of the City and of the West End'.[27] While in both St George's and White-chapel, there were improvements in housing in the late 1880s, at the end of the century, considerable poverty remained.

The industries of the East End

Much has been written about the alleged transformation of London from a manufacturing to a commercial city. As early as 1851 John Wheale claimed that London was 'a vast trading and commercial, rather than a manufacturing town.'[28] In fact, London had been the main manufacturing centre of the country for hundreds of years. But in the early nineteenth century, much of the industrial organisation was of a very basic type, based on craft workshops employing small numbers of people. The more offensive trades tended to be concentrated in the East End. Both Rosemary Lane and Petticoat Lane had contained street markets for many years. Petticoat Lane was the old clothes district. In addition to the street trades, seven main areas of industrial activity were important in the East End in the nineteenth century.

First, the docks consisting of London, St Katherine's, West and East India, and Millwall. The expansion of activity here was related to London's international trade. The age of the sailing ship led to casual labour and, in the 1850s, according to Mayhew, there were around 12,000 casual workers in London Docks. However, the introduction of steam reduced the numbers needed and, by the end of the nineteenth century, casual labour was marked by instability and uncertainty. Yet the East End remained 'the most notorious concentration of casual labour in Victorian London.' Stedman Jones has shown how much of London's economy was geared to seasonal production, and how central was casual labour to the growth of the East End labour market. It was 'a casual labour market of almost unparalleled dimensions' with a built-in tendency to perpetuate itself.[29]

The dock workers were mainly English and Irish. The coal heavers, or coal whippers, were almost entirely Irish. They unloaded coal from the ships onto barges. The term 'coal whippers' came into use when a whipping machine was introduced to 'whip' the coal up from the hold.[30] The docks and the riverside industries which grew up around the docks were at the heart of the economic as well as the cultural and political life of the East End. The Labour politics of Stepney was built around the riverside industries, and the Irish and their descendants were to dominate, and control, local politics until the 1960s.

Secondly, clothing. There were two main groups of tailors in the East End, the old established English traders and the Jewish immigrants. The clothes trade became increasingly concentrated in Whitechapel at the end of the nineteenth century, localisation reaching its peak about 1901 at the height of the sub-contract ('sweating') system. There were some Irish tailors south of Commercial Road, and an enclave of Germans in the Tenter Ground, while the warehouse district for ready-made clothes was in Houndsditch and Aldgate. By the end of the nineteenth century the trade had become entirely wholesale. In this transformation, the increase in female labour played a key role. In 1861 clothing workers formed over 10 per cent of the total labour force of London, and the concentration of tailoring was already established in Whitechapel.

Thirdly, boot making. Most of London's boot makers lived in the East End and Hackney, the largest number being in Shoreditch and Bethnal Green. David Schloss's study of 1893 showed the overcrowding and sweated conditions among the Jewish boot makers. Fifty-six per cent of boot makers were overcrowded. In 1891 38 per cent of all London's boot makers were in the East End.[31]

Fourthly, the furniture trade, which had spread eastwards from the City towards Finsbury and Shoreditch by the late eighteenth century. By 1846 the trade was concentrated in the districts around Curtain Road in Shoreditch and Virginia Road in Bethnal Green. Jews from Whitechapel were involved, though not to the same extent as some other trades. By 1911 the E2 and EC2 postal districts (Bethnal Green and Shoreditch) contained more furniture work than the West

End, and by 1939 E2 was well ahead. As late as 1958 most of London's cabinet makers and furniture makers were in the E2 district.[32]

Fifthly, tobacco. In the 1890s the East End and Hackney contained 76 tobacco manufacturing factories of which 49 made cigars only. (There were only 180 such factories in the whole of London.) The cigar trade had been exclusively Jewish in its origin, but by the late nineteenth century many of the workers in cigarettes were Russian, Dutch, Greek and German.

Sixthly, the silk trade, though this was in decline in most parts of the East End and even in Spitalfields itself where there was great distress between 1812 and 1816. After a revival in the 1820s, there was further distress, and this increased after the Treaty with France in 1860. By the 1890s there were around 900 functioning looms in East London, and the number of silk weavers had declined from 12,400 in 1861 to 4,900.

Seventhly, sugar refining was a key area of employment in St George's. But this too was declining, and, according to a Select Committee of the House of Commons, set up in 1879, was almost extinct.

Mission, philanthropy, social action and the settlement movement

The appearance of *The Bitter Cry of Outcast London* in 1883[33] brought missionaries, philanthropists, researchers and social reformers into the area. The Wesleyan presence was a direct result of the pamphlet. In the latter half of the century there was a massive growth of social concern about conditions in the area, and many organisations were founded in these years.

A major element in the history of the East End in the nineteenth century was the creation of the university settlement movement. Universities and colleges created centres, known as 'settlements', to seek to inform students about the realities of urban life, and to bridge the gulf between the academy and the communities of poor people. Toynbee Hall, the first of the settlements and the model for others, was founded in 1884, and was followed by Rivington House in New York City and Hull House in Chicago. As in Britain, the American settlements had close links with academic work.

By 1911 there were forty-five settlements in Britain. In the East

End today, in addition to Toynbee Hall itself, there are also Oxford House, St Margaret's House, and St Hilda's, all in Bethnal Green, Dame Colet House in Stepney, and others. Most of them owed their origin to Christian ideas and practices, but today they are secular organisations, although some of them retain vestiges of their Christian origin.

The settlements were originally of 'Oxbridge' character, founded by university colleges or 'public' schools. They tried to transport refinement and the culture of Oxbridge into East London. Later, some of them developed their own East End style. Thus the work of the Jewish philanthropist Bernhard Baron (1850–1929) led to the creation of the Bernhard Baron St George's Jewish Settlement. From the early 1930s Sir Basil and Lady Rose Henriques took over the work there, while Phyllis Gerson (1903–61) became warden of Stepney Jewish Settlement.

Toynbee Hall itself influenced Tawney, Beveridge (who was sub-warden in 1903), Attlee, and many others. Indeed it helped, indirectly, to shape the politics of the Labour Party, and Stedman Jones is probably correct in his assertion that 'Toynbee Hall has as much claim to be counted among the ancestors of the Labour Party as Methodism, Taff Vale or William Morris'.[34] Staff and members of the settlements were often in key positions in social service and social action.

Some of the settlements had close links with the 'Christian Socialist' revival. Thus Henry Scott Holland, founder of the Christian Social Union, was one of the founders of Oxford House in 1884, and of the F.D. Maurice Hostel in Shaftesbury Street, Shoreditch, in 1898. The first warden of Oxford House was James Adderley, a member of the socialist Guild of St Matthew. Other socialist Christians were not so happy with the settlements. Thus Stewart Headlam was contemptuous of the plans for an Eton College Mission in Hackney Wick in 1888,[35] while Tawney, who stayed at Toynbee Hall from 1903–6, and again in 1908 and 1913, came to see it as too paternalistic. Certainly Samuel Barnett, though he used the term 'socialism', saw nothing wrong with the class system, only with class antagonism. He saw religion as the one force which could turn antagonistic classes into fellow workers. The theology of a benevolent deity was closely linked to ideas of welfare and opposition to class struggle. Indeed Barnett spoke of the 'two nations', seeing 'the danger of collision' between rich and poor to be the great danger of the time. He saw the role of the settlement in part to be to help avert this danger.

Today, however, most of those religious and social traditions are in decline, and the settlement movement has been in crisis for several decades. Some believe that reform and transformation are possible, and see them as valuable resources for the future of social action; others see them as monuments to an age that has passed, and that the future can only lie with different models.[36]

East End poverty: continuing saga

Yet, as the nineteenth century drew to its close, the problems of East End poverty and deprivation remained. In 1806 William Hale had written of the concentration in the East End of the 'casual poor'. Hale claimed that

> the leading cause of that accumulation of extreme poverty which is to be found in the neighbourhood is the gradual removal of the more affluent people into other parishes, while their former dwellings here soon become divided and sub-divided into small lodgings which are immediately occupied by an accession of casual poor, and these, by residence, apprenticeships and other causes very soon gain permanent settlements in the parish.[37]

Over eighty years later, Mr Karamelli of the Whitechapel District Board of Works described Whitechapel as 'the resort of the residuum of the whole country and the refuse of the continent.'[38] Others were not slow to draw fearsome conclusions from the state of the area. In 1889 the socialist feminist Margaret Harkness, who wrote under the pseudonym 'John Law', put words into the mouth of a character in her novel, a parish doctor, which articulated the fears of many.

> The whole of the East End is starving. The West End is bad or mad not to see if things go on like this we must have revolution. One fine day the people about here will go desperate, and they will walk westwards, cutting throats and hurling brickbats.[39]

3

The coming of the Irish and the Jews

Several witnesses described them as forming a distinct community in the midst of the English and compared them in this respect with the Jews . . . Finding the natives unwilling to mix with them, they naturally herd together in particular quarters or streets of the large towns, and thus associate constantly with each other and have rarely any intercourse with the natives of the place, except those of the lowest class.

Poor Law Enquiry (Ireland), 1835[1]

I see no reason to doubt that there has been a substantial increase in the immigration of aliens into London in 1890, and an increase of that special immigration which has attracted so much attention of late years, that of Polish Jews, many of whom are in a state of great poverty, and some of actual destitution.

Mr Giffen's Annual Report to the Board of Trade, 1891[2]

The stereotype of the Irish

The Irish have always formed the largest immigrant community in England, but it was during the nineteenth century that their numbers grew dramatically. The Irish-born population of England and Wales was not large in 1795, but increased from 1.8 per cent of the population in 1801 to 2.9 per cent in 1851 and 3 per cent in 1861, while in Scotland the percentages were 4.8, 7.2 and 6.7. For the East End of London, the nineteenth century was the peak period for the Irish presence. In more recent years it has been most marked in other parts of London.

The nineteenth century also saw the formation of a type of anti-

Irish racist polemic which both fuelled later types of racial rhetoric and probably provided the historical basis for recent writing about the 'underclass'. Prejudice against the Irish people has deep roots within English history. When the Norman feudal lords invaded Ireland in the twelfth century, it was reported that they encountered a profligate, uncouth, impious, barbarous, rebellious and filthy people. This view of the Irish was promoted by Gerald of Wales whose *History and Topography of Ireland* was published in the reign of Elizabeth I and continued to be accepted as factually accurate for seven hundred years. A statute of 1413 had sought to remove both Irish beggars and Irish clerics from England. Christopher Hill commented, in reference to the Cromwellian period, that many English people spoke of the Irish 'in terms not far removed from those which Nazis used about Slavs'.[3]

Jonathan Swift, writing in the eighteenth century, suggested that by fattening up the children of the poor and selling them off as food, one would reduce the numbers of papists in the population, while John Curry in 1775 claimed that the Irish were 'considered scarcely human'. In the same year Richard Twiss wrote his account of *A Tour of Ireland* in which he described the population as 'a distinct race from the rest of mankind'. Similar sentiments were common in the nineteenth century. A poem in *Punch* in 1848 made a direct comparison between the Irish ('six foot Paddy') and blacks, including the line 'You to Sambo I compare'. Charles Kingsley described the Irish as 'human chimpanzees' while Thomas Carlyle spoke of them as 'a black howling Babel of superstitious savages'. Disraeli spoke of 'this wild reckless, indolent, uncertain and superstitious race'. The Irish were widely regarded as essentially lazy and work-shy. Thus an article in *Fraser's Magazine* in 1847 said that, of all races, the Irish were 'the most idle and the most fickle'. The Poor Law Commission claimed that the Irish were the means of communicating 'infectious disease'. And there was much more to the same effect.[4]

Irish migration and settlement in London

As early as 1629 there were protests in the City of London that the area had been troubled by 'a great many Irish beggars'. In the mid-nineteenth century the Marist Fathers who had moved into

Underwood Road, Spitalfields, were worried about the ignorance and superstition of the Irish immigrants. Others saw them as 'revolutionary agents'.[5] In 1818 an inspector of the House of Recovery, giving evidence to the Select Committee on Contagious Fever in London, identified Saffron Hill, Gray's Inn Lane, and districts in the St Giles area as the main settlements, but also mentioned Whitechapel. In fact there had been an Irish presence in the East End in the eighteenth century, and there were disturbances in Spitalfields in 1763, 1765, 1766 and 1769, and in Shadwell in 1768 which led to the capital conviction of seven coal heavers. During the Gordon Riots of 1780, chapels in Virginia Lane and Nightingale Lane in the Shadwell area were wrecked.

After 1815 the Irish in London were mainly Catholic peasants who had been driven from their land through crop failures. The *Report on Education* in 1816 described the Irish population in Shadwell as 'dissolute and depraved' though it acknowledged that they were not involved in begging. The Roman clergy at this time believed that there were around 14,000 Irish in Shadwell. Francis Place in 1816 stressed the poverty of the Irish, mentioning Ratcliff Highway among the poorest areas. Place noted that 'the poorest and most dissolute people in Spitalfields' were still of higher status than 'the mere Irish'.[6]

Between 1841 and 1861, over 60,000 Irish moved to London. The famine of 1846–7 followed the destruction of almost the entire potato crop, and a million Irish people died while another million went to North America. By 1880 two-thirds of the Irish-born were living outside Ireland. The mass emigration was without precedent, damaging the Irish economy and affecting every aspect of life in Ireland. The population of Ireland fell from eight million in 1841 to four million in 1961, while that of the south fell from six million to 2.8 million in the same period.[7] They were overwhelmingly a rural people for whom London was their first experience of urban life. Lynn Hollen Lees has rightly said that 'the Irish became an urban people when they left their homeland'.[8] The pattern was to be repeated a century later with the arrival of the immigrants from rural Bangladesh.

At the 1851 Census the Irish-born population in London numbered 108,548. The urbanisation of the Irish was aided by the demand for Irish labour in England in the manual sector (though there was also demand in the Kent hop fields and agricultural areas), and the Irish have remained a significant presence within the urban manual labour market from those years onwards.

The nineteenth-century documentation always associated the Irish with poverty and unhealthy conditions. The Poor Law Enquiry of 1835 noted the concentration of the Irish in the building trades and the existence of 'Irish quarters' where, they claimed, there was hardly any intercourse with the indigenous population. The Irish, the report felt, were a 'substratum' beneath a more civilised community. But Lyn Hollen Lees has stressed that the Irish were not 'locked into an urban ghetto' but formed rather a chain of Irish buildings and enclaves within English working-class territory.

The Irish in the East End

According to the Mendicity Report of 1815, most of the local Irish beggars were in Shoreditch, Spitalfields and Brick Lane, and 'some wretched places behind Whitechapel Church'. The report claimed that many subsisted 'entirely by prostitution and beggary'. It is not clear how reliable this report is. Indeed much of the mid-century data is highly anecdotal and inaccurate. One example is the writing of Rev. Samuel Garratt who delivered a lecture on 'The Irish in London' in 1852. Garratt saw the Irish as a 'pariah class'. His account is typical of many at this period, and it is likely that the origins of the modern 'underclass' idea lie, to a great extent, in the stereotypes of 'Irish quarters' from these years.[9]

However, while there were certainly concentrations in very poor districts, the Irish created 'not a ghetto but a string of settlements tucked into the tumbledown corners of working class London'.[10] The heavy concentrations were in St Giles (Camden), St Olave's (South London), Southwark and Whitechapel, and only in these districts did the Irish represent over ten per cent of the population. It is quite wrong therefore to see the Irish as 'a free floating underclass without roots in any one geographic area'.[11]

The districts of high density Irish settlement in the East End were between Rosemary Lane and East Smithfield, Goodman's Fields, and up to the border of Aldgate. The percentages were as high as 60 per cent on the south side of Rosemary Lane, and 74 per cent around Crown Court and Glass House Yard. But very few streets were entirely English or Irish, and there was probably more social intercourse than many accounts suggest.

In terms of occupation, the Irish were heavily represented in labouring, transport and construction. In a small study by Jackson of the 1851 census data, the largest groups of Irish in the East End were labourers, coal whippers and dock labourers.[12] As early as 1835 the secretary of St Katherine's Dock Company reported that the business of the docks could not have developed without the Irish labour.[13] There were also the 'street Irish', including the coster-mongers, discussed by Mayhew in 1861.[14]

In response to the Irish migration, Roman churches were founded in the East End – St Patrick's, Johnson Street in 1849, St Mary and St Michael's, Commercial Road in 1850, St Anne's, Underwood Road in 1855, and St Patrick's, Wapping in 1880.

The Irish in the census data 1841–61

The census data for 1841–61 for the East End both indicate the extent of the Irish presence and contradict the stereotypes. Contrary to much of the nineteenth-century writing, both anecdotal and 'sociological', there were few heavy concentrations in 1841 apart from Crown Court and King Street in St George's. In these districts the Irish presence had declined by 1861. The Irish-born were a mere 4 per cent of the population in St George's in 1841, and 7 per cent in 1851 and 1861. Whitechapel too was a very 'local-born area' in 1841. In Spitalfields the Irish were less than 5 per cent of the population, though there were a few heavy concentrations. In Goulston Court, over 50 per cent were Irish, and Goodman's Fields and Rosemary Lane had large numbers. In 1861 the Irish population was 141 in an area with a total population of 2,751.

The growth of the Irish population around the riverside districts of East London provided the infrastructure for local 'Labourism' in East End politics, and for the ministry of the Roman Church, which remained essentially an Irish immigrant Church until the 1960s. Although both the Irish population and the Roman Church have declined numerically in East London – as indeed has the Labour Party – the influence of that hundred-year period from the mid-nineteenth to the mid-twentieth century had a major influence on the area which has remained. Only with the total disappearance of the docks, and the partial disappearance of the working-class culture which was linked to it, did the Irish influence on the East End decline to the point of disappearance itself.

Early Jewish settlement in London

The Jews had been expelled from England in 1290, and again in 1609, and did not officially return until 1656. But there were at least 100 Jews in London in the mid-sixteenth century. In February 1657, some land at Mile End was leased for use as a Jewish cemetery, and it was in this year also that the first synagogue to be established since the expulsion of 1290 was created.

The earliest congregation of this resettlement in London was that of the Sephardim, a community of Spanish and Portuguese origin. At the accession of Charles II, this community numbered around thirty-five families, and by the end of the seventeenth century it had increased to several hundred. There were also Marranos, Jews of mixed ancestry who had become Christian, and by the mid-sixteenth century it was customary for all Marranos in London to be buried at St Dunstan's, Stepney. In 1696 Benjamin Levy acquired land in Alderney Road for an Ashkenazi cemetery, while the Sephardim obtained the freehold of a cemetery in Stepney in 1737. Soon after the Restoration, the Ashkenazi Jews formed the majority, their number increasing rapidly after the Bohemian persecutions of 1744–5 and the Haidamacch massacres in the Ukraine in 1768. By 1800 the number of Jews in London was estimated at between 15,000 and 20,000.

These early Jewish settlers were concentrated in a fairly small area in the eastern part of the City and part of what is now termed the East End. In 1695, for example, 70 per cent of the 850 Jews in the City lived in five contiguous parishes. In the small district of St James's, Duke's Place, they formed over 25 per cent of the population. The Great Synagogue had been founded in 1690 in Broad Court which later became known as Duke's Place, and a new Portuguese synagogue was built in Bevis Marks in 1701, replacing that of 1657. A secession in 1704–7 led to the creation of the Hambro Synagogue in Magpie Alley, off Fenchurch Street. In 1761 a further secession brought into being the New Synagogue in Leadenhall Street.

There were smaller communities in the East End in Rosemary

Lane, Gun Square and Cutler Street. The earliest synagogues in the East End were established in 1748 in Goodman's Fields and in 1790 in Houndsditch. By the mid-nineteenth century there had been little movement into Spitalfields, and few Jews lived east of Brick Lane. But in the 1850s and 1860s synagogues were established in Sandy's Row, Bishopsgate and Fashion Street, as well as the Dutch Synagogue in White's Row, the Society of Lovers of Peace (*Chevrat Ahavat Shalom*) in Whitechapel, and the Stepney Green Synagogue.

The Ashkenazi community did not begin to develop until the late seventeenth century. The geographical centre of this early community appears to have been Rose Alley, later known as Mitre Street, in Aldgate. By the end of the eighteenth century, the number of Sephardim in London was estimated at 4,000, about one-fifth of all the Jews in London. In 1795 Patrick Colquhoun estimated that there were between 20,000 and 26,000 Jews in England of whom 15–20,000 were in London.

In the late eighteenth century, there was a marked spread of the Ashkenazi communities from the restricted area around Duke's Place eastwards into the East End. The expansion was mainly in an easterly direction because of the City restrictions on retail trade. Petticoat Lane became largely Jewish at the close of the eighteenth century.

At this period Goodman's Fields was the most fashionable of the Jewish neighbourhoods, and Strype in 1720 described it as being inhabited mainly by prosperous Jews. Around this district were four streets containing elegant private mansions – Prescott Street, Mansell Street, Leman Street, and Ayliffe Street – 'where the elite of the ghetto held court'. Further north, Bethnal Green contained a settlement of Jews and there had been an attempt to create a small synagogue there in 1747. The Old Nichol (Boundary) district did not become Jewish until the 1890s. Wellclose Square contained some prominent Jewish people. Soon after the founding of the London Hospital in 1740, one of its five houses became known as 'the Jews' House'. Specifically Jewish wards were allocated from 1842 to 1853 and in 1860, and four new Jewish wards were added in 1904. During the middle years of the nineteenth century, various Jewish organisations were formed in the East End.

Jews in the East End in the nineteenth century

From about the middle of the eighteenth century the wealthier Jews had begun to leave the City for areas outside London. The gulf between the rich and the poor Jews grew wider, the poor often falling into a state of acute distress. It is from this period that the entry of poor Jews into the old clothes and peddling trades can be dated. In the East End 'Rag Fair' developed as the centre of the Jewish street trades. In 1832 some observers laid the blame for cholera at the doors of the street Jews.

In Whitechapel, the Jews were engaged in pencil manufacture, diamond cutting, and engraving. There were watchmakers, jewellers and silversmiths in most Jewish communities but relatively few Jewish tailors in the communities outside London. Those Jews who remained in London tended to begin as hawkers, and then progressed to stalls or proper shops.

The East End was the centre of the Jewish street trades. Mayhew, who devoted a whole section of his study to the 'street Jews', estimated that there were around 35,000 Jews in England, of whom 18,000 were in London. He went on to describe the nature and location of Jewish street trading as it was in 1861. They sold watches and jewels, shells, tortoises, parrots and foreign birds, cigars and pipes, and particularly cigars.[15] At this period, the Jewish manufacturing districts were Houndsditch and Aldgate, with jewellers of an inferior kind in Whitechapel and Houndsditch, and various manufacturers in Mansell Street, Great Prescott Street, Alie Street and Leman Street.

The competition from poor Irish immigrants was a significant factor in reducing the numbers of Jews in street trading. By 1850 there were probably only about 1000 Jewish street traders of all kinds in London out of a total Jewish population of 15,000. The combination of competition from the Irish, and the anxiety of the Jews to improve their status, led to a decrease in the numbers of Jews in street trades. In 1840 the Report on the Handloom Weavers noted: 'Buying and selling cheap, useful articles in the street is an employment which naturally falls to the weak and destitute; and a body of men like the Jews, in possession of fine physical condition, do not beneficially employ themselves in such an occupation.'[16]

Summing up the economic activities of Anglo-Jewry in 1850,

Lipman noted the beginnings of the growth of an artisan class, and of a professional middle class. Indeed, cigar making was more prevalent than tailoring among the London Jews of this period. In 1860 Whitechapel and St George's contained 2,294 Dutch and 894 Poles who were employed in what has been termed 'the oldest of immigrant trades'.[17] Tobacco remained more common as an occupation among the Dutch than among the East European Jews.

In 1859 it was estimated that the Jewish population of London was between 25,000 and 30,000, and that most of this population was composed of 'the poor'. Rev. John Mills, in a study of 1853, placed 3,000 in the 'upper class', 8,000 in the 'middle class', and 12,000 in the 'lower class'. Of the latter group, he claimed that 'many are in daily want of the necessities of life, and a still larger number scarcely able to obtain sufficient to support existence'.[18]

Between 1815 and the end of the century a Jewish middle class emerged. Jews were moving to the West End early in the century, and later a movement to the northern suburbs developed. The number of Jews in banking and commerce was growing, while those engaged in the street trades declined. Mayhew noted that Jews were still selling cigars and sponges in Petticoat Lane and elsewhere, but this was changing by mid-century. By 1860 the core of the Jewish community was a middle class of merchants and shopkeepers.[19]

In the East End there were still two distinct Jewish areas: Houndsditch to Middlesex Street, and Goodman's Fields, near Whitechapel Road. The latter contained the 'four streets' – Great Prescott, Alie, Leman, and Mansell Streets – residences of wealthy Jewish merchants. Probably two-thirds of London's Jews lived in these two districts. By 1850 the Jewish area did not extend far in an eastward direction, nor was there much movement into St George's. Knight's *London* of 1851 made no reference to Jews in a lengthy chapter on Spitalfields. There were few Jews in Mile End and Stepney Green. Between 1850 and 1880, the Jewish population of London increased by 125 per cent and after 1872 the majority came from Poland.

The immigration from Eastern Europe

The assassination of Tsar Alexander II on 12 March 1881 led to an attack on Jews in Elisavetgrad, and to a wave of terror throughout Eastern Europe. On 3 May 1882 the May Laws forbade Jews to settle outside the towns, and prohibited them from doing business on Sundays and Christian holidays. Intolerance increased, and in 1890 Jews were expelled from Moscow and Kiev. Emigration began in 1880, continued in 1881 and 1882, with a further wave in 1892. More left in 1899, and in 1903–4 after the pogroms at Kishinev and Homel. In 1886 alien Poles were expelled from Prussia, and in 1900 from Rumania. In 1895 *The Protocols of the Elders of Zion* appeared, a text which was to provide the basis for later 'international Jewish conspiracy' theories.

In 1880 the *Jewish Chronicle* estimated that of the Jewish poor 90 per cent were Russian.[20] By 1901 the number of 'Russians and Poles' in England and Wales was 95,425, and in 1911 this had grown to 106,082, with the majority in the East End. As early as 1881, 77.5 per cent of Russians and Poles in London were in the East End, and 82 per cent by 1892.

The Jewish Board of Guardians, founded in 1859, played a helpful role in providing social support, but was hostile to the immigration as such. Russell and Lewis said that English Jews were the main enemy of the Jewish immigrants.[21] The Board supported voluntary repatriation, and, between 1880 and 1914, helped 50,000 to return to their place of origin.

The Jewish quarter

By 1900 there was a geographical concentration north of Whitechapel Road, with a shift towards St George's in 1881, and towards Bethnal Green in 1897. However, Bethnal Green remained a 'Christian area' and was to remain a base for antisemitic, and, later, for fascist organisations. But it was Whitechapel which was to be 'the centre of immigrant life in every generation of Anglo-Jewish history'[22] – until quite recently.

By the beginning of the twentieth century, the Jewish population was heavily concentrated in Whitechapel where they formed between 90 and 100 per cent of the population. It was this geographical concentration which, according to Lipman, 'led to the exaggeration of the immigration into a national problem'.[23]

To the north, Bethnal Green remained very English and local-born, while to the south Wapping remained overwhelmingly Irish.

While the population statistics changed significantly over the next fifty years, as late as the 1950s the general contours of the three areas stayed essentially the same. Bethnal Green retained the 'kith and kin' character identified in the work of Willmott and Young, and symbolised in the rise to fame of the Kray twins: an area of tightly knit, often interrelated, families, very white, and containing few immigrants from elsewhere. Wapping, while the Irish ratio had declined, remained solidly white, an island community, and the descendants of the Irish formed the backbone of Labour politics. But in Whitechapel, the heart of the Jewish community, out-migration was continuing, and it was this process which was to characterise the future.

4
The Whitechapel ghetto, Anglo-Jewry and antisemitism

If you were in Whitechapel sixty-five years ago I don't suppose you would recognise where you were. First of all you would hardly see any Jews. There was a small Jewish colony between Bishopsgate and Aldgate High Street but it was not in the least obvious to the eye.

GEORGE LANSBURY, 1935[1]

The Whitechapel problem thus turns out to be European in scope . . . the East End Jews must be regarded as in effect an alien community.

RUSSELL AND LEWIS, 1900[2]

'Uncle, what's it like to be Jewish all your life?'
'S'all right,' he said.

DANNY ABSE, *Ash on a Young Man's Sleeve*[3]

The emergence of the Whitechapel ghetto

The migration of middle-class Jews away from the East End had begun in the early nineteenth century. But during the later years of that century the East End became the centre of a new Jewish community whose origins lay in eastern Europe. The concentration of this new community in Whitechapel reached its peak around 1900. In the years immediately preceding the First World War there was a movement into north, west, north-west and south London. After 1918 the dispersal intensified, and by 1930, when the Jewish population of London was about 200,000, less than half of them were living in the East End. In 1929 it was estimated that the Jewish population of the East London boroughs was 62,000 in Stepney, 13,000 in Bethnal Green, 48,000 in Shoreditch, and 4,800 in Poplar. During the Second World War and its aftermath, the Jewish population was further reduced, as indeed was the East End population as a whole. From the Whitechapel ghetto, Jews moved to Marble Arch, Regent's Park, Hampstead, Edgware, Ilford, Wanstead, and Woodford, as well as other parts of the country and the world.

In 1888 the *Jewish Chronicle* claimed that the concentration of Jews in Whitechapel had strengthened the belief that they were an alien race. It claimed that their practice of 'appropriating whole streets' had led to the view that the Jew was 'an alien in every sense of the word'.[4] Yet, while there were some sharp lines of demarcation between communities, the social intercourse between Jew and non-Jew was considerable. The strikes of dockers (mostly Irish) and garment workers (mostly Jewish) in 1912 created new links between Jews and Gentiles. Christians would often help their Jewish neighbours with Passover cleaning, and Jews often helped to arrange Roman Catholic processions.[5]

Whitechapel was the area of most intense Jewish settlement. In the early years of the settlement, very few Jews moved northward into Bethnal Green, which in 1881 was estimated to have only 925 'persons of foreign birth and nationality', compared with 160,000 in what was to become the Borough of Stepney. Writing later on antisemitism in Bethnal Green, Robb observed that 'Bethnal Green, being already overcrowded with local born folk, who were not prepared to make room for foreigners, was less hospitable to these people than Stepney, where their co-religionists formed a large part of the population'.[6]

Jerry White, in his study of Rothschild Buildings, noted that Bethnal Green 'had a consistently threatening reputation' for the Jewish inhabitants, citing one former inhabitant's words:

> Bethnal Green was a Christian area, and we avoided it because we were afraid of being beaten up. I remember a friend of my mother's coming up to us with his hat all bashed in, and he had been attacked at the end of Brick Lane going towards Bethnal Green. I remember somebody saying, 'Well, why did you go that way?' He

should have gone another way to avoid Bethnal Green. It had a
very bad name.[7]

This early reputation is an important factor in understanding the
role of Bethnal Green as a base for the building up of later racist
and fascist organisations in the 1930s and 1970s.

Later, as tenement dwellings began to replace the old slum houses,
there was a significant movement of Jews into such districts as the
Boundary Estate between Bethnal Green and Shoreditch. This district, the old 'Jago' or 'Little Nichol' district, had been entirely non-
Jewish until the slum clearance, but in 1900 Russell and Lewis's map
showed that some of the streets there had become 50 per cent Jewish.
Some writers have seen the former white inhabitants of the Jago as
forming a kind of 'lumpen' base for the growth of antisemitic
violence in the East End, but this is an oversimplified view. By 1901
the foreign-born population of Bethnal Green was 4,364 of whom
more than half came from Russia and Poland, and most of the
remainder from Germany, Austria and the Balkans. This figure
amounted to about 3.5 per cent of the population, though one
schoolteacher who taught in the Boundary Street district in 1919
claimed that 90 per cent of the schoolchildren at that time were
Jewish. One study of the 1920s and 1930s suggested that Shoreditch
(north of the Boundary) was only 0.1 per cent Jewish, Bethnal Green
about 5 per cent, and Stepney 85 per cent.[8]

A valuable guide to the growth of the Jewish quarter is contained
in the street classifications in the Booth Survey of 1892. Booth's study
of the streets included in the School Board District covered the years
1887–9, and showed the extent to which Jewish tailors in particular
had established themselves in the Commercial Street area. He noted
the presence of Jewish tailors in the area between Leman Street and
Whitechapel High Street, and also in Backchurch Lane, Commercial
Road and Leman Street, while in the district between Middlesex
Street, Commercial Street and Fleur de Lis Street were Jewish tailors,
general dealers, bootmakers, small tradesmen, cigar makers, cabinet
makers, labourers, hawkers and loafers. Booth noted the movement
of Jews into St George's, both in Commercial Road and in the
district between Cable Street and Commercial Road, which, he
claimed, was 'largely inhabited by Jews and Germans, tailors and

sugar bakers, etc, while the south mainly consists of a rather low waterside labouring population'.[9]

At the heart of the Whitechapel ghetto, as it developed towards the end of the nineteenth century, was Goulston Street. Here were concentrated refugees from the terrible overcrowding in Kiev where the streets of the Jewish quarter were not more than four feet wide and the tumble-down old houses seemed ready to fall down. So it was from even greater poverty that the immigrants came to the poverty of Whitechapel. Walter Besant, writing in 1901, referred to the East End Jews as 'the poorest of the very poor' and claimed that they occupied, almost to the exclusion of others, a triangular area of the East End, the area around Middlesex Street, Wentworth Street and the streets to right and left of them.[10]

Israel Zangwill, who began his *Children of the Ghetto* (1895) by stressing that the Whitechapel ghetto was 'of voluntary formation', went on to describe vividly the district around Fashion Street. Here, he said, were 'some of the vilest quarters and filthiest rookeries in the capital of the civilised world'.[11] Non-Jewish writers also described the area as dirty, and they tended often to blame the conditions on the habits of the immigrants. Thus a factory inspector, in evidence to the Sweating Commission, claimed that the habits of the people were 'very, very dirty'. Quoting this evidence, Montague Crackenthorpe, a leading critic of the immigration, claimed in 1892 that the immigrants 'lower the standard of living all round', reduce the wage rate, encourage sweating, and breed great discontent and inter-religious hatred.[12] Similar sentiments were expressed in 1886 in the *Pall Mall Gazette* which announced 'a *Judenhetz* brewing in East London', and published a letter which claimed that 'the foreign Jews of no nationality whatever are becoming a pest and a menace to the poor native-born East Ender'.[13]

One of the features of the ghetto which was a cause of angry debate throughout these years was that of sweated labour. The term 'sweating' probably owes its origin to Charles Kingsley's novel *Alton Locke* (1850). It became the name given to a system of labour in which the component parts of an article were handed out by factories to 'small masters' or sub-contractors. Sweated labour occurred in small premises, often basements or attics, with a small group of operatives working long hours for little pay. The East End was at the heart of the sweating system, and Jews were often blamed for the system. However, the House of Lords Select Committee showed that sweating existed where there was no foreign labour. Yet there is no doubt that the working conditions in the tailoring trade in the Jewish quarter of Whitechapel were appalling. Most of the workshops were very small. A study for the Booth survey showed that, of 901 coat-making workshops, 685 employed less than ten workers, while a report in *The Lancet* in 1884 showed that in Hanbury Street eighteen workers were operating in one room with damp walls and rotting roof. Many of the workers had respiratory illnesses. The situation only began to improve after the Factory Act of 1901.

The growth of the new Jewish community led to the foundation of many new synagogues and chevras, associations which functioned as benefit clubs as well as study centres. By 1892 there were thirty or forty chevras in the East End. Jewish charitable foundations and wealthy philanthropists played a vital role in building up the infrastructure of the area. A key figure in these years was Samuel Montagu, who helped to found both the Jewish Board of Guardians and the Jewish Dispersion Committee. The Board of Guardians certainly maintained links with poor Jews in the East End, and made a contribution to health care and welfare activity. However, its role in relationship to the improvement of conditions in housing and employment, as well as to the response to the anti-aliens campaign, is open to dispute, and has indeed been disputed. There was a vast cultural gulf between the rich influential Jews and the poor Jews in Whitechapel.

For example, for the most part, the Jewish leadership supported immigration controls and repatriation of 'undesirables'. The role of the *Jewish Chronicle* in this respect is a curious mixture of support for poor Jews and opposition to the immigration. Lord Rothschild said that 'we have a new Poland on our hands in East London', while N.S. Joseph of the Jewish Board of Guardians climbed on the anti-aliens bandwagon at an early stage.[14]

The early years of the twentieth century were years in which the East End Jewish community was coming to consciousness as a social unit. Awareness of social responsibility at all levels marked much of the discussion and writing in this period. For instance, it was becoming clear that there were serious problems relating to the welfare of Jewish orphan children in 'workhouses'.[15] By the First World War, local Jews were moving into the politics of Stepney.

Clement Attlee recalled that, when in 1919 he was elected to Stepney Borough Council, it was one-third Jewish and two-thirds Irish. But from the end of the war, the Jews were moving out, helped by the extension of the Northern Line. By 1929 East London contained only 60 per cent of London's Jews, in contrast to 90 per cent in 1889.

Relations with the local Christian churches were complex and varied. The Rector of Whitechapel, Rev. C.G. Hanks, writing in 1914, stressed that the Christian role was 'in its essence propagandist and proselytizing', though he also insisted that Christians should encourage Jews to hold fast to their faith unless they felt driven to accept Christian beliefs. The Rector of nearby Spitalfields was more pessimistic, and felt that 'extinction is the fate awaiting the church's work in Spitalfields'.[16] Other Christian groups were aggressively evangelistic. The London Society for Promoting Christianity among the Jews was based in Bethnal Green, but also had a hall in Goulston Street for 'aggressive evangelistic work'. The Hebrew Christian Testimony to Israel, founded in 1893, was originally based in Soho, but in 1901 moved to Whitechapel Road.

A related problem was that of Jewish children who came under the influence of Christian clergy as a result of being placed in institutions. The Jewish community was also concerned about the growing abuse of the Sabbath. So-called Jewish clubs would hold hockey matches on Saturdays and this led to minor controversies. The Jewish National Union was formed to secure Saturday rest for Jewish workers in the East End. But Saturday morning business grew in some of the Jewish markets. While to the outsider, the most marked feature of the Jewish community was its unity, many Jews saw fragmentation and disintegration. As late as the Second World War, the Mayor of Stepney could claim – though with how much accuracy is not clear – that 'English is not spoken at all by many of the people'.[17] But to many Jewish people, it was the loss of the Jewish social and cultural heritage which alarmed them most.

Out of the East End Anglo-Jewish community emerged a whole literary culture. The portrayal of Fagin in Charles Dickens' *Oliver Twist* had typified the literary characterisation, as well as much of the folk mythology, of the East End Jew in the mid-nineteenth century. Dickens himself was anxious to deny accusations of anti-semitism, pointing out that Fagin was a Jew, because at the time 'the class of criminal almost invariably was a Jew'. It was some time before Jewish writers presented an alternative portrayal to the common stereotype. The growth of the Anglo-Jewish novel closely paralleled the growth of the East End ghetto. Earlier novelists such as Julia Frankau and Amy Levy wrote about middle-class West End Jews, while, as late as 1933, when Joseph Leftwich published his collection *Yisroel: the First Jewish Omnibus*, the English pieces were mainly written by descendants of the pre-1881 immigrants. But the immigration from eastern Europe entirely transformed the character of Anglo-Jewry and its cultural portrayal.

The most famous novel of East End Jewish life was Israel Zangwill's *Children of the Ghetto* (1892). Zangwill's father had come from Rybinishki in Latvia, but Israel himself was born in London in 1864. 'I am a Jew, of course, and proud of it,' he pointed out, 'but I am not an alien. I am a pure Cockney. I was born in London within the sound of Bow Bells.'[18]

The East End figured prominently in the novels which emerged from the period after the First World War. They included Izak Coller's *The Five Books of Mr Moses* (1929) and Simon Blumenfeld's *Phineas Kahn, Portrait of an Immigrant* (1937). Other novels from the 1930s included Noah Elstein's *Plight of Pereretz* (1930), Simon Bluemfeld's *Jew Boy* (1935), and Wally Goldman's *East End My Cradle* (1940). Most of the characters in these novels were working class, and the themes were strikes, unemployment and political activity. In other novels of second-generation Jewry, non-Jews appear, and antisemitism and intermarriage had become key themes. Thus Louis Golding's *Magnolia Street* (1932) saw intermarriage as an answer to the 'Jewish problem'. Goldman's *East End My Cradle* was written against the background of Cable Street, the tailoring trade, and the imminent break up of the East End Jewish community, which was brought about by the Blitz. The decline of the East End as a Jewish cultural centre was reflected in the literature which that decline helped to inspire.

The anti-aliens agitation

The first recorded public meeting to mobilise opposition to 'alien immigration' took place at Mile End on 19 April 1887, and was chaired by Arnold White who was to figure prominently in the subsequent polemic.[19] White edited *The Destitute Alien in Great Britain* (1892). One of the contributors to this volume was Rev. S.G. Reaney, whose unrestrained language is typical of much of the polemic directed against the ghetto. He argued that

> before we are prepared to receive the motley multitude that comes from over the sea, and across the vast plains of Russia, with open arms, as political exiles, and as religious refugees suffering from high, noble and exalted virtues, for faithfulness to the faith of their fathers and to their God, we must know more about them, and we must assure ourselves that the only reason for their expulsion from Russia is because they are so pure and saintly and true to the best traditions of the remarkable race to which they belong . . .

Reaney went on to say that at times

> those who live and labour in the great East End feel hot and angry at the sight of the faces so un-English and the sound of the speech so utterly foreign, which crowd pavement and road on Whitechapel Waste, about the Minories, and all away down Commercial Street and Bethnal Green . . . In face, instinct, language and character their children are aliens, and still exiles. They seldom really become citizens . . .

Reaney concluded his reflections by expressing surprise that 'the depression has not turned to anger and that we have not had a "Jew-hunt" such as has been known abroad'.[20]

Throughout the closing years of the nineteenth century, the complaint that the Jewish immigrants had 'taken over' Whitechapel, and that an 'alien invasion' had occurred, was heard from many quarters. Sir William Marriott, Conservative MP for Brighton, commented in 1893 that 'there are some streets [in Whitechapel] you may go through and hardly know that you are in England'.[21]

The editor of *The Clarion*, after a 'pleasant Saturday afternoon' in the East End, described it as a 'strange experience because within half-an-hour's walk of the City Boundaries we were in a foreign country'.[22] The Bishop of Stepney added his own complaint in 1902: 'The East End of London is being swamped by aliens who were coming in like an army of locusts, eating up the native population or turning them out. Their churches were being continually left like islands in the midst of an alien sea.'[23] On the other hand, a writer in 1896 claimed that 'the ever-increasing Jewish population of White-chapel, apart from the social morass of the inner ghetto, is rapidly becoming Anglicised.'[24]

If 'Anglicisation' was occurring, Major Evans-Gordon, the MP for Stepney, had not noticed it. He wrote:

> East of Aldgate one walks into a foreign town. In the by-streets north and south of the main thoroughfares it is an exception to hear the English language spoken. The advertisements on the walls are in Yiddish and written in Hebrew characters. Notice of lodgings, etc, are in the same tongue. Nine-tenths of the names over the shops are foreign, and even where an English patronymic is seen, it is used for the most part by foreigners who have adopted it for purposes of their own.[25]

Evans-Gordon saw the arrival of the Jews, the 'alien invasion' as he called it, as a kind of disease. Another campaigner referred to the new Jews as 'the very scum of the unhealthiest of continental nations'.[26]

A constant claim was that the new immigrants were paupers. 'Alien immigrant' and 'destitute alien' were often used inter-changeably. Evidence from the Charity Organisation Society and from the Whitechapel Union does not bear this out, but the leaders of the anti-aliens agitation made this central to their case. Arnold White's symposium of 1892 attempted to bring together evidence to show that the immigrants were overwhelmingly 'paupers'. It is a familiar story which is repeated in our own day within the anti-immigrant rhetoric.

In 1900 Russell and Lewis claimed that 'race prejudice is strong' but they also noted 'the complete absence of anti-Semitic feeling'.[27] Others, such as Arthur Dalton, Rector of Stepney, believed that there was strong anti-immigrant feeling, and the *East London Advertiser* warned that 'the greatest industrial area in the capital city of Europe will be entirely populated by Yiddish speaking aliens'.[28]

The anti-aliens campaign entered parliament also as early as 1887. In March 1887, Captain Colomb, Conservative MP for Bow and Bromley, had attacked 'the immigration of destitute aliens without restriction',[29] and in February 1888 the government agreed to appoint a Select Committee of Inquiry. It used the phrase 'the immigration of destitute aliens'. However, the reports from the Commons (1889) and Lords (1890) did not recommend legislation.

In September 1890 the Association for Preventing the Immigration of Destitute Aliens was formed, with Mr Wilkins as its secretary and Arnold White as one of its leaders. In 1892 an Aliens Bill was prepared, but the return of the Liberals in July, and possibly the publication of Zangwill's *Children of the Ghetto*, delayed its introduction.[30]

The Conservatives, then as now, were committed to immigration control, and, on their return to power, they formed a Parliamentary Immigration Committee. In July 1894, when Lord Salisbury introduced an Aliens Bill, the East End was at the centre of the debate. In 1892 Thomas Benkin told the electors of south-west Bethnal Green:

> I consider the time has arrived when statesmen should consider measures which will directly benefit 'John Bull' without due regard to outside and foreign interests. I am in favour of stringent measures to prohibit the wholesale immigration of pauper foreigners. I warmly support the principle of maintaining 'Great Britain for the British'.[31]

As in most such campaigns, the anti-aliens agitators were anxious to deny that they were motivated by racialist or antisemitic feelings. Evans-Gordon insisted that his opposition was 'purely on social and economic grounds'. It has been said that 'the closer the agitators came to antisemitism, the more fervent were their denials'.[32] Terms such as 'undesirable aliens' were in constant use. Arnold White saw the world as dominated by 'the rich and powerful Hebrews who are really the rulers of the civilised world'. He warned of the importation of a 'criminal Jewish population', immediately going on to say that he was 'quite ignorant of the religion of these people'. These sentiments were repeated throughout the debates. H. Forde Ridley, MP for Bethnal Green South West, said in 1902 that the issue was 'foreign paupers and aliens as a whole', referring to 'Polish and Russian Jews'.[33] On 9 May 1901 Evans-Gordon founded the British Brothers' League to prevent any further immigration of 'destitute or undesirable aliens'.

Much of the anti-immigrant rhetoric was marked by warnings of deterioration. Harry Lawson, Conservative MP for Mile End, spoke of the 'backward march to physical deterioration'.[34] The Jewish immigrants were referred to as 'the scum of Europe', 'the broken-spirited physical wrecks which Northern Europe cares to dump down'.[35] It was claimed that most of them were 'nihilists and anarchists of the very worst type'.[36] At the British Brothers' League rally in Mile End in January 1902, the immigrants were referred to as 'rubbish', 'contents of dustbins', 'savages' and 'the scum of humanity'.[37]

As early as 1898 the Primrose League claimed to have collected 2,630 signatures in Bethnal Green in favour of immigration control. All the Conservative candidates from the East London constituencies used the anti-aliens issue in most elections from 1892 to 1906. In 1906 one advertisement stated, 'England for the English, and Major Gordon for Stepney', while an election address announced:

> Whitechapel, standing as it does at the very gates of the City of London, the centre of the Empire, was never destined to become a foreign pauper settlement. It is intolerable that we should have unblushingly dumped among us the very scum of the unhealthiest of continental nations.[38]

It was, the address added, 'an outrage to the district'. Captain Kyd, the Conservative candidate in Whitechapel, used almost identical words.

The Liberals espoused the aliens cause, but antisemitism was not absent from their circles. The Bethnal Green Liberal and Radical Club decided in 1901 that it would not admit Jewish members, while all but one of the East End Liberals petitioned the leadership in May 1905 not to oppose the second reading of the Aliens Bill. In the by-election in Mile End in January 1905, the only election to be fought solely on the aliens issue, the Liberal candidate Bertram Strauss, though he had opposed the Bill, still argued against the immigration of diseased, criminal and 'undesirable' aliens. Indeed, the Liberals argued against the Bill mainly because it would be ineffective rather than for any moral reason. (Winston Churchill in 1904 was an exception.) Trade unionists such as Ben Tillett were no better. 'Yes, you are our brothers,' said Tillett, 'and we will do our duty by you. But we wish you had not come to our country.'

The Aliens Bill, defeated in 1904, reappeared and finally received Royal Assent in August 1905. Bethnal Green Conservatives celebrated the occasion with a firework display and a mass distribution of 10,000 copies of the Royal Assent.

There is still debate about the fate of the anti-aliens feelings and of antisemitism in the East End after 1905. One view is that anti-semitism was moderately strong before 1900, flared up after 1902, and subsided after 1906. J.H. Robb, however, suggested that it might have been at its height in 1922 in Bethnal Green. The London County Council in 1925 wanted Jews excluded from all municipal housing.[39] Within a few years, the East End was to see the return of antisemitic rhetoric with the rise of the fascist movement.

The Jewish socialist tradition

Out of the East End experience emerged a series of distinctive Jewish radical movements. A key figure in the beginning of Jewish socialism was a non-Jew, Rudolf Rocker (1873–1958), whose underground work with immigrants between 1895 and 1914 made him one of the most influential figures within Jewish radicalism. He spoke and lectured in Yiddish, and was a founder of the Jewish Workers' Circle. During these years, mass meetings of the Federation of Jewish Anarchists in Whitechapel and Mile End were gathering crowds of up to 7,000. Rocker had first encountered Jewish anarchists in Paris, and, on arrival in London in 1895, he became acquainted with Enrico Malatesta. Rocker and his comrades met in the Sugar Loaf in Hanbury Street. One of his comrades was Aaron Lieberman who, on 13 May 1876, had founded the Hebrew Socialist Union in Gun Street, Whitechapel, the first recorded Jewish socialist group. It has been said that Lieberman 'changed the course of Jewish social history'.[40] His publication *Call to the Jewish Youth*, with its strong attack on private property, was a key document of Jewish socialism. Not surprisingly, the Jewish establishment, including the Chief Rabbi and the *Jewish Chronicle*, were fiercely opposed to him and his movement, and, after periods of imprisonment, he committed suicide in 1880.

In 1880, Morris Winchevsky and E.W. Rabinowitz published *The Polish Yidel*, the first Yiddish socialist paper, later to change its name to *Die Tsukunft*. The following year, *Arbeiter Fraint* appeared, edited by Philip Krantz, and issued from 40 Berner Street, home of the International Working Men's Educational Club. Berner Street was at the heart of East End Jewish socialism, and Jewish socialists were known as 'Berner Streeters'. *Arbeiter Fraint* was fiercely anti-religious and held a ball on the Day of Atonement from 1888 onwards. It had close links with William Morris and the Socialist League, and Morris, along with Kropotkin, attended the fifth anniversary of the club in 1890.

By 1891 the Berner Street club had become dominated by anarchists, and in April *Arbeiter Fraint* became an anarchist paper, adopting the description 'anarchist-communist' in 1892. Under Rocker's editorship, its office was in Chance Street, Bethnal Green. In 1903 it became the organ of 'Yiddish-speaking anarchist groups'. An *Arbeiter Fraint* Club opened in Jubilee Street in 1906. In all this activity, the East End was central, and it became 'the clearing house for the Jewish revolutionary movement'.[41] So, when, on 17 December 1910, three policemen were shot to death in Houndsditch, suspicion fell on Jewish anarchists. On 3 January 1911, the 'Siege of Sidney Street' took place. It was an attempt to identify those responsible, and it did help to discredit anarchism in the eyes of the public.

Jewish anarchists played a crucial role in the early trade union movement. There had been little organised union activity in the East End before 1889 when there was a strike of 10,000 London tailors. On 28 December 1889, the East London Federation of Labour Unions was set up, and all the constituent bodies were Jewish. In 1904 the Jewish Bakers' Union organised a strike. In 1912 the Jewish trade unions felt strong enough to challenge the sweating system, and in April the London Society of Tailors organised a strike in the West End. *Arbeiter Fraint* supported this, and called for a strike in the East End, which brought the clothing industry to a standstill. By 1914 the Jewish socialist movement was inseparable from Jewish trade unions. Rocker claimed that all the Jewish unions were started by the initiative of anarchists.

While *Arbeiter Fraint* was the best-known Jewish socialist group, there were others. In 1892 a paper called *Fraye Welt* was launched with a Marxist approach, linked with the Socialist Workers' Association, but this did not survive. In 1905 *Germinal* appeared, the organ of a group in Hanbury Street.

But the Jewish anarchist movement had died by 1914, not least because it was a Yiddish-speaking movement. By the 1920s, Jewish socialist activity had switched towards local struggles around housing. Campaigns for fair rents and for housing improvement spread from mainly Jewish blocks like Fieldgate Mansions to mixed ones like

Langdale Mansions, and at the heart of these campaigns was the Communist Party, which was almost entirely Jewish. It only became mixed as a result of links with Irish and English dockers such as Pat Colman and Bill Jackson, and with the Stepney Trades Council and Stepney Tenants' League. The role of the Communist Party in the East End was inextricably bound up with the Jewish socialist tradition.

One individual who played a major role in East End Communist activity was Sam Aaronovitch, born in 1919, of Lithuanian parents. Aaronovitch was educated at Christian Street School and could not remember a time when antisemitism was not present in the East End. He saw Cable Street in particular as a centre of anti-Jewish feeling, with Pell Street as a point of polarisation between Jews and Irish Roman Catholics. Aaronovitch joined the Young Communist League (YCL) in 1934. Out of the YCL came key figures such as Tobby Rosen and Max Levitas, who is still active in Whitechapel. In 1936 *The Times* noted a movement of Jews towards communism, and the membership of the Communist Party doubled between 1935 and 1937.

On 7 October 1931 Harry Pollitt was adopted as Communist candidate for Whitechapel and St George's. His adoption symbolised the growing influence of the Communist Party in the East End. But it was Phil Piratin who was elected as MP for Mile End in 1945, the only Communist member in England.

The rise of fascism

From 1935 onwards, organised fascism became a major issue in the East End. There were disturbances at meetings of the British Union of Fascists. Of course, antisemitism was much more wide-spread than the fascist movements. The *Sunday Express* in 1938 complained that Jews were overcrowding the country, trying to enter the medical profession, practise as dentists, and even as psycho-analysts. In November 1938 the paper offered 'A word of warning to British Jews'. Forms of the Jewish world conspiracy theory were very common, and Winston Churchill seems to have held a version of it.

The appeal of many of the early fascist movements was to the middle class, though the Imperial Fascist League (1928) had a branch in Hackney by 1934. But it was Mosley's movement which was to make inroads into the East End.

The British Union of Fascists (BUF) was formed on 3 October 1932, and adopted the black shirt in 1933. The East End was at the heart of its activities, the key area of its physical manifestation, without which it would never have become a movement at all. The rise of East End fascism was a kind of crystallising and focusing of a range of frustrations as well as of ideological currents of change.

Fascism in the East End was not uniformly popular. It became strong in Shoreditch, Bethnal Green, and Stepney, with very little support in Poplar or the Isle of Dogs. In Bethnal Green in 1921 over 87 per cent of the population were London-born. The *Evening Standard* reported, on 29 June 1938, that 'most of the trouble has occurred in the Bethnal Green district.' The two most important areas were Bethnal Green and Shoreditch. In Bethnal Green, there was a 'fierce village parochialism symbolised by the tiny terraced houses facing each other across narrow streets'. The key street was Green Street (now Roman Road) – 'the most fertile centre in East London'.[42] The first BUF branches in the East End were set up in Bow and Bethnal Green in 1934, while branches in Shoreditch and Limehouse followed. Shoreditch was the heart of the 'physical force' wing. Linehan refers to 'the radical racist populist orientation of the Shoreditch branch'.[43]

It is likely that between 1936 and 1938 about half of the national membership of the BUF was in the East End. There was activity from 1934 onwards. In July 1934 5,000 people marched from Aldgate to Victoria Park in an anti-fascist demonstration. On 9 September, although it was the eve of Jewish New Year when most Jews were in synagogue, 150,000 marched to Hyde Park to protest at a BUF rally. Within the East End itself, the first major fascist rally was at Victoria Park on Sunday 7 June 1936. *Action*, the Mosleyite paper, claimed an attendance of 100,000, while local newspapers claimed 30–50,000 and the police 5,000! The public meetings increased in the second half of 1936. East London police were present at 536 meetings in August, 603 in September, and 647 in October, while between 5 October and 8 November, almost 300 police per day were drafted into the East End. During this period the BUF claimed to have made 4,000 members in Bethnal Green, and they may have been even more successful in Stepney where Duckett Street was known as 'the fascist street'.

In a letter of September 1934 to the Home Secretary, Sir John Simon, the Commissioner of Police, admitted that the large police presence was 'creating the impression' that Mosley's movement was 'being permitted to develop under police protection'. He stressed that the military nature of the movement and the wearing of uniforms were critical, and urged the government 'to prohibit the wearing of uniform for political purposes'.[44] It was in fact two years later, on 16 July 1936, that the Home Secretary issued instructions to the police to take action to suppress the activity of the BUF. In that month Sir Percy Harris, the Liberal MP for Bethnal Green, again confirmed that there was a feeling that 'the police are acting in collusion with the fascists'.[45] Joe Jacobs, at that time a Communist Party activist, recalled that anti-fascists had to fight the police in order to reduce the violence.[46]

The street violence reached its peak in Whitechapel in 1936. Benewick has called it 'a siege of terror', while Cross saw the fascist activity at this time as being 'on a scale unprecedented in British politics'.[47] Much of the fascist activity was in entirely Jewish areas where there was no hope of making converts, and the only aim was provocation. During August 1936 there were 1,409 political meetings in London, of which 471 were communist-organised and 257 fascist. By October there were 1,473 of which 647 took place in the East End. On 26 September, *Blackshirt* announced that the BUF would march through Whitechapel on 4 October.

At first the Communist Party wanted to avoid confrontation, not least because the Young Communist League had organised a rally in Trafalgar Square on that day on the crisis in Spain. However, by 2 October the line had changed, and the *Daily Worker* proclaimed 'East End rallies against fascism'. At least 100,000 people opposed the fascist march, though it has been claimed, probably reliably, that the numbers blocking the entrance to Whitechapel grew to 250,000. Around 7,000 police were in the area, and at Cable Street occurred 'the closest approximation to a political street war in the Twentieth Century'.[48] Cable Street was the dividing line between the Jewish and Irish communities. The 'Battle of Cable Street' was, in the words of Father John Groser, 'a sign and a portent'. It showed that people could not be finally beaten down, and that 'when it came to a pinch they dropped their differences and united against a common enemy'.[49]

The 'Battle of Cable Street' holds a central place in East End mythology. It is a myth in the strict sense of the word: an event of imaginative power, a powerful symbolic reality, a subversive memory which inspires and gives confidence and hope for the future. But it is also myth in the popular sense in that it has come to be mis-understood, and there are a number of falsehoods, myths in the sense in which the word is used today. Thus it is still widely believed that the battle brought an end to fascist activity, drove Mosley out of the East End, was masterminded by the Communist Party, and was a struggle between fascists and anti-fascists which occurred at the heart of the Jewish community. All these ideas are false.

It was not a battle between fascists and the rest of the people. As one participant, Joyce Goodman, commented: 'We never saw a fascist all that day. We were fighting the police. They were just hitting everyone. There were women going down under the horses. Absolute terror.'[50] Cable Street was not the heart of the Jewish community but rather the boundary between Jewish and Irish neigh-bourhoods. The Communist Party's role was important but it was not the only organising force, and there was much spontaneous grass roots activity. Moreover, it is certainly wrong to see the Battle of Cable Street as marking the end of the East End fascist movement. After Cable Street, within three weeks, the BUF enrolled 2,000 new members, mostly from the East End, and there was a leap in total membership to almost 20,000 by late November 1936. A report by the Special Branch at Scotland Yard in November 1936 claimed that the BUF 'has been steadily gaining ground' in many parts of East London, and mentioned Stepney, Shoreditch, Bethnal Green, Hackney, and Bow as areas of 'strong support'. Since 4 October, the report claimed, there had been a number of very successful gather-ings. Indeed in the week after Cable Street, the BUF 'conducted the most successful series of meetings since the beginning of the movement' with crowds of several thousand, and on one occasion, when Mosley spoke at Victoria Park on 11 October, 12,000. The report argued that 'a definite pro-fascist feeling' had shown itself in the weeks after the battle.[51]

The atmosphere after Cable Street was confused, and it included celebration and tension. Yet the battle was extremely important in its effect on morale. It made many people see that fascism could be overcome, it gave confidence to thousands of decent people throughout the country, and it was to become an important *kairos* moment for future struggles. It also seems to have made sections of the establishment realise that there was massive opposition to the BUF, and to have strengthened the confidence of those critics of fascism within establishment circles. Within a short time, the climate was hardening against fascism. Lord Trenchard, the Commissioner of Police, had wanted uniforms banned for some time, and, according to one submission, seems to have wanted the BUF banned altogether.

> I am fully convinced that the present difficulties arise primarily from the existence and methods of the fascist party, and that the only really effective way of dealing with them is to put a stop to the present organisation and to prevent similar organisations being formed in the future.[52]

On 21 June 1937, all political processions were banned in the East End, initially for six weeks, but in fact the ban remained in force until 1940. On 23 May 1940, Mosley was arrested, the BUF headquarters were occupied by the police, and on 27 May the organisation was dissolved under the Defence Regulations.

Yet, opposition notwithstanding, it is clear that fascism was attractive to many members of the East End working class. As a result of recent work by Linehan and others, we know that the bulk of the membership of the fascist movement came from lower-class and lower-middle-class groups. The unskilled and semi-skilled were the largest single group (36 per cent) and constituted the social core of the movement. There were some key figures who acted as local leaders. Mick Clarke, the scoutmaster at St Barnabas Church in Bethnal Green, was one of these. His writings, according to Linehan, 'displayed a genuine nostalgia for the perceived passing away of an imagined more romantic notion of an East End based on mutual respect and the values of traditional English "fair play" '. Another key figure, J.E. Donovan, from Duckett Street, Stepney, saw Jews as the source of decline, and linked this with jazz and sex. One of the aspects which Linehan brings out in his detailed study of East End fascists is the way in which they manifested feelings of melancholy and dismal nostalgia, and he sees this nostalgia as being central to the whole appeal. There was an idealising of the past combined with a morbid fear of decay and degeneracy. Commenting on one well-known local fascist activist, he speaks of 'melancholy apocalyptic visions and the tendency to view society through the morbid imagery of illness, decay and death'.[53]

The events of 1934–6 did help to break the link between anti-semitism and fascism without, in the long term, bringing either to an end. Nevertheless, since Mosley, there has never been a fascist movement in the East End which has attracted such a high degree of support. In his study of antisemitism in Bethnal Green in the late 1940s, Robb referred to 'the apparent divorce between anti-semitism and fascism'.[54] Later fascist groups were to play down the antisemitic dimension in their public testimony, while it remained central to their ideology.

It is often claimed that antisemitism was not an essential part of the Mosley movement. The publication of Mosley's *My Life* in 1968 re-opened the debate. Here he claimed that 'anti-semitism was not our policy' and that 'the Jewish question had nothing to do with our progress'. He argued that unemployment was the key issue and that antisemites in the East End were a small minority. Mosley saw the attack by Jews on his meeting at Olympia on 8 June 1934 as a turning-point. Significantly, Mosley makes no reference in his book to the Battle of Cable Street, which does not even appear in the index, and there are few references to the East End campaign. Neither the East End, Stepney nor Whitechapel, which were so crucial to his campaigning, appear in the index, while Bethnal Green receives one reference on page 314. However, he did refer to the East End in a letter to *The Times* in 1969 in which he argued that the BUF were not in any way responsible for the Battle of Cable Street. Mosley's view received some support from his biographer, Robert Skidelsky, who claimed that the Jews must take 'a large share of the blame' for what happened. They were, he claims, 'obsessed by fascism'.[55]

Others who were present at the time presented a different picture. Piratin argued that there was a terrorist atmosphere, while an Anglican priest working in Shoreditch claimed that Mosley's speeches were 'an incentive to acts of anti-Semitism'.[56] A front page article in *Blackshirt* as early as 1933 opposed the Jewish 'organised interest'. A.K. Chesterton compared Jews to woodlice. Mick Clarke claimed that they were 'the lice of the earth and must be exterminated'. Mosley's language was filled with antisemitic terms – 'the yelpings of a Jewish mob', 'alien Yiddish finance', 'Jew-infested squalor', and so on. In 1934 he described his Jewish hecklers as 'the sweepings of the ghettoes'. An article in *Action* in 1937 claimed that 'anti-Semitism is intrinsically a normal reaction' to anti-social activities, and compared it to the human bloodstream when 'infected by a poisonous bacillus'. Even Skidelsky points out that Mosley's first antisemitic remark was made as early as 24 October 1932, while Mosley himself, questioned by Sir Norman Birkett in 1940, admitted that 'having looked at the Jewish problem, I developed what is called anti-Semitism.'[57] What is not open to doubt is that the East End campaign changed the direction and in a sense sealed the fate of the whole fascist movement.

The antisemitic dimension, however, did not originate in the East End. It was evident at Mosley's Albert Hall meeting in 1934 when he attacked 'little people who can hardly speak English at all' and who were 'the sweepings of foreign ghettos' (language which recalled that of Arnold White). Even earlier, *Blackshirt* in November 1933 had attacked 'unwanted aliens'. But it was in the East End that the antisemitic core of the movement was manifested most clearly and most violently. Skidelsky is incorrect in seeing the East End campaign as 'a separate episode', with little connection to the BUF, and his attempt to portray the East End fascist campaign as 'a kind of political Boys' Brigade' is not convincing.[58]

However, both Skidelsky and Joe Jacobs, former secretary of Stepney Communist Party, agree that the bulk of fascist organising was done on the edges of the ghetto districts, in non-Jewish areas.[59] Such areas, Bethnal Green, Shoreditch, and, much later, the Isle of Dogs were to figure in later resurgences of fascist movements in the East End.

5

From Cable Street to Brick Lane: racial minorities in the East End 1920–71

SARAH: Everything happens in Cable Street.
HARRY: What else happened in Cable Street?
SARAH: Peter the Painter had a fight with Churchill there, didn't he?
MONTY: You're thinking of Sidney Street, sweetheart.
HARRY: You know, she gets everything mixed up.

ARNOLD WESKER[1]

Whoever has walked slowly down Brick Lane
   in the darkening air and a stiff little rain,
past the curry house with lascivious frescoes,
past the casual Sylheti sweet-shops and cafes,
and the Huguenot silk attics of Fournier Street,
and the mosque that before was a synagogue
   and before that a chapel,
whoever has walked down that darkening tunnel of rich
   history
from Bethnal Green to Osborne Street at Aldgate,
past the sweat-shops at night and imams with hennaed
   hair,
and recalls the beigel-sellers on the pavements,
   windows candled on Friday night,
would know this street is a seamless cloth, this city, these
   people,
and would not suffocate ever from formlessness or
   abrupted memory,
would know rich history is the present before us,
laid out like a cloth – a cloth for the wearing –
   with bits of mirror and coloured stuff,

and can walk slowly down Brick Lane from end to seamless
   end,
looped in the air and the light of it, in the human lattice of
   it, the
blood and exhausted flesh of it, and the words
grown bright with the body's belief,
and life to be fought for and never to be taken away.

STEPHEN WATTS[2]

Social and political changes 1920–50

During the 1920s and 1930s material conditions in the East
End as a whole improved. *The New Survey of London Life and
Labour*, published in 1932, noted the 'diminished local concentration
and greater dispersion' of poverty. Overcrowding remained, although
districts in the west of London showed higher incidences than did
the East End. However, between 1921 and 1931, the percentage of
those in the 'Eastern Survey Area' who lived at a level of over three
persons per room rose from 2.8 to 3.4 per cent. Among the population of Stepney 19.3 per cent were identified as 'poor' (earning
about 38-40 shillings per week), though, in contrast to the Booth
Survey, low wages were not seen as a major cause of poverty at this
time.

The *New Survey* concluded that the percentage of persons in
poverty had 'greatly decreased in East London', as had the number
of 'poor streets', though 18.2 per cent of Stepney's population still
lived in such streets. There were pockets of poverty in Hackney
Road, in Limehouse, and elsewhere, and there were concentrations
of homeless people. The Census of Common Lodging Houses in
1926 showed that nearly half of the beds for women in London
were concentrated in a few 'low class' streets in Whitechapel and
Southwark.[3]

The area of East London which contained the most acute poverty
in the 1930s was Shoreditch. The Wenlock Ward, between Nile Street
and Murray Street, was 'a long persistent slum', with very high rates
of death from diphtheria and from violence.[4] The next poorest
districts after Shoreditch were Bethnal Green and Stepney, though

the Enumeration Districts (EDs) with the highest overcrowding in this period were not in the East End, but in St Luke's, Finsbury, Silvertown, and South-west Shoreditch. However, there was over-crowding in such streets as Pennington and Cornwall Streets in Wapping, and Romford and Goulston Streets in Whitechapel.

During and after World War Two, the population of the East End fell from 197,200 (1939) to 94,800 (1946). Many former residents left and never returned. In his study of Dagenham in 1958, Peter Willmott reported that 46 per cent of his sample were born in the East End. At the same time there were major plans to bring about 'urban renewal' within the East End itself. In 1951 the London County Council (LCC), using powers given to them under the Town and Country Planning Act 1947, introduced the Stepney–Poplar Comprehensive Development Area. The reconstruction of the East End was part of a large-scale vision for a new London, Sir Patrick Abercrombie's Greater London Plan of 1944, based on the assump-tion that the population, economy and local culture would remain stationary, an assumption which was soon proved to have been incorrect. The changing face of the East End was the subject of numerous articles. In 1953 *The Times*, for example, noted that travel and movement had broken down 'the traditional parochialism of East London street groups'.[5] However, for some time, the industrial centre of gravity remained in the area bordering the City, around Finsbury and the East End, though the distribution area for clothing had shifted to the West End.

Politically, the post-war scene in the East End was still coloured by the memories of fascism and antisemitism. The controversy over fascism became focused to an extent on the conflict between the Labour and Communist Parties. At the General Election of 1945, Stepney returned two Labour members, one of them the new Prime Minister, Clement Attlee, and one Communist, Phil Piratin. The advance of the Communist Party was carried further at the local elections in November 1945 when the party won all ten seats which it contested, and in 1946 the Communists also won the two LCC seats in Mile End. By 1947 the local strength of the Communist Party stood at one MP, two LCC councillors, and twelve borough councillors. The Communist Party in Stepney had the highest ratio of members per head of the population of any district in Britain – 1 per 175. When George Orwell's *Animal Farm* was published in

1945, *The Spectator* commented that it would cause outrage among the 'amateur Bolsheviks . . . of East Aldgate'. But at the General Election of 1950, mainly as a result of boundary changes, the Labour member Walter ('Stoker') Edwards was elected, and Piratin was pushed into third place by the Conservative candidate.

The outbreak of the Korean War in 1950 did not help the Communist cause. 'Stalin is dead in Moscow, Communism is dying in Stepney' announced a local paper. The enormous hostility towards the Communists from the Labour Party, Edwards calling the Communists 'our biggest enemies', was not without racial undertones, for the Communists were almost all Jewish while the Labour group on the council were mainly Roman Catholic and of Irish origin, often referred to as 'Murphy and sons and cousins'. At a Roman Catholic rally before the LCC elections of 1949, photographs of Cardinal Mindzenty were displayed, and the mayor denounced the Communist Party as 'anti-social, anti-Catholic, anti-Christian and anti-religious'. The Communists, in retaliation, claimed that Labour politicians were tarnished with antisemitism, and fought the Spitalfields by-election of 1948 on the slogan, 'Throw the anti-semites off the Council'.[6]

Communist members continued to be elected, mainly in Whitechapel, and the leading Conservative figure in the area, Joe Emden, resigned from the party in 1946 as a protest against Lord Winterton's statement (with reference to Phil Piratin) that 'we do not want the views of foreign Communists'. A year earlier, Father Fitzgerald, a well-known local Roman Catholic priest, was urging closer relations between Roman Catholics and Communists, an interesting phenomenon in the 'cold war' era.

Cable Street: the emergence of the 'coloured quarter'

Cable Street was mentioned frequently in the popular literature of the East End from the late nineteenth century onwards. Sir Walter Besant, in 1901, referred to its 'street companies', armed with clubs, iron bars and knives. In the 1930s the *New Survey* commented on its 'unsavoury reputation'.[7] While the term 'subculture' was not fashionable until the 1960s, the reality to which it referred was well established in the East End by the end of the nineteenth century. The building of Rowton House in Whitechapel in 1892 in a sense set the seal on a long process by which the district became a home for large numbers of homeless and rootless people. By the time that Jack London's *The People of the Abyss* was published in 1903, the district contained large numbers of rootless people. Edith Ramsey was writing reports on 'the derelict in Whitechapel' in the 1920s.

From about 1940 attention was directed on the changing racial composition of the district, and on the growth of a cafe quarter. From about 1947 to the early 1960s the media focused frequently on the squalor of what they often termed 'London's Harlem'. In 1953 *The Times* referred to 'a new and disturbing problem in the Cable Street area' – the fact that black men had been 'corrupted by women and political agitators' and formed 'a disgruntled and for the most part unemployed colony'.[8]

A good example of the crude stereotyping of Cable Street was Roi Ottley's *No Green Pastures* (1952). Ottley, a black American, wrote:

> Today, down by London Docks, in about a square mile of back streets, there exists a dismal Negro slum. The neighbourhood . . . abounds with brothels and dope pads in old tumble-down buildings. Few slums in the United States compare with this area's desperate character, unique racial composition, and atmosphere of crime, filth and decay.

He went on to write of the cafes with their 'native music', knives and murders. But none of the cafes had 'the good-natured exuberance of a Negro tavern in Harlem'. They rather 'resembled the Casbah in Algiers – mysterious, sinister and heavily-laden with surreptitious violence'.[9]

Ottley's account is not untypical. An English writer in 1961 called Cable Street 'the filthiest, dirtiest, most repellently odoured street in Christendom',[10] while in the same year, a journalist wrote of it as 'Hell's Gate'.

> I know Harlem with its strutting negroes and its hopped up whacky citizens. Best of all I know Spanish Harlem, that square mile in New York that is called Hell's Gate where the young gang leaders prowl and where every kid of 14 and up is a potential murderer. All these areas in New York border on Central Park which after dark has become a No Man's Land. Nobody who is not a nut would dare to walk in any of these places after sundown.

After my tour last night I am beginning to feel the same way about Stepney.[11]

The comparison with Harlem and East Harlem occurred in many articles. (Not only in articles – there was a cafe in the street called 'Little Harlem Cafe'!) Other writers tended to romanticise the street. In 1960 *The Observer* printed a major article entitled 'Cablestrasse' by George Foulser, a merchant seaman, who wrote of the atmosphere of Cable Street.

> It is a place with an atmosphere of its own, a combination of British and overseas traditions. From all over the world people have travelled to settle in Cablestrasse; to live and work together as peaceful fellow citizens. They are an object lesson in living for other people everywhere.

The street contained 'the most racially mixed crowd of people in Britain bar the people of Tiger Bay in Cardiff'. He played down the accounts of violence as relics of the past.[12]

In fact accounts of violence, always linked with race and prostitution, go back to 1947 when it was claimed that there a 'gang war' between West Africans and other black men, mainly Jamaican. In 1947 a petition signed by 3,000 people was presented to Stepney Council, protesting about the moral and physical dangers, and urging the council, the Home Office and the Food Ministry to act against the conditions and the cafes. A group of local clergy claimed that the picture in the petition was 'grossly exaggerated' and deplored the implicit blaming of the black population.

But the flavour of the 1947 coverage of Cable Street was uniformly sensational. The following examples are typical.

> Seamen all over the world know of Cable Street, and if their tastes lie that way, make for it as soon as their ships dock. Some of them are coloured boys, just off their first ship. A few months ago they were still half naked in the bush.

> The girls who haunt the cafes and pubs are not local girls, they come from South Shields, Newcastle, Cardiff, Liverpool; many of them are on the run and some have escaped from remand homes. They are safe in Cable Street. Most of them are teenagers, they get drunk, and the coloured seamen they are with get jealous.

> Stepney folk have already decided that unless authority steps in, 'war' will be declared . . . Stepney is determined that this dangerous element must be wiped out.[13]

There were the usual stories that police only walked in pairs in Cable Street, though one paper printed a photograph of a solitary policeman in Cable Street at night. Even the better-informed sections of the press referred to 'this other Harlem'.[14] Perhaps the most balanced and thoughtful account was Patrick O' Donovan's talk 'The Challenge of Cable Street', broadcast on BBC Radio in February 1950. O' Donovan pointed out that the publicity related to a very small section of the street:

> The majority of the street deeply resent the name it has been given. It's been a bit of a field day down there for journalists, and only a couple of blocks at one end are involved. The rest is as decent a street in which to live and die as you will find in the whole County of London.

Nevertheless, O' Donovan noted

> a sense of old hopelessness and of poverty that has ceased to struggle. It's as bad as anything I have ever seen in London . . . I think these few hundred yards are about the most terrible in London.[15]

As well as newspaper articles, there were various reports. Captain F.A. Richardson wrote one on *Social Conditions in Ports and Dockland Areas* in 1935 which located most black residents in the Canning Town area, and claimed that 'these types probably attract women of low type, particularly the Indians'. Three years after Richardson's report, Hindustan Community House opened at 79 Lambeth Street, but it was bombed during the war and soon closed.

However, towards the end of the war, there was a renewed concern about the conditions of the black community in Cable Street. In 1944 a 'Committee investigating problems concerning coloured people in Stepney' met, and Mrs Phyllis Young was commissioned to write a report. Later that year her report, *Investigation into Conditions of the Coloured Population in a Stepney Area,* appeared. It was a poorly researched document, but it provided a starting point for the later and more substantial work by Michael Banton, and for the work begun in 1945 by the Society of St Francis, an Anglican Franciscan order. Mrs Young began her report with the curious observation: 'Down by London Docks in the Borough of Stepney there is an area of just under a square mile of back-street slums in which at any given moment during the past three months at least 698 coloured people could be found.' She then went on to produce percentages based on 'particulars obtained of 130 of the male resident coloured population'. Her report contained a number of extraordinary calculations, such as: 'During the past three months, the daily average floating population, not including casual visitors, has been 298.' However, while her statistics were of little value, and at times absurd, Mrs Young's report was an interesting source of impressions of the Cable Street area in the early years of the immigration from Africa and the Caribbean. She believed that colour prejudice had increased since the First World War and pointed to the decline in black residents of the Sailors' Home in Dock Street. Mrs Young claimed that there were about 400 black people in Stepney, of whom 80 per cent were seamen or cafe workers, argued that prejudice had increased, and called for increased welfare provision, and for the establishment of a 'community centre for coloured people', and a hostel for one hundred men.[16] None of these happened, but one of the results of her survey was the arrival of the Society of St Francis, a community of Anglican Franciscans, in 1944. They moved into 84 Cable Street where they remained until 1963.[17]

The structure of the black communities 1940–60

Black people were not, of course, new to the East End. Records of the Sailors' Home in Dock Street, founded in 1835, show that for the first ninety-one years of its existence, 14,766 black men lived there, but almost all of them did so before 1918. After disturbances in that year, black people ceased to use the home, and until 1939 the main black district in East London was in Canning Town, to the east of Poplar. However, between 1944 and 1948, several hundred West African seamen settled in Britain's dockland districts, including the East End. Many belonged to the Kru and Ijo tribes, and had come from Sierra Leone, Ghana, and the Gambia. Among the Gambians was a group who had been 'pilot boys' (boys employed to 'pilot' European seamen to prostitutes) and entered the delinquent subculture in the East End.

According to Edith Ramsey, in an unpublished memorandum on 'The coloured population in Stepney', dated February 1950, 'the west end of Cable Street and the streets leading off it is now a "coloured quarter".' This seems to be the earliest use of the term 'coloured quarter' in relation to Cable Street, and the term was taken up and popularised by Michael Banton in his book of that title in 1955. Ramsey says that the community was mainly West African, West Indian, Maltese and Indian. At 10.00 p.m. on 3 February 1950, Ramsey claims to have counted 112 black men within a two hundred yard stretch of Cable Street. Those whom she describes as Indians were in fact mostly Pakistanis from Bengal, and many of them were in touch with the welfare department of the Pakistan government. Ramsey's memorandum, like all her writing, contains many sweeping generalisations and expressions of racial prejudice. For example, 'I believe every West Indian carries a knife as a weapon, and the occasional outbreaks of razor slashing are due to West Indians.' On the other hand, many of her claims were accurate and reliable. Thus her claim that there were forty Somalis in the Cable Street district was confirmed by the 1951 Census.[18]

In 1955 Michael Banton's *The Coloured Quarter* was published. While its title contributed to the confusing stereotypes of black communities in Britain, it remains the most detailed study of the Cable Street district in the post-war period. Banton himself recognised that Cable Street was 'no coloured ghetto but a depressed working class neighbourhood', and, for black immigrants, a reception area. During the period of his research – 1950–2 – he estimated that there were 400–500 West Africans and West Indians in the district, and that by 1951 the figures were 145 West Africans and 174 West Indians. (The 1951 Census reported 118 and 179 respectively.) Most of the West Africans were former stowaways. There were very few women.[19]

The Somalis have been an important presence in the East End for many years. In 1951 there were forty Somalis, all male, in Stepney, and fifty (forty-seven male, three female) in London as a whole. Ensign Street was the centre of the community, though no African names appeared there until 1950. In 1942 most of the residents had

Jewish or Maltese names, but by 1951 the Somali presence was evident.

The names listed in the 1959 *Post Office Directory* for the west end of Cable Street indicate the racial composition of the area.

Koiki, Freimuller, Azzopardi, Mackay, Vella, Tendler, Lacome, Mackay, Garfield, Hassan, White, Lerner, Nathan, Howard, Kroo, Strunkey, Kenter, Danziger, Cohen, Mill, Gauci, Freedman, House, Taylor, Cohen, Caplan, Broer, Marsolini, Zelinsky, Feigenbaum, Freedman, Coleman, Kaiser, Wansofsky, Brady, Prodromov, Jacobs, Dansick, Aranzulo, Hassan, Grima, Frendo, Mifsud, Galanis, Chase, Gromofsky, Eisen, Henny, Gold, Schulmann, Lawal.

By the 1961 census the East End was no longer a major area for Africans, apart from Somalis. The largest numbers of Nigerians were in Islington and Wandsworth, and Wandsworth also contained the largest communities from Ghana and Sierra Leone. While one study in 1964 still referred to 'a Gambian cafe in Cable Street' – the Rainbow Café – by this time the East End no longer played a major role in the life of West Africans in London.[20] In fact Commonwealth immigrants were more heavily represented in Lambeth and Paddington than in the East End. There were only 1,599 West Indians in Stepney in 1961, and in 1964 there were only six East End schools where the West Indian pupils reached two figures. But the Indian population grew from 371 to 905 between 1951 and 1961, and the Pakistani from 309 to 799. The 1961 figure was certainly an under-estimate. By 1964, according to the electoral lists, Princelet Street and Old Montague Street were the main centres for the Pakistani community.[21]

A recurring concern throughout this period was that black people might be manipulated by political agitators. In 1949 a group of local workers claimed that 'they form in East London a discontented minority, and ideological writers have seized their opportunity'.[22] Edith Ramsey was particularly worried about communist influence on Africans, though, as she admitted in 1950, there was only one West African member of Stepney Communist Party – Stephen Ocquaye of 14 Pell Street. But she warned that an organiser of a 'Somali Communist Party' had been recruiting in Stepney.

By 1967 the old 'coloured quarter' had gone. But this is to anticipate the dramatic struggles over housing in the late 1950s and early 1960s.

Cable Street, slum clearance and the cafe society

In 1920 the Medical Officer of Health for the City told a Guildhall Inquiry that conditions between Houndsditch and Middlesex Street 'could not be made fit for human habitation otherwise than by the wholesale clearance proposed'.[23] Although a newspaper article of 1934 had announced 'Old Spitalfields is disappearing now', much of the old property remained until the late 1960s.[24] In 1939 a writer in *Toynbee Outlook* claimed that the housing problem in the East End was the most serious in Britain. In that year there were rent strikes in Brady Street, Langdale Mansions, and elsewhere.[25]

In 1945 the London County Council (LCC) accepted the task of comprehensive development, and in 1951 a large part of the East End was defined as a Comprehensive Development Area. Communist councillors played a key role in the housing agitation after 1945, helping East End squatters to occupy empty flats in Kensington and Marylebone. There was agitation for requisition notices on empty premises, for the building of new flats, and for prosecution of landlords who did not repair property.

By 1961 the housing conditions were more serious. Over half of the households in the East End had no access to a bath, and over 60 per cent lacked or shared basic amenities. A former chief city planner for Chicago 'could not believe his eyes' when he saw Spitalfields in the 1960s.[26] Black residents hardly existed within local authority housing. In 1966 there were twelve black families as borough tenants.

The Cable Street and Spitalfields districts in particular deteriorated. The *East London Advertiser* claimed in 1960 that the LCC had 'turned a blind eye' to Cable Street and Spitalfields.[27] A report to a sub-committee of the LCC in June 1961 described the property in the west end of Cable Street as being in a declining state.[28] The LCC had announced demolition on 4 May 1961, and the *Daily Mail*, describing Cable Street as 'the toughest street in Britain', quoted Norman Pritchard, chair of the Housing Committee, as saying that 'large scale demolition had started'. In fact, very little changed until 1967.[29]

Papers from the LCC in the early 1960s led to optimistic claims about the demolition and redevelopment of Cable Street. Headlines included 'Changes in Cable Street', 'Death sentence for Cable Street, E1, and they all rejoice', and 'The end of Vice Mile'. In 1962 there were promises that the area would 'come down in the near future'.[30] In fact most of the area remained as it was until 1967.

A key figure in the demolition of the slum housing in Cable Street was Father Joe Williamson, described as 'Stepney's turbulent priest'. A flamboyant character, with little concern for factual accuracy, but with a tremendous passion for justice, Williamson achieved more in his relatively short time in Cable Street than more thoughtful and polite activists did over a longer period. Williamson's correspondence was merciless, and he bombarded everyone from the Queen and all the Royal Family, press, radio and television, through to all local councillors, with constant letters. If the replies were unsatisfactory, he would publish them on the front page of his magazine, *The Pilot*. Aided by an expert photographer, his churchwarden Frank Rust, he circulated photographs of rat holes, excrement, and crumbling walls throughout the country. Yet by 1960 the Minister of Housing, Henry Brooke, was still saying that the property might be dealt with 'during the next five years'.[31]

In 1960 and 1961 an obscure street called Sander Street became national news. Here a row of slum property had become a continuous brothel. In October 1960, the magazine *Today* ran a feature, focused on Williamson, entitled 'Hell is my parish' which began 'Housing Minister Henry Brooke merely deplores the situation in Sander Street and surrounding areas. The London County Council by its failure to pull down the derelict property has become landlord to a vast and shameful brothel.'[32] The LCC held an all-night sitting, ending at 8.42 a.m. on 1 March 1961, and seriously considered libel proceedings. But it was clear that Williamson would have delighted at the chance to put his case in the Central Criminal Court, and would happily have gone to prison. They pulled down the property instead, while Williamson, informed by his 'moles' in County Hall of their intentions, knelt on the pavement, surrounded by the national media, and recited the Gloria![33]

Cable Street was not so fortunate, and the campaigning had to continue. In 1960 the fiery Communist councillor Solly Kaye said, 'Areas like Cable Street have got to be rescheduled by the LCC and tackled immediately', but his equally dynamic Independent colleague Edith Ramsey lamented that there was 'no hope of any change in the foreseeable future'.[34] Williamson, despairing of the local MP, Walter Edwards, whom he once described as 'no more use than a sick headache', invited any MPs to visit the area, provided they were willing to address the issues publicly. One who did was John Mackie, Conservative MP for Enfield East, who spoke in a Commons debate in 1962, telling the House that he 'saw no sign of anything being done in the area.'[35]

The Guardian also asked: 'What on earth . . . is happening in Cable Street? . . . Not one brick has been laid upon another.' Conservative ministers were keen to ally themselves with Father Williamson, and Sir Keith Joseph, then Minister of Housing, told the House of Commons in July 1962 that 'when we read Father Williamson's papers and realise that it is Cable Street that we would be pausing at, how could any government or anybody wish to pause?' But that is exactly what happened.[36]

Throughout the campaigns and debates, little attention was given to the position of black people. It is significant that in its evidence to the Milner Holland Committee on London housing, Stepney Council devoted just one paragraph (out of thirty-seven) to its immigrant communities, only mentioning Pakistanis who, their paper claims, were 'quite content' to live in overcrowded conditions. While the Milner Holland Report made it very clear that immigrants were an extreme example of London's housing problem, not their cause, the LCC valuer in Stepney in 1963 claimed that 'most of the overcrowding is caused by immigrants who are often used to a different way of life.'[37]

The cafes which were at the centre of the Cable Street subculture were not all new. One Arab cafe had been there since 1919. Nor were they all involved in drugs and prostitution. One Somali cafe took legal proceedings against Associated Television in 1963 about suggestions that they were involved in prostitution.[38] But the cafe area was also the prostitution area. David Downes's study of delinquent subcultures in the East End showed that prostitution offences in 1960 only occurred west of Sidney Street, with Hessel Street, Cable Street, and Sander Street being the main locations. Downes's work showed that, while Spitalfields and Cable Street accounted for only 22.7 per cent of the population of the East End, they accounted for 40–60 per cent of crime.[39] Prostitution grew in the East End in the period 1957–60. In 1946 there were two convictions for prostitution. In 1955 there were 585, and in 1957 795. The women involved were much younger than in London as a whole. The British Social Biology Council study of 1955 coined the term 'Stepney problem', and referred to Stepney as 'a reception area for young unsettled girls'. It described Cable Street as a young prostitutes' district.[40] Data from the early 1960s show that a high proportion of the women were mentally ill, had alcohol problems, or were runaways. As in the late 1940s, it was still true that 'mentally, physically and socially, they were in a lower grade than the ordinary prostitute'.[41]

In 1960, in the East End, prostitution accounted for more female offenders than all other offences combined. But prostitute activity was confined to an area west of Whitechapel Station. Spitalfields was not a major centre, the main locations being Cable Street, White-chapel Road, and Commercial Road. Half of all convictions for immoral earnings in 1960 occurred in the south part of Cavell Street, a short street close to the London Hospital. Most of the prostitutes encountered in this period were nineteen or twenty years old. The majority were not local, and there were many from Liverpool and Ireland. According to Downes, twenty-one was the peak age. In 1960, out of fifty-one prostitutes charged, fifteen were aged under twenty and thirty-one were aged seventeen to twenty-one. Only two of the fifty-one were local. Sixty per cent were from outside London, but none were from outside Britain, and none were black.

The west part of the East End also contained large numbers of 'social deviants'. Although Harold Macmillan, Prime Minister in 1961, claimed that there was no special concentration of mentally ill people in the area, the data were strongly against his view. The mental hospital admission rate for men was three times the national average. In the East End as a whole, the prevalence of schizophrenia was over twice the national average. It was 'a retreat for the schizo-phrenic patient'. Here too were concentrations of crude spirit drinkers and the heart of the docklands drug traffic.[42]

The history of Cable Street raises a number of issues which are of continuing importance in Britain. Two are of particular signifi-cance. First, the deeply entrenched question of segregated housing.

Cable Street was not a ghetto in the historic sense, but rather an enclave, a dockland black community, ghettoised in the sense of being more or less confined, through discrimination and the working of the housing market, to this small area, yet lacking the infrastructure and the political and religious organisation of, for example, Harlem, Brooklyn or the South Side of Chicago.

Second, the problem of political disconnectedness and fragmentation. The 'mainstream' parties were entirely white with the exception of the Communist Party which did have two black members, both African. None of them managed to make effective inroads into the growing black communities any more than did their national organisations. The historic association between black workers, of African Caribbean and Asian origin, and the Labour Party developed later. So, while there were friendly societies, supportive networks along national, tribal or clan lines, and a few attempts at wider community activity, there was no effective pressure group or campaigning organisation, political or religious, which could enable the voice of the Cable Street black community to be articulated, let alone heard.[43]

Racist and anti-immigrant polemic in the 1950s and 1960s

The years after 1946 also saw an increase in racist and fascist activity in East London. In 1947 Stepney Council called for legislation to forbid the propagation of antisemitic or fascist activities. The Communists were concerned at the lack of government action against fascist activity, though Edith Ramsey took the view that fascism would die out if it were left alone. The Council of Citizens of East London on 26 October 1948 claimed that antisemitism was much less acute. Colour prejudice was seen as occasional and sporadic, and racist rhetoric was common among political leaders. The local MP, Walter Edwards, blamed the growth of 'vice' on the Maltese, 'these filthy so-called British subjects', while Lady Ravensdale described the clients of the local prostitutes as 'mostly coloured, pouring in like ants'. Edwards strongly supported immigration control, while Stepney Conservative Association moved a motion in favour of control at the party conference in 1958.[44]

Fr Williamson too argued for controls, claiming (without any evidence) that 'this is one part of London where coloureds are outnumbering whites' and that 'the threat of race violence is imminent'. Until the housing situation was solved, all immigration should cease. Support for Williamson came from various sources. Beverley Nicholls, writing in the *Sunday Dispatch* in 1961, began by saying of Cable Street: 'I have walked through the dirtiest slums in Marseilles, toured the ramshackle shanties of the Southern States of America, plunged into the most scabrous alleys of Calcutta, for sheer filth, Stepney beats the lot.' From this demonstrably absurd claim, Nicholls went on to his central thesis. 'This is a black problem . . . through all the squalid tangle of this dustbin area stalks the figure of the coloured man.' He asked, 'Is there such a thing as being a little too colour-blind?' But, he argued, 'they flood in, the duped and the doped', and 'they get a corner of a cellar and they gather their fellow rats around them.' His article was reprinted as a leaflet in support of Williamson's work.[45]

Meanwhile small fascist groups were emerging. The British National Party could not hope to compete with Nicholls' rhetoric, but its newspaper *Combat* announced, 'Stepney vice is a black problem', and called Stepney 'a stinking cess-pit that is a Mecca for every black pimp and dope addict who steps off the immigrant boat'. The BNP, who described themselves as 'a Nordic racialist movement', praised Williamson as 'one of the few churchmen who have the courage to speak out against the vice problems brought in by immigrants'. An East London branch of the National Labour Party, another fascist group, was formed on 29 May 1958 at the Carpenters Arms in Cheshire Street. At the beginning of 1960, swastikas appeared on the walls of Stepney Green Synagogue. Meanwhile, Mosley was attempting a comeback, focusing on the Hackney area, and an alliance of Jews and Christians led to the Yellow Star Movement Against Fascism.

The emergence of Brick Lane

By the early 1960s Cable Street was dying as a social centre for black communities. Brick Lane, Princelet Street and Old Montague Street, to the north of Whitechapel Road, were taking over as centres for the Asian people. The cafes were moving, and so were the prostitutes. A new community, mostly from East Pakistan – later to become Bangladesh – was moving into the area. Brick Lane, once the heart of the Jewish ghetto, was to become the focal point of this new community. But unlike Cable Street, Brick Lane was to develop as the industrial, commercial and culinary centre of a large and well-organised community. After the creation of Bangladesh in 1971, Brick Lane became the home of the London Bengali restaurant business, and by the 1990s it had become known throughout the country as 'Bangla Town'. But this is to anticipate the material in Part Two. By 1967, when the old 'coloured quarter' in Cable Street was finally being demolished, the Brick Lane area was becoming increasingly populated by people from East Pakistan (as it then was). It was this community which was to become the largest minority group in the East End of the future.[46]

Part 2

Doing theology
in the community

6
Urbanism and its discontents

The city is a fearful place for temptation. Vices have an opportunity to thrive there as they cannot do in the country. In a rural village there are few openly vicious men to lead the young and unwary to ruin. But in a large metropolis there are great numbers of them on the look out at the corner of every street, and thousands fall into their webs of vice every year . . . Cities are the greatest centres of evil.
Elements of Success (Victorian book of advice for young men)[1]

Cities are good for us.

HARLEY SHERLOCK, 1991[2]

In Part One I examined in some detail the history of the part of East London in which I live and work, and within which I try to be a theologian, one who reflects on the word of God in this specific context. I begin Part Two with an attempt to describe the urban context, internationally, nationally and locally, and the role of the Christian communities within it.

The urban 'explosion'

Whether the language of 'explosion' is correct or not in relation to the development of cities, and of urbanisation, it is undoubtedly correct as a description of the study of, and fascination with, cities. Following Louis Wirth, I have used the term 'urbanism' to indicate not simply the existence of cities, but also a certain lifestyle, commitment, even state of mind. Whether we recognise it or not, we are all, more and more, urban creatures, and the future of the city is our future. It is not surprising that there is a concern about cities. Scarcely a day passes without a new study of the state of cities and their future prospects. The media report on the changing face of cities. There has been, since the late nineteenth century, from the days of Patrick Geddes, Peter Kropotkin, and Ebenezer Howard, a growth of urban studies as an academic discipline. This growth accelerated and developed at various stages in the twentieth century with the Chicago School of Urban Sociology, and the work of Ruth Glass and others in London in the 1950s. In contrast to that period, there are now centres for urban studies in many universities, and in many urban areas.

In recent decades there have been two major streams of urban studies, one focusing on economic and political issues, and one, post-structuralist in ethos, focusing on issues of culture, diversity, and so on. There has been a considerable input from radical geographers, in contrast to the earlier work which was dominated by sociologists and town planners. Historians, artists, architects, linguists and literary critics are among the many groups for whom the city has become an important area of reflection.[3]

The history of the East End of London is part of the world history of urbanisation, and it is right to view that history as being, on the whole, fairly recent. What we call the 'urbanisation of human life', the concentration of populations in urban areas or growths out of, and dependent on, urban areas is a phenomenon of recent times, of the nineteenth and twentieth centuries in particular. Yet it would be a mistake to study cities as if there were no earlier history.

There were cities in the ancient world. Ur apparently contained many thousands of people. Babylon contained eleven miles of walls, while Rome, in St Paul's day, was a city of immigrants, and contained the first high rise apartments. While they differed dramatically from modern cities, many of the features which they exhibited were the same. For instance, they too had 'red light districts' where prostitutes functioned, centres for 'pubs' and drinking houses, problems with water and sewage. The earliest cities seem to have developed about six thousand years ago. However, archaeological work has led to the conclusion that the concept of 'city' was used vaguely about a wide range of settlements.[4] There was considerable growth of towns and cities in the Middle Ages, and between 1050 and 1300 the population of Europe trebled.[5]

However, it is in the twentieth century that we have witnessed the growth of a language of urbanism, a language characterised by what Ruth Glass called 'verbal incendiary devices' – 'urban explosion', 'exploding cities', 'the urban time bomb' and so on.[6] Much attention has been devoted recently to the idea of 'megacities', and it has been said that these are likely to increase from fourteen to twenty-seven by 2015, especially in the 'Third World', even though most people will still live in smaller urban areas. Asian countries build a city of the size of London every six months. The world's tallest buildings now are not in Chicago and New York but in Kuala Lumpur and Shanghai.

Much of the language of urbanism is extravagant and lacking in precision. Today, it is often said, over 90 per cent of the British population is 'urbanised'. And, it is often assumed, this is a new reality. But what does this mean? To speak, for example, of 'unprecedented' urban growth is to ignore the experience of the eighteenth and nineteenth centuries when cities such as Manchester grew at a far greater speed than many modern cities. There are certainly precedents. And there are real problems in the definition of 'urban'. In global terms, many of what are termed 'urban centres' are in fact farming areas adjacent to cities. There are problems of boundaries. What, for example, is the population of London? If we define London in terms of the old Greater London Council boundaries, it is about 6.4 million. But if we follow international definitions, and speak of the 'metropolitan area', the figure comes to 12.5 million. The 'East London' area, if one includes Thurrock and Dartford, has a population of 2.5 million, larger than that of most great cities. By 1950, 64 per cent of the population of the USA lived in urban areas, and by 1990, 51 per cent lived in thirty-nine cities. But the majority of the population in fact were suburban.

So there are problems of definition, and concepts are changing. The growth of suburbia and of 'edge cities' has led some to speak of an 'exopolis' where the strength of urban life is not at the centre but at the periphery.[7] There are problems related to population growth and density. For example, in Europe, during the twelve centuries from the sixth century till around 1800, the population did not reach above 180 million. But from 1800 to 1914 there was massive growth to around 460 million.

Then there are problems about the nature of the economic base. Many British towns and cities were built around a single industry or small cluster of industries. Thus in 1851, two-thirds of the population of Oldham worked in coal, cotton and engineering, while in

Northampton half the population made shoes. Meanwhile London was growing at the expense of other British cities. In 1640, 10 per cent of all English people lived in London. But during the eighteenth century, London began to decline as other cities grew.

The changes in the economic base have been particularly important in areas which were dependent on one industry, but they have also affected cities such as London. Until the middle of the nineteenth century, London was the greatest manufacturing centre in the country. From then onwards, the population declined until very recently. However, London has started to grow again, and there were population increases in boroughs such as Westminster, Kensington and Chelsea, and Tower Hamlets from 1991 onwards. But population increase has taken place alongside social polarisation and economic dislocation.

Movement within the south of England has also been important. The growth of the South occurred at the same time as a massive out-migration from London. There was, for example, no significant immigration into London, or even the South-east region, in the 1950s. These areas grew more slowly than did England and Wales as a whole. Between 1965 and 1979 only three regions – East Anglia, the South-west and the East Midlands – gained population through migration, while the South-east lost 247,000. By the 1970s the highest proportion of employers, managers and professionals were located in the South-east. Thirty per cent of Britain's population lived in 12 per cent of the surface. But the population of the South-east region declined in 1972–3.[8]

The 1991 Census data showed that, during the previous decade, the rural areas had increased in population at the expense of the cities. While Greater London had lost population, the rural areas had gained 366,000. By 1985 it was possible to draw a line from South Wales to the Wash. South of this line was an area of population growth, new housing stock, and relative economic prosperity. North of it was an area of economic and social deprivation and industrial decline. This has, in recent years, become known as the 'North–South' divide, and, while it has been identified in over-simplified form, it has been for some time the primary dimension in variations of economic health.[9]

The strongest growth of jobs has been in small towns and rural areas, a development which has been described as 'counter-urban'.

The major area of growth in Britain was in East Anglia. Cambridge increased its population by 12.5 per cent between 1981 and 1991, while Milton Keynes grew by 39 per cent (41 per cent between 1981 and 1988).[10]

The role of immigration

The role of immigration has been important in the growth of cities since the Industrial Revolution. In Victorian Britain, more people died in cities than were born in them, and cities were constantly renewed by immigrants, though these came mostly from other parts of Britain. Writers constantly claim that 'the history of London is the history of its immigrants',[11] but this is only partly true. Internal migration was more significant. Between 1851 and 1911, for example, many of England's rural counties lost population to the cities. I have shown in Part One that both internal migration and immigration from outside Britain played important roles in the life of East London, and this was true of London as a whole.[12]

However, today, the effects of wars and revolutions, of poverty and economic hardship, of persecution and changes in the global economy, have made international migration a central part of human life and work. The world of settled, static communities with clear boundaries has gone for ever. In European countries, the foreign-born populations have grown since 1950. By 1992, that of Germany had grown from 1.1 to 8.6 per cent, Luxembourg from 9.8 to 29.1 per cent, and Holland from 1 to 5.1 per cent. Paris is now the second largest Portuguese city in the world, while in Switzerland foreign-born residents account for over 16 per cent of the population.

In North America, Los Angeles is home to over 400,000 El Salvadorians, and David Rieff has called it the capital of the Third World. There are more Salvadorians in Los Angeles than there are in San Salvador. By 1998 Latinos had outnumbered 'Anglos' in Los Angeles County. In New York, the Bronx area witnessed an increase of 87.8 per cent in its population of Asian origin between 1980 and 1990, while Hispanics increased by 32.4 per cent. There are now estimated to be 32 million Latinos in the USA and this may increase to 59 million by 2025. The Latino presence has already led to a significant transformation of urban space.[13]

Early in 1999 it was predicted that immigration would be a key issue for the American presidential election, and it has figured in recent political debates in Britain and elsewhere in Europe, not only in Germany and France, but also in Italy.[14]

Urbanism: decay, decline, division?

The rhetoric and literature of urbanism is marked by a demonology, but also by a sense of the importance of the city, even its superiority. Shelley described hell as 'a city much like London', while there is a strong anti-urban streak in some of Dickens' novels – *Bleak House* (1853), *Little Dorrit* (1857) and, in relation to Manchester, *Hard Times* (1854). 'Having pioneered urbanisation,' wrote Martin Wiener, 'the English ignored or despised cities'. English history is marked by a great deal of nostalgia for an idealised moment when the typical Englishman was 'a thatched cottager or country squire at heart'.[15] However, nostalgia for an imagined past is often linked with a vision of some imagined future for urban life. There has been a sense that somehow 'urban man' is superior to 'rural man', that the city is a source of cultural richness and diversity, and so on. Much recent work in urban sociology and urban geography has focused on cultural transformations and shifts. Richard Sennett has argued that one of the major benefits of the city is that, through its diversity and strangeness, it enables us to become more complex human beings.[16] But there is nothing inevitable about this.

Similarly, in the history of visions for the future of cities, there is a mingling of apocalyptic hope and disaster. While the image of the 'New Jerusalem' was common among an earlier generation of politicians and planners in Britain, this has given way in some quarters to the view that the city is a doomed ecosystem, incapable of ever being a community or even an environment for community. It is suggested by some that we can no longer use the term 'city' in its older sense of 'a limited and bounded structure which occupies a specific space'. Now 'the urban' has become 'an all-devouring monster that is engulfing both "city" and "country" '.[17]

However, alongside the symbols of 'explosion' and of 'megacities', the rhetoric of urban studies in recent decades includes an equally frequent use of the concepts of 'decline', 'decay' and 'division'. Recent books on the city include titles like *Clichés of Urban Doom*, *The Urbanisation of Injustice*, *Voices of Decline*, and *Divided Cities*.[18]

There has, of course, contrary to popular misconceptions, been a persistent decline in population in British cities since the exodus from the cities began, in the case of London in the 1840s. Between 1981 and 1991 all of the major British urban conurbations declined in population, some of them dramatically, such as Merseyside which experienced a population drop of 9 per cent. Within Inner London, only the East End increased, because of the Docklands development (see below) and the numbers of children born to Bangladeshi women.

The decline of inner urban areas is not peculiar to Britain. One of the most dramatic examples of inner urban decline, virtually collapse, is Detroit, the birthplace of the factory assembly line, the high industrial wage, and the affordable family car (as well as Motown!). Since the 1960s, Detroit has lost half of its population, the most dramatic example of such decline in the world, with the possible exception of Beirut. ABC TV called it 'America's first Third World city'.[19]

In the case of London it has been clear for years that the most striking social problems have been due to population decline, not growth. It has been the decline in population combined with the continuing existence of London as an employment centre which has created severe problems of housing and homelessness. Between 1951 and 1961, while the population declined, the number of households increased. The decline in these years was not accidental but was encouraged by planning policies, for example, by the fact that London, unlike other cities, was not allowed to advertise for new workers.[20]

Decline has occurred also in the economic infrastructure of cities as a shift has taken place from manufacturing towards service and information. The decline, and in many cases the collapse, of the manufacturing sector, was noted many years ago, along with the phenomenon of 'deindustrialisation'.[21]

Linked with the theme of urban decline is that of social polarisation. Thus Andrew Davey has written: 'Inner London experiences extreme deprivation within sight of centres of political and financial power. In the shadow of the towers of commerce lie communities where very different stories are being lived out.'[22]

The idea of polarisation goes back a long way in urban studies. The sociologists of the Chicago School wrote of cities in terms of residential segregation, 'the Gold Coast and the slum'. John Nash, the architect of the Regent's Park development (1814–37), was not the first to recognise class divisions, but he probably was the first to make their maintenance, and even strengthening, the object of planning, and to design methods of separation. In the early 1960s there were certainly 'areas where a polarisation of the society of Inner London is visible: rich and poor directly confront one another'.[23]

However, by 1973 the above writer was warning about the uncritical use of the term 'polarisation', and pointed out:

> Inner London is not being 'Americanised'; it is not on the way to becoming mainly a working class city, a 'polarised' city, or a vast ghetto for a black proletariat. The real risk for Inner London is that it might well be gentrified with a vengeance, and be almost exclusively reserved for selected higher class strata.[24]

Never were words so prophetic.

Urban policy and projects

Much early urban policy had been shaped by the belief in the need for dispersal of population from the cities. By the 1960s, legislative changes were increasingly motivated by political concerns. The Greater London Council was created in the hope of increasing the Conservative vote, and was later abolished for the same reason. Since then, many urban initiatives have been taken by non-accountable agencies. The list is almost endless. We have had urban development corporations, enterprise zones, task forces, city action teams, urban programmes, estate action programmes, and so on. We have had Urban Aid, the Urban Programme (1968), and numerous others with similar names. They come and go, leaving confusion and unfinished work.

The early policies were an incoherent mixture of social pathology and anti-poverty ideologies. The radicalism of the Home Office's Information and Intelligence Unit led to its closure in 1976, and the Community Development Project met the same fate. It took structural injustice seriously, which then led to a reaction in favour of a 'culture of poverty' approach, with a focus on personal moral behaviour. In 1977 Peter Shore, a Labour minister, initiated a programme for 'regeneration' of the inner areas.[25] Thus the language of 'regeneration' entered the political vocabulary, where it remains.

More recently, we have had City Challenge. One of the conclusions of the evaluation of this project was that comprehensive
regeneration could not occur if it were simply imposed on local
communities, a fairly obvious conclusion, one might have thought.
It would seem that some lessons from this have been learnt by 'New
Deal for Communities', the most recent government programme.
In the East End, for example, there was considerable difficulty in
relationship between Bethnal Green City Challenge and the local
council which only improved after the third year.[26] The most recent
urban initiative has been the Urban Task Force under Lord Rogers.[27]
It remains to be seen how a future government responds to this.

The long list of short-term urban initiatives, and urban failures,
is depressing. But one of the most striking features of recent years
has been the erosion of the whole idea of common or public ownership, which was central to the thinking of the Uthwatt Committee
of 1942, and which led to the nationalising of development rights
under the Town and Country Planning Act of 1947. It is highly
unlikely, if not impossible, that there can be justice in urban life
without a return to the idea of common ownership of land.[28] Yet
the commitment to the idea of the 'private' is now so entrenched
that it will take a revolution to transcend it.

The changing face of the East End of London

All of the issues raised in urban policy are manifested in the
recent history of the East End of London. Anyone who has lived in,
or observed, the East End over the last half century will be aware of
the dramatic changes – the collapse of the economic base, the closure
of the docks, the arrival of gentrification and luxury housing, the
resurgence of organised racism, the destruction of old communities,
and, looming over it all like Babel, the huge bizarre symbol of
Canary Wharf. In the last twenty years the changes in the East End
have included population, class, industry and housing. Between 1966
and 1971 there was an 18 per cent loss of population, and in the late
1980s Tower Hamlets was the only London borough with increases
in population.

The collapse of the economic base has been devastating. Between
1961 and 1971, jobs in Greater London fell by 10 per cent, and
manufacturing jobs by 25 per cent. Tower Hamlets lost one-fifth of

all its jobs. The numbers of docks workers fell from 25,000 in 1960 to 4,100 in 1981, as the docks closed in the late 1970s. In these developments, the East End manifests more general trends as cities become centres of information, consumption and business, rather than of directly employed labour in the manufacturing field. It should be stressed, however, that the dominance of the 'knowledge economy' has been greatly exaggerated, and that much of the rhetoric about the 'information super highway' and 'information city' is extremely unsophisticated and misleading.

A major problem for us in East London is that most of the people with higher educational qualifications move away. This is clear from the census data for Barking and Dagenham from 1981 to 1991. Here there was an increase in educational qualifications, but the ratio of residents with such qualifications remained the same, 3.5 per cent of the population. Most of those with qualifications had moved out of the area.

At the centre of recent East End changes has been the phenomenon of 'Docklands'. In an editorial of 6 September 1991, *The Times* observed that 'the area has been a battleground of economic ideologies and the price has been paid in poverty'. On 29 January 1971 the *East London Advertiser* warned that a construction company was building eleven town houses on the Isle of Dogs, and that it was now 'the "in" thing to live near the river'. The community activist Ted Johns was cited: 'The frightening thing is that this is just the start of what is bound to happen in the future . . . The riverside is gradually being taken away from the East End, and this must be realised before it is too late.' Ten years later the London Docklands Development Corporation (LDDC) was created.

It was too late, though local groups put up a good fight. Yet the developers won, and the artificial construction called 'Docklands', dominated by the monstrous phallic-capitalist symbol of Canary Wharf, arose to dominate the landscape of East London. The geographer Darrel Crilley called it 'a bastion of privilege, towering over the vernacular of East London'.[29] Sue Brownill in 1990 was scathing about the LDDC and Canary Wharf as 'another great planning disaster' and 'a major failure in inner city policy', while in his Reith Lectures of 1995, Sir Richard (later Lord) Rogers described Docklands as 'a chaos of commercial buildings linked by an amusement park train.'[30]

The lack of real (as opposed to rhetorical) consultation, the insensitivity to and, most of the time, contempt for, the local residents, the concern for profits more than for a good and wholesome community, the imaginative and visionary failures, the weakness of the transport infrastructure, and so much more, are integral to this history. They represent a microcosm of the world.

So this area was transformed into the largest development in Europe. As Janet Foster says in her recent study, 'those who developed Docklands did not take into account the prevailing context' – not surprisingly since local people were 'incidental rather than integral to the development . . . a peripheral rather than integral part of the development process', 'The community was the last to be consulted and the first to be discarded.'[31] As a former cabinet minister said, in my presence, they were only 'the latest layer of dust'. It has been claimed that the development went forward with less scrutiny than would have been needed for an illuminated sign outside a fish and chip shop in East India Dock Road.[32] Foster brings out the complexity of the situation in what is now called Docklands, itself a new connotation implying new ideologies and a new conceptual framework. But four old issues are still paramount: jobs, housing, health, and 'community'.

Between 1961 and 1971 jobs in Greater London fell by 10 per cent, and manufacturing jobs by 25 per cent. In the East End, because of the closure of the docks, the position was particularly serious. In 1991, after ten years of the LDDC, unemployment in the Isle of Dogs area stood at 17.2 per cent. Half of the jobs in the LDDC area were in relocated companies. By 1992, when Olympia and York, the developers, became bankrupt, the vacancy rate in the new offices was 58 per cent.

The costs in physical and mental health have been enormous. At Gill Street Clinic, close to Canary Wharf, by the early 1990s, 10 per cent of patients suffered from asthma and disorders of the upper respiratory tract. Dust and atmospheric pollution have been crucial, and serious health problems have continued among residents of what has been rightly called 'the biggest building site in Europe'.

The demand for decent and affordable housing has been at the heart of the whole saga. The East End experience is part of the whole story of housing in Britain where there has been a decline in total expenditure from 6.8 per cent in 1966 to 2.6 per cent by 1990. In

East London, almost all the housing built has been private and at the luxury end of the private market. In the first ten years of the LDDC, not one house was built for rent on the Isle of Dogs. The racism which erupted in 1993, with the election of a British National Party councillor for the ward which contains Canary Wharf, has deep historic roots, but the competition over housing was central to that moment. Foster gives a good account of this episode in a chapter appropriately entitled 'It all turns very nasty'. It was nasty from the start.

What the coming of the LDDC did was to bring much of this history to the surface, and focus and polarise it in a particularly painful and aggressive way. Vanessa Houlder of the *Financial Times* once called the Canary Wharf exercise 'the most costly disaster in the history of UK property development'.[33]

One of the most frequent complaints about urban life in East London, as in many other places, is that of 'the collapse of community'. The East End, the heart of Cockney London, is renowned for its sense of community. It was here, after all, that 'community studies' began with Willmott and Young's *Family and Kinship in East London*, and daily one is told stories of how, in the 'old days', 'we all looked after one another', and the East End was the friendliest place on earth. So it must have come as something of a shock to discover that, in a recent study of 'friendly neighbourhoods', Tower Hamlets appeared as the least friendly district in the country. In fact, London as a whole does not figure very high in terms of quality of life. It came thirty-fourth in the world scale, with Vancouver, Berne, Vienna and Zurich way ahead.[34]

One of the assumptions in much discussion of 'community' is that it is based upon residential proximity. But this is increasingly not the case. The geographer Doreen Massey has suggested that there have been very few areas of Britain in recent years where 'place' and 'community' were profoundly intertwined in this way, areas where community was inseparable from residence, but she cited the Isle of Dogs, the cotton towns, and the mining areas as three major examples of such areas.[35] In the Isle of Dogs, one often hears the expression 'a true Islander'. While the concept of an 'Islander' remains a little elusive, it is certainly true that, to some old residents, people from as close as Poplar were seen as foreigners. Many of the old tightly-knit urban villages of London such as Hoxton, Bethnal

Green and Notting Dale (all of them areas where I have worked) were districts with low rates of movement, strong patterns of kinship, and fierce levels of xenophobia and racism. It is not surprising that it was in these areas that Sir Oswald Mosley found much of his support for the fascist movement, and the first two are still targets for fascist activists.

There is a really big problem here in relation to East London where there is so much nostalgia and talk of a world we have lost, the true spirit of the East End, family and kinship, the days of the Kray twins, and so on. The language of 'community' evokes sentiments and memories of both a real and an idyllic past, and may be the precursor for a real regeneration of corporate life, or for something resembling a grass roots fascism. How does the church relate to all this? This was the central issue in the recent crisis about the nature of the church *vis-à-vis* community on the Isle of Dogs in the build up to, and the aftermath of, the election of Derek Beackon of the British National Party. (See Chapter 8.)

Linked to this changed character of 'community', one of the major changes in the East End in recent years is the dramatically altered nature of the housing stock and of the residential population itself. Only forty years ago the East End contained one of the highest ratios of manual workers in the country, and the majority lived in local authority housing. Many people believe that council housing will die out by 2010, and local authorities until recently were forbidden to add to their housing stock. By 1981 the council still owned 82 per cent of the housing stock, but this fell to 58 per cent in 1991. Meanwhile the percentage of owner occupiers increased from 4.6 to 23.3 per cent.

The most striking changes have occurred in Spitalfields, Wapping and Canary Wharf. Between 1981 and 1991, 81 per cent of new housing in the LDDC area was private, and most of it at the luxury end of the private market. The conversion of St Katherine's Dock in the 1970s included an international hotel and the World Trade Centre, while nearby Tobacco Dock was made into a retail centre and luxury housing. Meanwhile in these, and other, parts of the East End, there is a population of extremely wealthy new residents, and luxury flats are being built in districts formerly occupied by working-class families.[36]

It is clear that at least 75 per cent of the local population cannot afford the private property which has been built. The stark contrast between this property and the housing conditions of poor people is horrifying. Forty-four per cent of the housing stock in the East End is unsatisfactory. In Spitalfields Ward, 28 per cent of the households live at a density of over one person per room. Yet houses in Fournier Street, in the heart of that ward, are selling at £1 million. Land and property have become very expensive, and they have become battlegrounds. The wishes, needs and values of property developers increasingly collide with those of residents, as in the current struggle over the future of the Spitalfields Market site.[37]

Inequality and health in the East End

'Inequality in health provision will become more marked,' warned Will Hutton, in his important work *The State We're In*, 'and the health of the poor will become worse'.[38] Our experience in the East End is that this has been the case for some time, and is now extremely serious. Again, our local data simply focus and reinforce a pattern which is seen in western cities as a whole. The numbers of poor people living in cities has doubled over the last ten years. By the end of 1999 it is estimated that the figure would be a billion. The relationship between poverty and health in western cities is well documented, but the documentation makes little impact on political change. In Washington, DC the infant mortality rate is higher than that of Nepal, and in Harlem in New York City it is higher than in Bangladesh. In parts of Liverpool the death rate for coronary heart disease and lung failure is over twice the national average.

Research has consistently shown the strong links between income gulfs and health. Health inequalities in Britain reached their lowest level in 1951, but have been increasing since then. As the gaps between communities have grown wider, so the incidence of ill health has increased. It is clear that the more equality and cohesion there is, the more likely it is that the population will be healthy. The Black Report of 1980 was very emphatic about this, but health inequalities continued to widen, as Sir Donald Acheson showed in his report in 1998. Social location is crucial to social and personal health.[39]

Certainly the gap has widened between the East End and the rest of Britain. The death rate is 14 per cent higher, the illness rate 27 per cent higher, than the average for England and Wales. The asthma rate is 80 per cent higher. Damp housing is a major factor in health, not least in the incidence of depression. In one study in 1989 over 72 per cent of people reported that they lived in damp rooms. The leading cause of preventable death of under 65-year-olds in the area is cardiovascular disease (coronary heart disease or stroke). In October 1994 there were 410 people with tuberculosis in the East End, and possibly 4,000 carriers. Death rates among unskilled men were twice that of professionals in the early 1970s, and by 1998 had become three times. In 1980 Tower Hamlets was the only London borough in the top ten highest death rate areas in Britain, and in 1999 had the highest child death rate in England. In the East End the death rate was 14 per cent higher, and the illness rate 27 per cent higher than the national average. In September 2000, it was top of the list in government data as the most deprived area in Britain.[40]

Agenda for an urban theology

What is a theology which considers the issues arising from the urban scene? What kind of theology should this be? Reflection on urbanism and its discontents leads us to conclude that an urban theological agenda must take seriously a number of key issues. These need to be at the forefront of our minds when considering schemes of 'regeneration' or proposals for redevelopment of a neighbourhood. I believe that they are issues on which Christian theology has a great deal to contribute but also where significant areas of agreement and practical co-operation are possible with people from other traditions of faith and of ethical reasoning.

The LDDC experience is certainly a warning of what may happen when property developers are given free rein, and there are many signs that all these mistakes are being repeated. Yet we are bound to ask: Are they 'mistakes'? Or does it depend on what your perspective is? From the perspective of a poor, inner-city resident, the whole operation may seem unjust and irrational. But 'Whose justice? Which rationality?' (as MacIntyre would say – and did say!). Is it a case of 'Their morals and ours' (as Trotsky put it)? We are in the arena of conflicting sets of values, conflicting ideologies, conflicting ways of reasoning.[41]

It is important too to remember some earlier history, the history of 'planning' and of 'urban renewal'. Much of the language which is used – development, renewal, regeneration, etc. – was acquired many years ago and became part of a kind of kit. Often it is assumed, without critical examination, that concepts mean the same thing to different people, and that words are interchangeable –'regeneration' and 'redevelopment', for example. As long ago as 1959 Ruth Glass noted that 'there is an international alphabet of physical planning and it tends to be used all over the world, even in circumstances in which it is incomprehensible'.[42] Since the 1980s the metaphor of 'regeneration', with its religious overtones, as well as its links with the earlier social Darwinist rhetoric of 'degeneration', has taken over from that of 'reconstruction' (post-1945) and 'renewal' and 'redevelopment' (1960s and 1970s).

In Britain neither deferential hierarchical capitalism nor the newer forms of unaccountable quangos, managerial elites and bureaucratic empires are particularly stable. They have not led to the 'culture of contentment' identified by Galbraith but rather to a culture of insecurity. Galbraith's thesis contrasted the simmering discontent of the 1930s with what he called a culture of contentment today. Yet it is not so simple as this, and clearly there is a good deal of discontent. One of the most worrying aspects of current capitalism in Britain and elsewhere is the rise of the unaccountable quango and the breakdown of accountability. Decisions affecting human lives are increasingly made by remote bodies over the heads of local democratically elected councils. The history of the LDDC itself is the classic example where the Toronto-based property developers Olympia and York were selling property in New York City in order to pay for the developments in London's East End. In spite of the rhetoric of 'consultation' and the commitment to 'social housing', this movement of 'regeneration' has been dictated by international developers, unaccountable to anyone.

Local churches have played an important role in resisting these forces, and the record of the Anglican Church in Docklands at the time of the election of the fascist councillor Derek Beackon in 1993 is an excellent one. Indeed, one geographer has commented that the role of the Church is to focus on 'the fusion of the spatial and the spiritual, the sense of place and the sense of justice'.[43] But this is a call for really hard work.

Among the questions which urban theologians must face are these.

1. What is a good city?

The Christian rhetoric here is ambiguous, with a lengthy anti-urban polemic on the one hand, and a vision of the city of God, the holy city, on the other. Christianity was, in origin, an urban movement, so much so that the words 'pagan' (people of the countryside) and 'heathen' (people of the heath) were used in contrast to the urban Christians. In St Matthew's Gospel, the word *polis* (city) is used twenty-six times, in contrast to *kome* (village) which occurs only four times.

The presence of the Church in cities is itself a theological statement. It assumes the goodness of cities, since, were cities considered as intrinsically evil, it is arguable that the Church should manifest this position by removing its presence from them as a testimony and a sign of renunciation. However, though many Christian trends do contain a strong anti-urban element, mainstream Christian thought has – at least in its theory – valued the city as a site of justice and as a place where holiness can be nurtured. Again, the Church's presence in the city assumes the potential for the 'salvation' (transformation, even 'regeneration'!) of structures.

Yet the city is also a site of injustice, oppression and dehumanising forces. Decisions about the future of cities, about 'regeneration', for example, are often made without any serious regard for the common good. The private good of a particular company, their ability to offer financial deals to the local authority, often accompanied by token gestures to 'social housing' or 'urban renewal', are substituted for sustained moral commitment. The City of London is an extreme version of this position, which is in fact much more widespread. In this square mile, dominated by the global market, much of it occupied by American and Japanese banks, there is little or no attempt to link global finance, the needs of London, and the views of its residents. It is a central task of urban theology to question, undermine and expose the false values which put profits before people, private gain before public good, and ultimately the success of enterprise before the welfare of the city and all its people.

2. How can inequalities of wealth and power be reduced?

Inequalities of wealth and power are most visibly manifest in cities. Sociologists have spoken of an 'urbanisation of injustice'.[44] This is not a situation which Christians can simply accept as part of the unchangeable structure of life. Schemes which serve to increase the wealth of the rich, and to marginalise further those who are already deprived, must be resisted.

From the perspective of the East End, I have never known a time in the last four decades when the gap between rich and poor was so wide. We now have an influx of the wealthy. They do not live alongside the poor, indeed they have little contact with them. They have taken over territory, in Spitalfields, Wapping, and the Isle of Dogs, which previously housed poor people. But the new rich live in a world of their own, guarded by technological security devices, protected by the heavy wooden shutters of gentrification. Will this also happen in current developments?

3. What is a just immigration policy?

As we have seen, immigration plays an increasing role in the life of cities, not least in its employment structure. Yet the presence of immigrants is determined by the operation of legislation which is often, in intention and in practice, racist. It is also clear that immigrants are often employed in situations of extreme insecurity, and financial and personal exploitation. Urban developments which depend upon immigrants for cheap labour, but damage and inhibit their prospects for a life of dignity and security must be resisted. Government policies aimed to combat 'social exclusion' operate alongside other policies – on asylum, immigration and refugee welfare – aimed to promote it. More will be said on these questions in Chapters 8 and 9.

4. How can North and South work together?

While the conventional idea of a 'North–South divide' is oversimplified, there is enough truth in it to be a source of concern and commitment. Recent attempts to deny the divide are not supported by academic research data. Christians in different regions of the country need to develop methods of sharing of ideas, pooling of resources, and developing areas of common action. The image of 'breaking down the wall', central to the theology of the Epistle to the Ephesians, is important in relation to divisions within countries, and there is immense scope for co-operation across these divides. Manchester, Liverpool and Barnsley can offer much to, and learn much from, London, Croydon and Milton Keynes.

5. What can we learn from the USA?

A lot – but we usually learn the wrong things. My impression is that we have tended to follow American urban policies mainly in those areas where they have most conspicuously failed. (Drugs policy is the classic example.) We can learn much from the regeneration programmes of other European cities, and need to exercise caution and ideological suspicion in what we learn from the USA, where levels of poverty, racial and social segregation, and disparities of wealth are much greater than here.[45] One important aspect of the situation in the USA, however, is that the role of churches in the inner city is increasingly being taken seriously by the media. Between 1996 and 1998, for example, a number of journalists raised the question of whether churches would make a better job of managing the inner cities than government agencies have done.[46] We need to be in touch with this debate and learn from our comrades in the USA. Churches working in urban environments can, and need to learn from one another, sharing their insights, frustrations, joys and struggles across national boundaries. This is why, for me, the weeks I spend each year with American Christians are of immense local value in the East End of London.

6. What is community?

Can communities of the older type be recovered? Michael Young and others claim that they can, that recovery is possible. But there is real danger in 'looking backwards'. We need to do far more work on this. While it is true that the old 'urban village' model of closely-knit communities, and of many extended families living in close proximity, has largely disappeared, there are parts of the East End and of other towns and cities where a strong neighbourhood sense is still present, though the danger of the further breaking up of such communities is a real one. Concentration on the 'neighbourhood church' has become more, not less, relevant in many places.[47]

7. How do we cope with unemployment and loss of value?

There is widespread hopelessness about job prospects, while insecurity has risen among those who are economically active. Nor is this sense an irrational one. The Organisation for Economic Cooperation and Development has claimed that the chances of prime age male workers becoming unemployed have risen in all major member countries except the United States. For many people, the chances of ever entering into full-time employment are low, and for years now many young people have left schools without any hope that they will ever get a job. But this is not the whole story: there is also a loss of confidence in the ability of 'the system' to deliver the goods, a sense that things are falling apart.

The collapse of many traditional areas of work has led to a major crisis of identity. Loss of jobs often leads to loss of dignity, sense of worth, and sense of direction. Undoubtedly new types of work are emerging, but we are at present in a transitional period where there is a loss of older commitments to full employment and, so far, inadequate ways of structuring and shaping new understandings. In this climate the 'regeneration' of devastated neighbourhoods, which is perceived only to introduce new employment opportunities for the already prosperous, is bound to lead to further bitterness, frustration and social conflict. The Church's verbal commitment to human dignity and value must be concretised in actual situations and practices.

8. How can we work for a sustainable city?

One frequently used piece of political jargon, more or less obligatory in some circles, is the phrase 'joined up'. Yet much urban policy is clearly not joined up at all, but rather a jungle of assorted interests, proposals, and plans which serve competing interests. In this context, what meaning has the concept of 'sustainability'? Cities do not automatically thrive and flourish. Collapse and disintegration are not unknown. Attention to sustainable environments and sustainable developments must be at the heart of regeneration schemes.

Take, for example, the issue of pollution. The North American experience shows that toxic and hazardous waste sites are invariably in poor areas. Sumter County in Alabama contains the largest hazardous waste landfill in the USA with toxic materials from forty-six states and some foreign countries, while the South Side of Chicago contains the greatest concentration of waste sites in the USA.[48] In London many deaths occur each year which are linked to traffic pollution.

The issues of pollution are becoming more serious by the day. The lifestyles of urban people in the Northern hemisphere are the major factor in planetary degradation. The problem of uncontrolled carbon dioxide emissions is a major threat, and it is likely that many of the earth's self-healing systems have now been irreversibly degraded. One writer has called this 'the planetary equivalent of AIDS'.[49]

9. How can we promote more adequate health care?

The evidence of relationship between poverty and ill health is enormous, not least in Tower Hamlets. One major issue for Christians in urban areas is that of food. The relationship between the human body and good, nutritious food is a key element in the Christian tradition with its stress on incarnation and on the sacramental character of material things including food. The acts of eating and drinking are at the heart of Christian liturgical life. Yet many inner city areas are dominated by junk food.

In Rochester, New York, in 1998 a campaign to establish a good grocery store was launched by Allison Clark and a group of Christian activists. They called their project 'The Politics of Food'. The recent history of the area had been one of decline in accessible stores – supermarkets had fallen from forty-two in 1970 to eight in 1994 – and the rise of 'convenience stores' serving junk food, as one local Methodist minister put it, 'high priced, high salt, high cholesterol, packaged frozen dinners and pizzas requiring a microwave or an oven and a landfill for all the trash they generate'.

Are 'regeneration' schemes likely simply to lead to more junk food, more multinational McDonald's/Burger King, etc.? What are the wider health implications of developments? The most abiding memory of the Docklands era for many has been the levels of dust, and the increase of asthma.

The omission of health from regeneration is damaging, an omission which work at the King's Fund is trying to rectify. Health does not figure in most regeneration schemes. Most papers on regeneration ignore health. A search of Medline, a database of recent health research, and other Internet sources showed that almost all the references to regeneration were to the repairing of human tissue. When the Department of Health launched Health Improvement Programmes, it apparently did so in unawareness that in other areas of government, HIP stood for Housing Investment Programmes![50]

It is, incidentally, important to help medical students to understand what are curiously termed the 'non-medical factors' in sickness and health. (Are not most of these factors non-medical?) Of the 5,600 residents of St Mary's Ward in Whitechapel, where I live, about one-quarter are doctors, nurses and medical students attached to the Whitechapel site of the Royal London Hospital. For several years I was involved with the 'community module' at the London Hospital Medical College, an attempt to help medical students understand wider social, economic and political issues. Such programmes need to be developed and expanded if 'healing' is to acquire authentic social meaning.[51]

10. How is housing to be transformed?

In the Spitalfields district of East London, the home of the largest Bangladeshi community in Britain, the Spitalfields Small Business Association (SSBA) has been active in purchasing and developing land for both social housing and industrial development. Led by a community activist and former architect, Kay Jordan, and a Bengali veteran Tassaduq Ahmed, the SSBA is now the biggest Bangladeshi-based community group in Britain, owning £18 million of property, including houses and flats. Its work in the most overcrowded ward of Britain has been a model of good practice and of co-operation between communities and interest groups. How can this be developed, and what are the forces which get in the way of developments such as this? Churches have a good record in the housing field, and groups such as the Catholic Housing Aid Society

(CHAS) and the Churches' National Housing Coalition are examples of first-class work rooted in excellent research, while 'secular' groups such as Shelter grew out of work done by churches in Notting Hill.

11. How can we tackle issues of literacy in the context of strengthening human potential and agency?

Literacy is far more than learning how to read and write. It is about understanding, about articulation, and about self-confidence. It is about acquiring the ability to engage with ideas, to argue, and to debate matters in the public arena. It is about over-coming the indignity and disability which attaches to the inability to take part on such matters, and about the tremendous sense of liberation and 'empowerment' which comes with progress in them. Paulo Freire in Brazil and Chris Searle in East London are examples of people who have pioneered good work in this field.

12. How can we strengthen and renew the significance of place?

Walter Brueggemann is right to see that 'a sense of place is a primary category of faith' and that we need to take very seriously the issues of rootage, belonging, location.[52] Theology must stress the crucial importance of the earth, the material environment. A major influence – some would say the major influence – on the thinking of the British Prime Minister Tony Blair was the Scottish philosopher John MacMurray. At the heart of MacMurray's thought was the belief that the economic order must serve the personal, and that a good political and economic system must provide for a rich personal life. How do developments stand up to these principles?

More and more today the sense of place is being eroded by globalisation and the consequent loss of roots in any concrete location, and by the monochrome character of many cities. A major task of Christian theology is to help recover a sense of place. Of course, there is a continuous polemic which began with the Jewish prophets which questions the whole notion of 'sacred space'. Space is only sacred when it serves the will of God.[53] Yet, as the legendary Sheffield pastor Alan Ecclestone wrote: 'Soil reflects soul. The ravaged earth of old mining areas, the dust-bowls created by reckless cropping, the squalid litter left by departing crowds, the desolation of decaying inner city areas, all testify to the impoverishment of the Spirit.'[54] The work of Agenda 21, which developed from the Earth Summit in Rio in 1992, has made limited inroads on environmental issues in local communities, but there is so much still to be done.

A factor which is important here is the role of what have been called 'anchor institutions', institutions which can provide stability in the midst of turbulence, but which can also prevent communities from moving forward in more calm and changing times. The evidence does show that churches have played both roles at different times. So this raises the question of the church as a symbol of continuity and of roots. In American cities such as Atlanta, Dallas or Memphis, where the rate of change in terms of property and design has been enormous, the only familiar buildings from the past are often Baptist churches. In London, in the nineteenth century, some churches were crucial to their neighbourhoods, landmarks, symbols of the community. The theology of the future will need to move beyond the limitations of both the 'spiritual' and the 'human', and deepen its concern about, and commitment to, the future of the material world. Of course this will involve an enrichment and expansion of both spirituality and humanism, and it can only start at the local level with the care of the ground on which one stands.

Finally, we must reject the view that there is only one theology – pure, spiritual, universal, aloft – which is valid for city and suburb, rich and poor. Denys Turner has pointed out that what brings Christians together in the affluent suburbs cannot be solidarity in Christ unless it also brings them together in solidarity with the residents of the inner city. I am sure there are parallels in the social teachings of other faiths. The gospel cannot be good news unless it is first bad news for those whose power and wealth diminish and humiliate others.[55]

7

The captivity and liberation of theology

The important questions to be asked by theology . . . are: who should do theology, and where, and in whose interest, and for whom?

J.B. METZ[1]

The most important thing is to keep doing theology.

KARL BARTH[2]

A 'paradigm shift' in theology?

The word 'theology' has a complex and confusing history, and it is necessary, therefore, before we examine the nature of theological work in contemporary urban society, to consider the ways in which the word, and the ideas behind the word, have been used in earlier times.

The word was used in pagan antiquity to mean a study of the myths about the gods. It occurs in the writings of some early Christians such as Clement of Alexandria and Hippolytus, but its use is infrequent in Christian circles before the Council of Nicea in the fourth century. By the time of Basil of Caesarea, *theologia* had come to mean God in the very heart of God's being – as contrasted with *economia,* which referred to God's activity in the world. In the writings of the Cappadocians, theology was often a synonym for the Holy Trinity. In these early writers, there was no sense of the modern split between intellectual work and spiritual work, between study and prayer. Theology was itself seen as spiritual activity. In the classic definition of Evagrius Ponticus, a theologian was one whose prayer was authentic. The essential unity between theology and what later came to be called 'spirituality' is evident by the fourth century.

Gregory Nazianzen, for example, emphasises purity of heart and inner calm as the prerequisites of the theologian, and sees breathlessness as the principal enemy of theological life![3]

Since those days, the discipline of theology has undergone major changes and developments. Some writers have argued that theology is in a state of decay, but my sense is that we have moved beyond this moment towards one of change, calling for discernment and discrimination.[4] I will concentrate here on recent changes, and suggest that some kind of 'paradigm shift' has taken place. The concept of a 'paradigm shift' has become fashionable as a result of the work of the late Thomas Kuhn on scientific revolutions. I want to suggest that, while the term can be used in a simplistic and imprecise way, 'paradigm shifts' have been occurring, for good or ill, in the whole understanding of what it is to 'do theology'.[5] It is therefore worth examining some of the ways in which theology has been understood, and the ways in which these have been challenged. While I refer to recent shifts, it is essential to realise that in many cases a current change in outlook reflects a return to an older tradition as much as a movement towards a newer one.

1. Theology had come to be seen as a primarily cerebral discipline.

For many centuries in the West, theology had come to be associated exclusively with intellectual activity within the context of the university or seminary. The notion of theology as science grew up within the foundation of medieval universities. The idea of theology as a purely intellectual discipline seems only to have appeared with Peter Abelard (1079–1142). After him came scholasticism, and, while both Aquinas and Bonaventure stressed the integration of theology and spirituality, the gap widened in the epoch after them. By the thirteenth century theological work had shifted from the *lectio divina* of the monasteries to the disputations of the cathedral schools and universities.[6]

Karl Barth famously defined theology as a rational wrestling with mystery.[7] However, in recent decades, we have seen the spread of theological activity of other kinds, and there is a realisation that theology is 'more than the work of the mind',[8] where mental activity plays a part alongside other approaches involving feelings, the visual arts, the imagination, and the affirmation of insights gained outside the academy and the world of formalised theological education.

2. *Theology had come to be seen as an elitist discipline.*

This is linked closely with the first point. In order to be a theologian, on this view, one must have gone through a process of inculturation which would include training in the classical languages, entry into a subculture associated with common rooms, academic conferences, sherry parties, and becoming familiar with the notaries of the subculture. Only those who have entered this subculture, and who have produced a certain number of articles in learned journals, are recognised as theologians. Members of the subculture often cite one another's work, often referring obliquely to members of other similar academic disciplines, making references hardly at all to the existence of theological reflection beyond the elite borders.[9]

One of the features of such elites is their incestuous quality. Members write for one another, cite one another's writings, develop languages which only make sense to the initiates, and, consciously or not, exclude those who are not initiated from access to the conversation. There is also the class aspect of all this. Walter Rauschenbusch observed in 1907 that 'eminent theologians, like other eminent thinkers, live in the social environment of wealth and to that extent are slow to see.'[10] His words are still true to a large extent.

While there is evidence that such elitism is being eroded, albeit slowly, two warnings should be addressed. First, the strength and resilience of such elites should not be underestimated. The potential to sustain elitism and to exclude is still very strong. Second, there is evidence that in recent years new elites, new jargons, new forms of exclusion have developed, and many of those involved are young people. Feminist theology has done a great deal to undermine hierarchical understandings and to break down the split between the academy and the world beyond, but it must be stressed that feminist theologians are by no means immune from the seductive power of capital and the appeal of academic security and status.[11]

So there has been, and needs to be, a stress upon the participants. We hear now of 'public theology', a term coined by Martin Marty in 1974.[12] The Jewish thinker Irving Greenberg has said that 'no statement, theological or otherwise, should be made that would not be credible in the presence of burning children', while Donald Nichol also claimed that the physical presence of children was a necessity in good theological work.[13] Others have stressed the need to democratise theology, recovering the idea of theology as 'the people's work'.[14] There is abundant evidence that who you are, and where you stand, affects what you see, and theological work will change as those taking part in it are different people from different contexts.

Two other matters arise at this point. The first is that theology has come, in popular discourse, to be a synonym for irrelevance, and there is no doubt that, to a large extent, the Christian community has only itself to blame for this caricature.[15] The second is that it is conventionally assumed that the only theologians are academics.[16] The bourgeois dominance of theology in the West has also meant, for example, that the idea that theological debates should always be polite has been taken for granted. But we know that important conversations are often impolite and conflictual, indeed that intellectual life itself, not to mention life as a whole, is marked by tension and turbulence.

3. Theology had come to be seen as a preparation for some other form of activity, rather than a way of life, a habitus.

However, there have been shifts here also. Thus Elaine Graham, Professor of Social and Pastoral Theology at the University of Manchester, points out that theology does not consist of abstract propositions, but is a performative discipline within which knowledge and truth are realisable. It involves the pursuit of realisable social strategies. 'The praxis of the faithful community constitutes the character and wisdom of theology: it is the means by which Christians purposefully inhabit the world and the vehicle through which the community itself is formed and ordered.'[17]

The idea of theology as a preparation for some other form of activity raises its own problems. While some respondents to the Commission which produced *Faith in the City* noted that their college training had 'positively unfitted them for work in urban areas', the critique of the seminary model seems to have waned in favour of complementary and parallel models – non-residential

ministerial training courses, locally ordained ministry schemes, with
the seminary still seen as the superior model.[18]

4. *Theology had come to be seen as in some sense 'pure'*
and, while threats to it were recognised, such threats were
perceived as solely intellectual, as was their rebuttal.

In some areas of theological thinking, a wedge has been
driven between conviction and 'objectivity'. Theologians, on this
view, are neutral investigators; the beliefs of the theologian are, it is
thought, if not abandoned, at least best suspended. The American
theologian James McClendon rightly observed that in convictional
work of any kind, involvement of the person is natural and appropriate: it is disengagement which needs to be explained and which
calls for justification.[19]

However, the place of conviction, even bias, in theological work
has come to be valued and stressed in recent years. The shift to an
engaged theology began several decades ago. As long ago as 1966
Harvey Cox wrote of the need for theology to serve the prophetic
community: 'For this reason the place of theology is that jagged
edge where the faithful company grapples with the swiftest currents
of the age. Any "theology" which occurs somewhere else or for some
other reason scarcely deserves the name.'[20]

Today more theologians are questioning the idea that theology
can ever be pure and detached. Elisabeth Schussler Fiorenza, for
example, sees feminist theological work as the work of troublemakers,
resident aliens, destabilisers of centres.[21] Theology, many thinkers
stress, must be committed, messy, in the midst of imperfection
and brokenness. So there is more emphasis on neglected aspects of
theological work such as the centrality of care.[22] Recently too there
has been more stress on the pastoral character of theology itself,[23]
and on theology in the midst of action. 'In the midst of action we
are theologians'.[24]

Also under attack is the professionalisation of theology, its self-
containment within clearly defined and compartmentalised boundaries. On the contrary, argues Graham Ward, 'theology's business has
always been to transgress the boundaries'.[25] My experience is that
theology is challenged, threatened, called into question, by the
struggles, pains, dilemmas and tribulations of actual living people

and communities. It is in one's own context that the positions one holds are called into question or shown to be inadequate, strengthened, or even abandoned. Theology flourishes and is most authentic when it abandons its 'purity' and lives in interaction and dialectical engagement both with other disciplines and with the concrete struggles of people.

5. Theology had come to be seen as an individual pursuit.

It is probable that the idea of an individual theologian, as indeed of an individual at all, was a product of the eleventh century. St Anselm seems to have played a key role in introducing ideas of self-awareness into prayer and reflection.[26] Yet the life of the mind involves social discourse. One American bishop has stressed that 'theological training is a community effort . . . theological education is something that is localised within the life of a community . . . These two insights, localised education and education that is culturally relevant, are going to be the two paths, two highways, that will carry us into the Twentieth Century.'[27]

Theology is a corporate project. Schreiter speaks of 'the community as theologian, while Marcella Althaus-Reid has claimed that 'nobody *is* a theologian. We *are* theologians in community and dialogue'.[28]

6. Theology had come to be seen as disconnected from prayer, spiritual discipline and the pursuit of holiness.

In the East, as we saw above, the unity of 'theology' and 'spirituality' was assumed from early times. It is purity, according to St John Climacus, which makes a person a theologian. To this day the title 'theologian' is reserved in the Orthodox liturgical calendar for three people of outstanding holiness and spiritual insight – St John the Evangelist, St Gregory Nazianzen, and St Symeon. In Orthodox understanding, all theology is essentially mystical, and its aim is *theosis*, deification.[29]

In the West, St Thomas Aquinas is often portrayed in iconography holding a flaming sun. He burns with light, the sun burning through him, a clear example of how theology was seen as spiritual. It has often been pointed out that Aquinas's last word was silence.[30] But, it seems, by about 1300 theology had lost the ability to express ecstasy. The gulf between theology and spirituality was widening, and theology came more and more to be an activity purely of the intellect.

In Britain, there have been writers who have stressed the integral link between theology and the 'spiritual life' for many years. Martin Thornton, for example, was very emphatic on this point,[31] while, in the USA, Edward Farley has consistently underlined that theology is a state of the soul. More recently Mark McIntosh has also emphasised this,[32] as have other writers, many of them influenced by Hans Urs von Balthasar.[33] One of the clearest statements has come from Gavin D'Costa who argues that 'good intellectually rigorous theology . . . can only be done within the context of a praying community' and that 'cohabitation with God through prayer is a prerequisite for doing theology'. This draws on Rowan Williams' view that the subject matter of theology is one who prays.[34]

I suggest then that we are truly experiencing a paradigm shift in theology, though much of it is still at the level of thought and talk, rather than action. However, much theological work is increasingly taking place outside formal academic structures, and it is important to take seriously the recent resurgence of local theologies.

Doing theology locally

The term 'contextual theology' is, of course, tautological, for the very idea of a non-contextual theology is an absurdity. Yet it has become popular for a justifiable reason: that much past, and some present, theology has failed to recognise its own contextual character, limitations and often privileged status. Such theology has been offered as if it were a kind of universal pattern of thought, unrelated to any earthly material structures of class, gender, race, social and cultural position, and so on. One gets the impression from some academic theological writing that it could have been written on the moon, since there is no explicit acknowledgement of what some writers curiously term the 'non-theological factors', in other words, the actual material context within which it came to be written. For this reason, if for no other, the term 'contextual theology' will remain in currency for the foreseeable future.

The idea of a contextual theology, in its recent use, is associated with South Africa and with the Institute of Contextual Theology in Johannesburg, but it quickly spread in other parts of the world.[35] It is a common term among 'Third World' theologians. In Canada, Douglas John Hall speaks a similar language, emphasising the need for contextual theological work within the North American context, while Mark McIntosh calls for 'a more embodied and contextual model' of theology.[36]

Of course, theological work, like any other disciplined activity, is not determined by its context but it is shaped by it.[37] Where one stands does affect what one sees. Nor is a context purely geographical, but it is at least geographical. Physical location is a critical element in theological work. However, there are other significant factors such as the interests of those doing the work. Black theologians have pointed out that theology is not a universal language but reflects the interests of specific groups. Much white theology reflects the interests of dominant groups.[38]

At the intellectual level, the spread of the theme of contextuality is a rejection of the Enlightenment notion of an Archimedean point from which one can attain a kind of pure vision, the Cartesian idea that truth is best reached in a state of abstraction from context. There is no such point, no such state, and so contextuality in theology, as elsewhere, is part of a widespread critique of the ideas of 'objective rationality'.[39] Here theological thinking shares some connections with thinking in science and philosophy from Michael Polanyi to Alasdair MacIntyre and many others.

A key document in the development of local theological work in the Roman Catholic tradition was the letter from Pope Paul VI to Cardinal Roy entitled *Octogesima Adveniens*, issued in 1971.[40] In this document Paul stressed that there was no overarching social theological position which could be applied to, or injected into, any and every situation. Rather each community had to engage with, struggle with, and reflect upon, its particular context, in the light of the received tradition and the local situation. Paul emphasised the need for analysis of the situation in the light of the gospel, and the use of the social teaching of the Church as a source for principles of reflection, norms of judgement and directions of action. Paragraph 4 was crucial: 'In the face of such widely varying situations, it is difficult for us to utter a unified message, and to put forward a solution which has universal validity. Such is not our ambition nor is it our mission.' Out of Paul VI's letter came a stress on social analysis. The Jesuits took this up at their 32nd General Congregation in 1975 when they urged 'the most rigorous possible political and social analysis' and the need to link analysis, discernment and committed action. The same stress is found two years later in the Third Inter American Conference of Religious at Montreal in 1977. It was popularised in an important study *Social Analysis: Linking Faith and Justice* by Joe Holland and Peter Henriot which was greatly influenced by the work of Paulo Freire. Holland and Henriot proposed a four-fold pattern, involving insertion into the local situation, social analysis, theological reflection, and pastoral planning. Their approach was developed by such groups as the Centre for Spirituality and Justice in the Bronx, New York.[41] Some of these approaches go back to the idea of the 'pastoral cycle' and the 'See, Judge, Act' method which originated with Fr Joseph Cardijn in Belgium.

My own experience of working with this kind of model leads me to the following conclusions for contextual theological work. First, it is vital to understand the immediate local, as well as the wider, context in which we are working, and not to see it as a neutral backcloth to 'the real work'. We need to be asking: What is going on? Where are we? What are the forces that shape us and threaten us? Where are the points of leverage and areas of hope? Second, we need to reflect on the content of our experience. Theology is about feelings and hopes as well as thoughts. Third, we need to go to the resources of Scripture and tradition and let them challenge the present. Fourth, we need to scrutinise the tradition in the light of our past and current experience. Fifth, we need to recognise that nothing is fixed and final, and that all is in movement. This is all done best in groups of people working together, supporting, criticising, challenging one another, within a framework of common discipleship and common struggle.

In recent years there has been an increase in the numbers of people, individuals and communities, who have chosen to pursue their theological reflection outside of academia. Some examples which come to my mind are:

(i) The setting up of the Mirfield Centre under the direction of Bridget Rees, to promote theological reflection in a very multi-racial and multifaith part of West Yorkshire. Sadly Bridget's work was brought to an end by the organisation which set it up, but both the work and the way in which it ended contain important lessons and warnings for the future.[42]

(ii) Mary Beasley's work with homeless people in Birmingham, which has included theological reflection with students at Selly Oak, Queen's and Oscott Colleges. This is an example of contextual theology rooted in concrete practice with marginalised people.[43]

(iii) The growth of regular theological reflection among those working with homeless people, much of it associated with such groups as the Catholic Housing Aid Society (CHAS) and the United London Ecumenical Action with the Single Homeless (UNLEASH). The UNLEASH Theology Group brings together, on a regular basis, Christians working in the area of homelessness to think through their theology in practice.

(iv) The tremendous upsurge of theological work within the groups affected by HIV and AIDS. This needs to be fully documented, but the work of CARA in London, and of groups in Scotland, are important examples.

(v) Jim Hart and INCIT, a Liverpool-based project, and its use of census data as an aid to the practice of local experiential theology. Jim's work has helped to bring together statistical data and pastoral ministry, and there have been developments from this in other areas.

These, and many others, are examples of what can happen when theology 'escapes from the rarefied atmosphere of academia and bursts into the community'.[44]

Although people have been pursuing theological work within a local context since the beginnings of theology as a discipline, the notion of a 'local theology' as such is fairly new, and is associated with the work of the Chicago theologian Robert Schreiter. His study *Constructing Local Theologies* (1985) is of crucial importance to the work which shapes this book, and his later writings have developed the themes. Schreiter stresses 'the new intensification of the local'.[45] He points out that local theologies in recent times were born as a result of an ethnification process, grounded in the particular experience of communities and movements. It has been suggested that local theology has more of the character of 'wisdom' than of a system.[46]

Other writers have emphasised how central is the theme of 'the local' to all theology and indeed to all Christian consciousness. Rowan Williams has stressed that 'local Christian communities . . . speak of God with a marked local accent' and that 'no one learns their Christianity without a local accent'.[47] The stress on the local Christian community as the locus of theological work is found also in the work of Elaine Graham, who sees theology as a 'transforming practice', a discipline involving practical social strategies within a 'faithful community'.[48] Laurie Green, now a bishop in eastern England, is another person who has underlined the need to do theology 'at a pavement level'.[49] What is really central here is that theology 'lies at the heart of Christian identity'.[50] Yet it is clear that many activist Christian groups are weakest in this area.[51]

One example of local theology was a project initiated by Church Action on Poverty between October 1989 and September 1992, called Action of the Church Towards a New Social Vision (ACTS), for which I acted as theological consultant. Its aim was to 'discover the faith resources for its critique of the prevailing values and for the creation of alternative theologies which are being developed and used by those on the margins'. Based in Manchester, the project developed ways of enabling local people to articulate and discuss their theology in relation to their specific experience of life in poor neighbourhoods. The two employed workers, Craig Russell and Jonathan Dale, determined to avoid dominating the project and causing it to fail, put great effort into ensuring that it really did enable the voices of ordinary people to be expressed and heard. ACTS worked in the Barracks Estate in Salford, Hulme and Moss Side in Manchester, Hattersley, and some estates in Yorkshire and the North-east. It was also involved in the 'Health for All' campaign in Ancoats which was formed to resist the closure of the casualty ward of the local hospital.[52]

These are only a small number of examples of the explosion in local theological work. In almost all cases, local theologies are ecumenical and 'post-denominational' although they often involve and may receive financial and other support from denominational structures.

Urban theology

The idea of a specifically 'urban theology' antedates the terms already used, 'contextual theology' and 'local theology'. While the latter have roots in South Africa, Latin America and the work of Robert Schreiter in Chicago, the idea of an urban theology is much older. However, there has been a resurgence of interest in recent years. The editor of a reader in urban theology published in 1998, Michael Northcott, complains that 'modern academic theology has become divorced from the life and worship of the Church and especially from the spiritual and cultural struggles of urban Christians to discern the way of Christ in the life of the modern city.' Northcott calls upon Christians 'to chart a new path in urban theology and to exemplify a new way of doing theology in Britain'.[53]

The origins of urban theology lie in North America where, in 1892, Dr Graham Taylor, Professor of Social Economics at Chicago Theological Seminary, set up the Chicago Commons, a settlement house, laboratory and training centre for community ministry. It was the first of a series of urban initiatives of which perhaps the best known was the Urban Training Centre, set up in Chicago in the 1960s. Earlier, in the 1940s, the East Harlem Protestant Parish was established in New York, with close links with Union Theological Seminary.

In Britain, Sheffield has been a key site for urban theological reflection since the days of Alan Ecclestone, Roland Walls and Ted Wickham. Wickham's study *Church and People in an Industrial City,* published in 1957, was a landmark in the study of Christianity and working-class life, though its conclusions have not been accepted uncritically. Out of Sheffield too came the Sheffield Industrial Mission, the precursor of many other projects within industry, and much theological work has emanated from these initiatives, not least the pioneering work of Margaret Kane in North-east England.[54]

Urban theology in Britain since the 1960s is associated particularly with the work of John Vincent and the Urban Theology Unit (UTU) in Sheffield. Not that Vincent has been alone, but he has undoubtedly been the giant in this field, and his prolific writings over the years have been very influential. The work of the UTU has been of tremendous importance, and we all owe a great deal to it. Inevitably, it has certain weaknesses. It has been very much dominated by Vincent's own thinking and writings, and has, until recently, shown little if any interest in or understanding of race, of cultural diversity, or of feminist issues. It has been very white, and shaped by a particular theological outlook within liberal Protestantism. On the other hand, it is difficult to exaggerate the contribution which Vincent and the UTU have made to the understanding of urban theology, and there are thousands of people throughout the world who have been helped by this project in Sheffield.[55]

In addition to the UTU, there have been other significant movements of urban theological work, including the Evangelical Urban Training Project developed in Liverpool with Neville Black and others. Out of this work has developed Unlock, and Jim Hart's work at INCIT. Also in Liverpool is the Merseyside Churches' Urban Institute, co-ordinated by Hilary Russell, and based at the Centre for European Urban Studies at Liverpool John Moores University. There is the long-established Passionist Inner City Mission led by Fr Austin Smith, and, more recently, a network of urban clergy working in urban priority areas has emerged, who publish a newsletter called *The Edge*.

The former Urban Ministry Project, based in South London, was inspired by, and to some extent modelled on, the Urban Training Centre in Chicago. In the 1970s the Evangelical Coalition for Urban Mission was created. In 1975 a project began in East London called START. The key figure in it was a Church Army sister, Audrey Shilling, and it focused its attention on issues affecting the Church in the Stepney Episcopal Area, with a base at Oxford House, Bethnal Green. At the time of writing, there is a plan for an Urban Programme for the Anglican Communion.[56]

Some of these groups lay emphasis on 'the urban' as 'the most privileged context for doing theology', and many of them have recently begun to devote much of their attention to links between the global and the local, and to the issues raised by globalisation.[57]

The relationship between academic and contextual theology

An important question is how the 'academic' theologians relate to local theologies. Some would write off academic theology as irredeemable, and academic theologians as unregenerate,[58] but most of us who are involved in contextual, local theological work welcome co-operation with the academy, while recognising that not all people there are likely to be of much use to us.[59] Ernest Kasemann in 1973 made an important comment in relation to the work of the late Archbishop Helder Camara in Brazil. 'I do not know Dom Helder Camara personally . . . but were my work of no possible help to him in his troubles, I would not remain a New Testament scholar'. More recently, Chris Rowland has stressed the 'need for contextual theology and conventional theology to share their agenda'.[60]

Some developments within the academic world have already been found to be helpful at street level. The interest in 'practical theology' has brought together people from academic and non-academic environments.[61] It remains to be seen whether the movement known as 'Radical Orthodoxy', associated with John Milbank, Catherine Pickstock and others, can transcend its present commitment to linguistic obscurity and learn to express itself in a language which makes sense outside the rarefied subcultures of Cambridge. But it has been a significant influence in the last few years, and has attracted many young people. It is not without its critics, who have spoken of its 'suicidal sectarianism' and see it as more gnostic than orthodox.[62] Yet one of the aims of this school is to bring about 'the end of theology's long intellectual marginalisation',[63] and it has certainly done this to a limited extent. One of its key figures, Catherine Pickstock, has expressed pleasure at 'an increased presence of theology in the domain of public debate'.[64]

Very different is the group around Ian Markham at Liverpool Hope University where a conference took place in September 1998 stressing plurality, inter-faith dialogue, and a 'new theological vision'.[65] Again, the future is open. Whatever happens, it does seem important that theologians in academic and non-academic frameworks retain the closest possible contact with one another in the coming years.

The prospects for contextual theology

What, in the meantime, do we need to do to get on with doing theology at the local level? Seven elements seem to me to be important in the light of our experience in East London, and I will enlarge on some of them in the coming chapters.

Firstly, we need to see each small local Christian community as the locus for theological activity. In Schreiter's terms, the community is a theologian.

Secondly, this activity need not only be an intellectual one – though undoubtedly the intellect will be involved. But theology does involve other types of human responses, and poetry, art, music, and so on can be forms of theological expression.

Thirdly, theological work must involve a cross section of the people in terms of age, class, culture, and so on.

Fourthly, theological work is ongoing activity. It does not have a clear end point.

Fifthly, theology is messy. It is confronted by issues and crises – in the world, in the parish, in the neighbourhood, and in our own personal lives – to which it does not have simple and clear answers. It has therefore to live with mess and incompleteness.

Sixthly, prayer is central, and without a prayerful, contemplative base, the whole activity fails.

Finally, theology does involve belief, for it is concerned with truth. Many years ago Alasdair MacIntyre complained that liberal theologians were giving atheists 'less and less in which to disbelieve'.[66] The justified reaction against fundamentalisms and forms of religious arrogance cannot lie in the abandonment of truth claims. There lies a real captivity. Liberation lies in theology's fundamental openness to the reality of God.

8
Theology, race and plurality

O travellers
hold fast the hammer, pick up the shovel,
sing in unison, and advance.
        KOBI NAZRUL, 'The Song of the Worker'[1]

Stony the road we trod, bitter the chastening rod
Felt in the days when hope unborn had died.
Yet with a steady beat have not our weary feet
Come to the place for which our parents sighed?
        JAMES WELDON JOHNSON, 'Lift Every Voice and Sing'[2]

It is important to recognise at the outset that racial, cultural
and religious diversity is in most places the norm rather than the
exception. This has been true in many areas for many years, in some
for thousands of years. In Britain's cities, there is immense variety of
ethnic origin, and of religious belief and practice, and this has spread
to many other parts of the country. When people speak of a 'plural'
society, it is this situation among others, to which they refer. To
recognise the plural character of British society is not the same as
to adopt a philosophical or theological position called 'pluralism'.
Whatever position we adopt, the plural character of our society is
beyond dispute.

The East End is one of the most racially mixed areas of the world.
In 1991, 42 per cent of the population in Newham, and 36 per cent
in Tower Hamlets, were from ethnic minorities. Over thirty-seven
languages are spoken in East London. (On the other hand, one only
needs to travel east on the District Line to Barking and Dagenham
to find an overwhelmingly white area. Here, in 1991, 93.5 per cent
of the population were born in the UK.)

The largest minority community in the East End originates in
Bangladesh, formerly East Pakistan. 'Bangla' means Bengal, 'desh'

means land. Bengalis are the fifth largest linguistic group in the world, with 120 million in Bangladesh, 120 million in India, and about 10 million elsewhere. In Bangladesh around 88 per cent of the population are Muslim, with over 10 per cent Hindu. Buddhists account for 0.6 and Christians 0.3. Since 1988 Islam has been the 'state religion'. There is a rich literature in the Bengali language, and, while Rabindranath Tagore is the most famous Bengali poet, and played an important role in shaping the language, there are many more writers within a long history.

Many Bengalis emigrated during the early 1960s, just before and after the passing of the Commonwealth Immigrants Act of 1962. Much of this immigration was linked to a 'beat the ban rush', and it has been argued that the legislation which was introduced allegedly to prevent an increase helped to cause it. Almost all the Bengalis in the East End are from the Sylhet region, which, under British administration, was part of Assam Province. There had been some Sylheti restaurant workers here as long ago as 1873. There are tight kinship networks. In East London, the Bangladeshi population forms 61 per cent of the population in Spitalfields, while in the area as a whole Bengalis comprise over 54 per cent of children in schools. Many Bengalis moved into the old clothing trades, while others work in the restaurant business for which the Brick Lane area is famous.[3]

The East End also has a rich and complex history of 'faith communities'. St Botolph's parish was, until quite recently, mainly Jewish in population as was that of Christ Church, Spitalfields. The famous map by Russell and Lewis of 'Jewish East London' in 1900 can still be bought at the Eastside Bookshop in Whitechapel Road, and shows a 95–100 per cent East European Jewish population in the Whitechapel and Spitalfields area, which is now mainly Muslim. There is a small Buddhist enclave in Bethnal Green, around the Globe Road area, and, as one moves north into Hackney or east into Newham, the proportions of Christians from Africa, the Caribbean and elsewhere, and of Hindus, Sikhs and other faiths, increases significantly. In Newham in 1994, there were 198 congregations and 77 religious organisations, centres or communities, while in 1995 it was estimated that there were 25–30,000 Muslims, 20,700 Hindus, 4,150 Sikhs, and 15–18,000 Christians.

In terms of inter-faith relations, there are creative and positive elements in this history as well as very destructive and negative ones. One bookshelf in St Botolph's is devoted entirely to Christian–Jewish dialogue and witnesses to a long and continuing activity here. On the other hand, the East End historically has been, as I have shown in Part One, one of the strongholds of organised antisemitism. Arnold White and Major Evans-Gordon, the British Brothers' League and the British Union of Fascists, the National Front and the British National Party are all part of our history.

Today the majority of the Jewish population has moved. The old synagogue at the corner of Brick Lane and Fournier Street, once a Huguenot church for the silk-weaving community, is now a mosque, one of eight in Tower Hamlets. The old East London Mosque, which I knew thirty years ago when it was an old house in Commercial Road, frequented by the small but concentrated Somali community, has now been replaced by a magnificent structure in Fieldgate Street. Thousands worship on Fridays, and the Young Muslim Organisation is the biggest religious youth movement in the East End. The mosque is an important social and cultural centre, and has recently established an excellent reference library and bookshop, and a room where students can do homework and other studies.

The Christian presence in East London

The Christian Church has been a significant presence in the East End of London, as in most inner urban areas of England, for several hundred years. In some neighbourhoods, churches were crucial to the life of the locality, though in others they were less significant. They played a key role in many neighbourhoods as sources of care, and providers of resources, clubs, and financial help through a network of church-based charitable trusts. In some districts, before the creation of the National Health Service, the church provided nurses and midwives, as in the parish of All Saints, Poplar where a parish midwife was a member of the staff team and where the Nursing Sisters of St John the Divine, an order of religious sisters who were all trained nurses and midwives, became a much loved and valued part of the local community.

However, it is arguable whether the Anglican Church, in particular, has ever been in the truest sense indigenous. At the national level it is a minority Church with around 2.9 per cent of the population attending it. Within East London, while its membership in most areas has consisted, and still does consist, mostly of local people, the leadership has been imported. It has always been essentially a bourgeois institution, present to 'do good', more manifestly 'at home' elsewhere. Its social role has focused on service more than advocacy, on personal pastoral care more than directly political intervention, though there are very significant exceptions to this.

'Mainstream' (almost entirely white-led) church congregations in urban areas often contain high representation of people in social classes 2 and 3 – teachers, nurses, students, and so on. Skilled manual workers and council tenants are very conspicuously absent, owner-occupiers often dominate. In one outer estate, in the 1980s, 77 per cent of the Anglican congregation were owner occupiers though only 8 per cent of the population were such, and, while 48 per cent of the population were semi-skilled, the figure in the congregation was only 10 per cent. The figure for unemployment was 47 per cent, but only 8 per cent of the congregation were unemployed.

In the Forest Gate district of East London in 1988, 70 per cent of church members were owner-occupiers and only 3 per cent council tenants. In nearby Canning Town, where 97 per cent of the population were council tenants, less than 2 per cent of council tenants attended the churches. This position certainly needs to be modified here and there, and the position with other denominations and traditions is different. Yet in general it is correct: the Church in England is not an integral part of most urban areas as some Churches are, for example, in many parts of the USA.[4]

Throughout the Middle Ages, the whole of the East End was in the parish of St Dunstan, Stepney. During the seventeenth century, new churches were built in Aldgate, Bethnal Green, St George's in the East, and elsewhere, and, as a result of the Church Building Act of 1818, more churches were built. But, it has been argued, churches have been 'planted' in the East End in a colonialist way, often with the intention of bringing order and civility to the people. Christ Church, Spitalfields, built by Nicholas Hawksmoor with the intention of cowering 'the mob' into submission by its grandeur, dominated the scenery around Commercial Street and Fournier Street, as it still does. But the impact of organised religion seems to have been slight. Booth summed up his study of the Spitalfields churches at the end of the nineteenth century:

> On Sunday morning the parish churches are practically empty. In the evening they gather together more or less a congregation consisting of middle class people, some of whom come from a distance and maintain in this way an old connection with others of the same class from the neighbourhood.[5]

W.D. Davies, Rector of Christ Church, said in 1903 that the district was becoming poorer and that those with money were moving elsewhere. Another writer observed that in Whitechapel 'religious influence, despite the number of churches and chapels, was ineffective, so far as the very poor were concerned', while Samuel Barnett, Vicar of St Jude's, Whitechapel and founder of Toynbee Hall, admitted in 1877 that his church was 'comparatively empty' and that 'few of the East End places of worship have a congregation'. In 1879 Bishop Walsham How observed: 'The church is nowhere in East London.' Booth, describing the churches in Hoxton at the end of the nineteenth century, noted that 'We find everywhere small congregations – sometimes hardly any congregation at all.'[6]

Anglo-Catholicism was one of the most significant traditions in East London's religious history. Yet many of the parishes were maintained by non-residents. At St George's in the East, where the riots occurred in 1860, the rector admitted that the population consisted of 'those very classes who are alas! almost universally alienated from attendance upon the services of the church'. The church had an average of forty communicants each Sunday.[7] St Saviour's, Hoxton, in the 1860s has been described as 'dreadfully respectable' and supported by many non-Hoxtonians. Inhabitants of the parish were rarely seen except as recipients of charity. By 1900 it 'had lost all contact with its real constituency'.[8]

Yet in some parts of the East End the Anglo-Catholics were the first to realise that the vicarage was quite out of place in the slum, and their model of priests living in community could have been the beginnings of a whole new approach to pastoral ministry. But, while some churches really did become churches of poor people, Anglo-Catholicism too became bourgeois and respectable. It is sometimes claimed that the Anglo-Catholic movement was radical in its origins, and the 'slum priest' tradition is seen as the prime example of this radicalism. Neither of these claims can be substantiated. The only issue on which the original Oxford Movement could be seen as 'radical' was that of its resistance to the state, and this did not last long, while the social radicals within the East End and other deprived areas, though important, were always a minority.[9] However, one feature of Anglo-Catholicism which was important was its stress on beauty, colour, drama, and a certain flamboyance in worship, and this appealed to many working-class people.[10]

The Roman Church, in the East End as elsewhere, was an immigrant Church, and remained so until very recently. Many Roman Catholics in London longed for their life in Donegal, Poland, Goa or the Caribbean. The Church was not active in social and political affairs until the 1960s. Even then it was the religious orders, not the parishes, who pioneered social and political action. There was a significant shift under the late Cardinal Hume when the National Pastoral Congress of 1980 stressed the parish's concern for the whole neighbourhood, and official Roman Catholic views moved 'from charity to empowerment'.[11]

As late as the 1980s almost half of English Roman Catholics were first or second generation immigrants and, at the end of the 1970s, a sociologist described the Roman Church as 'a fortress church, organised very largely around ethnic parishes, with a largely passive and deferential laity governed by an authoritarian clerical bureaucracy'.[12] This was hardly surprising, for Pope Pius X in 1906 had said: 'As far as the multitude is concerned, they have no other duty than to let themselves be led'[13] – which they did! But the consequences were in the end disastrous. The Roman Church is now in serious decline. Mass attendance in England fell from almost two million in 1965 to just over one million in 1996, and the shortage of priests is well known.[14]

The church presence in the East End was dominated by Anglicanism, and increasingly after the 1850s by Anglo-Catholics. However, one of the results of the publication in 1883 of *The Bitter Cry of Outcast London* – described by one writer as 'the most important single piece of writing about the poor that England has ever seen'[15] – was the increased Methodist presence in the East End. *The Bitter Cry* had emphasised the failure of the churches to respond to the growth of poverty. Two years later a Wesleyan movement began in East London, based first at City Road in Shoreditch, and

then in Cable Street. The *Methodist Times* called it 'the most significant and important event in the modern history of Methodism'. Yet
three years later the *Methodist Recorder* was asking, 'What is Methodism doing for the East End? Slowly, deliberately, sorrowfully, in
reply, comparatively little'.[16] Booth certainly discovered little support
for Methodism among the poor.[17] However, in 1896, within a three-
quarter of a mile stretch of Ratcliff Highway, there were at least
seventeen churches and missions.[18]

Today many of these churches are in decline. The growth areas
are elsewhere. In 1998 in Newham there were 294 faith-based organisations of which 181 were Christian congregations and 20 were
mosques, while Hackney's directory of Christian churches in 1996
had over 200 entries. Of these, the most striking groups, in terms
of growth, were the black-led churches, mainly, though not
entirely, of Pentecostal type.

The evangelical sociologist Greg Smith, whose immense research
on Newham has contributed much to our understanding, wrote a
fascinating paper entitled 'The Christ of the Barking Road' which
captures something of the atmosphere of this area, the most easterly
part of East London before one moves into the Essex suburbs. Here,
in the four kilometres of Barking Road, there are forty-four places
of religious activity, as well as shops indicating religious motivation.
Close together here we find His Grace Photos, Amazing Grace
Groceries, Signs and Wonders Hair Salon, Mount Zion General
Store, Faith Electronics, Saraswati Newsagents – and the Old English
Pawnbroking Company! The Islamic Centre (a former synagogue)
is flanked by a bookmaker on one side and Calvary Charismatic
Baptist Church on the other. Greg Smith comments:

> The church too has changed over the last three decades from a
> tiny dispirited remnant of white old ladies to a lively, growing
> and noisy multitude. Our fellow travellers in both mainline and
> independent churches are the people of the Two Thirds World: it
> is now African, Asian, Latin American, Pentecostal and Catholic,
> prosperous professional and poverty stricken, global and local and
> all mixed up.[19]

Here, as in many other inner city areas, the growth area
for Christianity is among churches of African and African-
Caribbean origin. The failure to welcome, and in some cases the

explicit rejection of, black people by the Anglican and other churches left its effect in the massive growth of the black-led Pentecostal and Adventist churches. As mass religious movements among urban blacks in Britain, they are a post-immigration, post-racist phenomenon. Some of them, having their origins in American fundamentalist missions to the Caribbean, had a theology which was otherworldly, escapist and pietist, rooted in the racially segregated world of Tennessee and other southern states, and ill-equipped (and unwilling) to engage with racism, either theologically or politically. Only in recent years has this begun to change.[20]

In the urban areas Pentecostalism has been stronger on social organisation than on social critique. It has created structures which have enabled entrepreneurs to develop, and financial schemes which have been valuable to lower income groups. But the churches have been uncritical of global captivity, sometimes supporting the prosperity gospel. Yet here also changes are likely, and there are moves towards a political theology for the black Pentecostal churches.[21] Between 1981 and 1991 attendance at Christian churches in the E16 district doubled, and most of the increase was Pentecostal. Studies by John Oliver in Canning Town show that, while only around 2.8 per cent of the population were churchgoers, one quarter of these were black – in a mainly white area.[22]

In spite of all this, there is one important point that needs to be said in support of Anglicanism. There is no place in England which is not within an Anglican parish. There are around 780 Anglican schools on housing estates, and often they are the only community buildings in the area. No other organisation 'has such a ubiquitous and self-sustaining structure'.[23] Moreover, Anglicanism in England has no sectarian tradition (though there are signs that it is now growing, under the influence of consumer capitalism disguised as theology). As a result, in many urban areas Anglicans have a stronger social theology and basis for community engagement than some other Christian groups.

The Jewish presence and antisemitism

The East End Jewish background, discussed in Part One, remains of critical significance for our present practice even though the Jewish presence is now much smaller. That history, however, is still our history, and Christians in East London need to learn from it if we are to contribute insight and wisdom 'for the living of these days'.

First, dialogue and co-operation between Jews and Christians must continue and develop. At St Botolph's, the London Diocesan Council for Christian–Jewish Understanding has its base. The Council of Christians and Jews is one of the most dynamic movements in British religious life, and one of the few religious groups which takes its youth section, and therefore its future life, seriously. The Jewish Socialist Group maintains good links with secular and Christian socialist networks.

Second, it needs to be recognised that neither 'Judaism' nor 'Christianity' are monolithic systems. Marc Ellis has argued that Judaism and Christianity in their institutional form must disappear.[24] Certainly both traditions are experiencing turmoil and change, and the exploration of common ground is vital.

Third, the Christian roots of antisemitism are well documented. The response of the Churches in Germany to antisemitism was appalling and helped to prepare the way for Nazism.[25] The question of antisemitism remains critical. Between 1984 and 1992 there was an 85 per cent increase in antisemitic incidents in Britain. We have also seen the growth of such white supremacist groups as Christian Identity. I have been privileged to take part in some meetings of the American Jewish Committee in which Jews, Christians and others have come together in response to the resurgence of 'hate crime'.[26]

Fourth, the theological issues raised by Auschwitz and the experience of extermination need to be constantly in the hearts and minds of Christians as well as Jews. Alan Ecclestone argued that the Holocaust 'sought to expunge from the life of Europe any witness to a religious component by which its behaviour might be judged'.[27] The recent reappearance of the 'holocaust denial' movement also calls for active oppositional work by Jews and Christians.[28]

The contribution of Jewish people to radical political action and thought in the East End was one of the most dynamic aspects of our history, and Christians have a great deal to learn from this Jewish radical tradition.

Engagement with Islam

By 2015 Islam will be the second largest religion in the USA. In Europe it is estimated that there are between 8 and 10 million Muslims – 2 million in France, mostly from North Africa, and 3 million in Germany, with the Turkish people as the most significant group. It is estimated that there are around 1.5 million Muslims in Britain, mostly from the Indian sub-continent, particularly from Pakistan and Bangladesh.[29]

Islam is a world faith which manifests itself in different forms in different places. People who are viewed in the western media as 'Muslim leaders' may not necessarily be popular among Muslim groups elsewhere. For example, Saddam Hussein was not popular among many Muslims in Pakistan because he took the side of India over the Kashmir issue. However, later he was seen as a champion of the poor, a symbol of Third World defiance. This, of course, made no difference to the racist attacks on children with the name Hussein in schools in East London and elsewhere during the Gulf War.

The appearance of anti-Muslim feelings and behaviour in Europe is well documented. It has been said that 'if Islam is the second religion in France, the first is the fear of Islam'. The Runnymede Trust and others have used the term 'Islamophobia', which has led some Christians to suggest that there is also 'Westophobia' within Muslim communities.[30] There has also been considerable writing in recent years about conflict and clashes between Islam and the West. In a Gallup Poll of 1989, 37 per cent of people said that international Christian–Muslim conflict was likely in the next decade, while in a poll in the USA, 45 per cent believed that Muslims were anti-American. The theme of the 'clash of civilisations', first raised by Bernard Lewis, was brought to wider attention in the writing of Samuel Huntington. Since then, Willy Cleos, Secretary-General of NATO, has said that militant Islam is the most serious threat to the security of the West. Others have spoken of a 'new cold war'.[31] It has been claimed that relations between Christians and Muslims is 'the explosive issue which must come to dominate theology in the twenty first century'.[32]

What we have in Britain is a 'fragmented Islamic tradition',[33] and situations vary from place to place. In East London, the early Muslim groups came from North Africa, particularly Somalia and the Yemen, West Africa, and the Indian sub-continent. Today most Muslims here are Bengali. Bengali Islam is seen as syncretistic and impure by strict Sunni Muslims. For example, in Bengali Islam there is a stress on the pir, or Sufi elder, and there is often a master–disciple relationship, not entirely unlike that of the role of the spiritual director in Christian tradition. In one study, almost 29 per cent of Bengalis had a pir or guru. (Interestingly, while it is now not unknown for spiritual directors in western Christianity to charge fees, one of the tests of a true pir is that, if offered money he will reject it!) There are also in Bangladesh close links with surrounding Hindus.

More will be said later about principles of inter-faith co-operation, but it should be mentioned that much progress has been made in East London, in the churches through the work of individuals such as the Anglican priest John Webber and the Roman Catholic Servite priest Joe Collela, and through involvement of Christians and Muslims in active work over local issues.

Critical literacy and the Kobi Nazrul experience

It is impossible to discuss the future of theology and inter-faith relations without doing so within the wider framework of debates and struggles about the nature of education. My years in East London have made me realise how much theologians have to learn from people, Christian and non-Christian, who are working in the field of education, from primary to adult. One person who influenced me greatly in the 1970s was Chris Searle, a teacher in several local secondary schools. Searle, in all his work, stresses the central importance of history in understanding a community.

> I sat for hours in the local history room of Mile End library, reading the literature proudly published in the Women's Dreadnought, in Lansbury's Labour Weekly, in the East End News, and in the mass of trade collections of poetry and fiction, that gave the heartbeat of the struggling communities, not only of the past, but of the one which surrounded me beyond the library walls. I found a whole new literacy, a new curriculum of poetry and life embracing each other for the betterment of those whom it served, and I was

determined to make this noble and purposeful use of language and the imagination the centre of any 'English' teaching in my classroom.[34]

However, Searle did not only recognise the importance of history. He saw that education was about transformation. It could not be seen as a neutral and objective preparation for transformation. Education on that view was a prelude to change, not the process of change in itself. So, for many teachers, 'education was about knowledge detached from action, rather than knowledge as the inseparable guide and dynamic of action'.[35]

The dismissal of Chris Searle from a Church of England secondary school in Stepney is one of the most tragic and deplorable episodes in the recent history of the Church in East London, one in which clergy from St Botolph's, Aldgate and St Dunstan's, Stepney were equally involved. In that episode, described in his own writing and that of others, there lies a fundamental conflict between two incompatible views of the nature of education, the role of the church, and the politics of change. I see no evidence that the lessons have been learned, and, as far as the establishment is concerned, it is part of past history. Yet no part of history is past. It is a living continuum, and those who ignore the past are likely to repeat it – and do.

The work of Searle and others is linked with the interest which grew up in these years in the work of Paulo Freire on critical literacy. While Searle does not write as a theologian or even as a Christian, his understanding of education is close to that of some of the exponents of local theology. Schreiter, for example, using almost identical words to Searle, sees theology as 'a pedagogical process liberating consciousness and inciting to action'.[36]

Yet the local church is way behind, woefully behind, in the field of adult education, as Stanley Evans noted as long ago as 1962, pointing out that 'there is no single organisation, outside the church, concerned with adult education, which would conceive it right to have two discourses delivered to people every week, where there was neither taking of notes nor asking of questions or discussion, and seriously expect the people to assimilate and digest what was said.' He went on to stress the centrality of conversation, discussion and debate in education.[37]

For me, having done very little work with young children since the early 1970s, it has been a great privilege to become involved in a small way with them in the East End. Kobi Nazrul Primary School is the newest primary school in Tower Hamlets, and is named after Kobi Nazrul Islam (1899–1976), one of the most famous Bengali poets. In addition to the school, there are two Bengali restaurants and a community centre named after Kobi Nazrul.

The school was officially opened on 1 May 1996. Since then it has had remarkable results in literacy and numeracy. This is particularly important in the light of data from the Basic Skills Agency's first national survey of adult literacy and numeracy, released in March 1998, which showed that Tower Hamlets had the worst level of adult literacy in the UK. In Tower Hamlets as a whole the schools obtained the second worst examination results in the UK in 1994. Only 18.5 per cent of pupils obtained five or more GCSEs with grades A–C. In 1999 Tower Hamlets came eighth from the bottom for reading levels among eleven-year-olds. By contrast, at Kobi Nazrul, where 95 per cent of the children speak a language other than English at home, in the late 1990s all the seven-year-olds reached Level 2, the standard expected for their age, and half reached Level 3.

The school has adopted the 'Success for All' programme which originated in Johns Hopkins University in 1986, and this is proving very successful. But the school has also realised the crucial importance of building a sense of strong community between teachers, pupils and parents. Work in the USA and elsewhere has shown that, in the reasons why pupils do well at school, family background is more important than teachers, resources or size of class. While we are still concerned about the numbers of children who never speak English at home, the progress has been impressive, not least in the area of self-confidence and inner strength of character. While media attention has focused on literacy and numeracy, this work has been a unique opportunity to be involved in education for a multi-faith society, and to promote understanding between Christians and Muslims in a tightly contained neighbourhood between Commercial Road and Whitechapel Road.[38]

In a context such as ours, issues of faith within the school are complex. Under the 1988 Act, religious education in schools should be 'wholly, mainly, broadly Christian'. But what does this mean in our context? Kenneth Clarke, a former Minister, told Chief Education Officers in 1991 that the syllabus could not confine itself exclusively to religious education based on Christian traditions. The position is difficult, and we often feel that government officials have little understanding of our situation or are imprisoned within legislation and bureaucracy. Sometimes we can feel rather hopeless about the possibility of progress. I felt that this was important to address at the opening of the school in 1996. This is part of what I said:

> But we know, and we need to remind ourselves, that despair and hopelessness get us nowhere; that if things are to get better, there has to be commitment and struggle. And a school is a place of preparation for this, a place where people can learn to live together, grow together, and out of that experience become people who can help to build a world based on equality and justice. A school can be a place where a new generation of men and women of principle and commitment are trained for the struggle of human life.
>
> Kobi Nazrul was a very important man, a poet and a visionary. He was ahead of his time. He saw the importance of the role of women and he saw the power of children in society. He saw the need to break through barriers based on race and class and religion, and to build a more human world. And I want to end with the chorus of one of Kobi Nazrul's poems which seems very suitable for May Day, 'The Song of the Worker'. There could be no better motto for this school, which carries his name, here in Tower Hamlets: hold fast the hammer, sing in unison, and advance.

Some principles for engagement

Out of our experience here, some insights have emerged which we should share. First, it is essential to recognise and learn from the spiritual strengths of other traditions. For example, within Islam there are areas of what we would call 'spirituality' from which we could learn a great deal. There is a sense of belonging to a strong community, the *umma*. The mosque is a crucial centre and source of new life. There is the stress on fasting, prayer, almsgiving (as an obligation of justice), and pilgrimage – all of these neglected by western Christians. There is a concern with the physical dimensions of prayer – bows and prostrations – which puts incarnational Christianity to shame.

Take, for example, the issue of fasting. A central element in Islamic spirituality is the practice of the Ramadan fast. It was once said of Bengali Muslims that 'they never give up fasting as long as they have life in them'.[39] The close proximity, in 1999 and 2000, of Ramadan to the secular preparation for Christmas made the commitment of the Ramadan fast more startling than usual in London. In Sainsbury's in Whitechapel, the contrast between the immense sales of food to the 'Christian' customers and the dedicated fast of the (mainly Bengali) assistants was immensely moving and dramatic. As with the Orthodox Christians of the East, Muslims know both how to fast and how to feast, and Ramadan ends with the feast of Id al-Fitr, a celebration in which sweets are shared and new clothes are worn. This is a spirituality which is essentially corporate, physical, homely and rooted in hospitality and comradeship.

Inter-faith dialogue must be a spiritual activity, and, for Christians, this must include penitence, and a recognition of the evil in our own history. (Of course, Muslims and others have much to confess, but that is their responsibility.) St Bernard of Clairvaux, for example, claimed that Christ was glorified in the death of Muslims. It is important too to approach people of other faiths with reverence, awe and immense respect. The late Max Warren said that the first step in inter-faith conversation was to take off one's shoes.

We must build on the traditions of justice in the faith traditions. The Koran condemns the neglect of the orphan and the poor (89:18-21) and insists that the just share their resources with beggars (51:17-19). It attacks the amassing of wealth (92:5-11). The issue of money and the just use of money is crucial to our future work together. The work of the Grameen Bank in Bangladesh and its system of micro-credit is one from which Christians could learn. The bank lends to around 2.4 million people in the 93,000 villages in Bangladesh, and 94 per cent of its borrowers are women. Through its work, there has been a strong emphasis on the place of health and nutrition as well as on the fundamental question of monetary justice.[40] Christians, according to the Koran, are the 'closest in friendship' or 'nearest in affection' to Islam (Koran 5:82, 9:29). We need to work together in the cause of justice.

Second, it is essential to see that things are changing. Cultures are not unified or static. In the diaspora situation of religions and cultures, many elements are changing, things are going into solution, things which were once thought solid are melting into air. Of course, the theme of journey is central to Islam, but it now appears in a form not anticipated by earlier generations. Akbar Ahmed has referred to the Muslim intellectual as existing in 'a state of despair, torn between an ideal world he cannot order, and a reality he cannot master' – a state of exile.[41]

For most Muslims, life in Britain is their first experience of life in a society where Islam is a minority religion, while, in the 'Christian' West, we are seeing a residual Christianity, with a collapse of the symbolic framework, but also with new forms of Christian presence emerging.

On the whole, Islam has not coped easily with dissent and diversity, although there are hints in the Koran that diversity of faith may be God's will, and that there must be no compulsion in religion. But now in East London, everything is coming under scrutiny. Bangladeshi Islam is having to rethink the position of women as feminism has made its impact. For example, surveys have shown that most Bengali girls see sex education as an important part of their life. Then there is the issue of homosexuality. In some Muslim areas, there is a demand for gays over the age of ten to be executed, and for lesbians to receive life imprisonment. Yet there are now organisations for gay Muslims, such as Al-Fatiha, founded in the USA in 1997, and Homan, a gay group for Iranian Muslims in Britain. It has been claimed that 75,000 of Britain's 1.5 million Muslims are gay.[42]

In this situation of flux, positions which people take can be surprising. Thus in 1992 many apparently conservative Muslims in the East End supported – and sold – Taslima Nasreem's novel *Lajja* (*Shame*) in spite of the hostility to her in Bangladesh. The novel was written after the destruction of the Babri Mosque at Ayodha. There is discussion of an Islamic theology of liberation.[43] And, of course, many key issues are being raised by children in our multi-faith society. A colleague has looked at the questions raised by children in one district, and no doubt in thousands. They include:

Is Jesus stronger than Allah?
Are we Christians or are we English?

Will Parmesh go to heaven?

Aleisha's a Hindu. So do we have to get her a Christmas present?

Third, we need to take care in our use of the word 'fundamentalism', a term not known in Islam. Yet the most publicised aspect of Islam in the western media concerns the growth of 'fundamentalism' with its implication of warfare, and there is an assumption that the warfare model might be reproduced locally. Actually, while 'holy war' ideas arise from time to time, this is not a key influence in Britain, nor are most Muslims here 'fundamentalists', though there are spin-offs from the media coverage.[44]

Fourth, our experience is that co-operation and mutual learning often start with immensely practical issues, whereas 'inter-faith dialogue' which is not concretely based in local action tends to be a rather disconnected middle-class activity without roots in the communities. A real and growing dialogue is more likely to grow from local co-operative action. Thus the issue of female circumcision (or, as it is better called, female genital mutilation) has become a major issue among Somali women and others. The Black Women's Health Action Project, based in the East End, has been the pioneering group in this field, and Shamis Dirir one of the key figures, and it has brought together numerous groups and individuals.[45]

Then there is the question of drug abuse. In the early 1990s the Maze Drugs Project, which I chaired, worked closely with the Young Muslim Organisation (YMO) over this issue. We based some of the work on a very successful anti-smoking campaign, run during Ramadan by the YMO, and developed it into an educational project on the use of other drugs, based on the Ramadan calendar. Combined with this we held the first of a series of conferences on drug abuse in the Bengali community, attended by 350 people. The day was run bilingually, in English and Bengali, and was aimed at Bengali parents. It was held in the mosque, with breaks for the 1.00 p.m. and 3.30 p.m. prayers. Out of this has grown a good deal of co-operative work involving Muslims, Christians and others.

A movement which also has taken root around practical issues is Community Organising, a movement committed to broad-based solidarity between organisations and communities. The movement began with the work of Saul Alinsky (1909–72), and much of the early work focused on churches. The Nehemiah Project in Brooklyn emerged from the local churches. In Britain the Citizens Organising Foundation was formed in 1988. Communities Organised for a Greater Bristol appeared in 1990, and Merseyside Broad Based Organising in 1992. In the 1990s also came TELCO, The East London Community Organisation.[46]

Fifth, it is best to begin with issues on our own doorstep. In a survey in 1995 92 per cent of people in Newham believed that people of different faiths should work together on issues of human need, and we need to build on this goodwill. The work of John Webber, inter-faith advisor in the Stepney Episcopal Area, has been important in getting local work off the ground. Work by the chaplaincy team at the London Hospital has led to increased inter-faith dialogue and common action around the approach to dying and death. The work of the Servite priest Joe Collela and the 'One for Life' project has focused attention on the importance of silence, for sharing pastoral concerns and work together on common problems and needs. For several years a small group at St Botolph's looked at approaches to dying and death in a multi-faith context.

In fact much progress has actually been made in the East End. There is, after all, a wealth of accumulated wisdom and expertise here, going back over a hundred years. As in so many fields, I suspect more theological exploration and inter-faith encounter may be going on in primary schools (or some of them) than in churches, synods and groups of adult Christians. I hope we can make some quiet progress in looking, as all good theology must, at what is actually happening among communities.

Sixth, networking across continents can be immensely useful. In rural Wiltshire there has been a link for over eighteen years with a Muslim fishing community in Gunjur in the Gambia. The educational resources which have been developed from this link are now used in 1,600 primary schools in Britain, and have led to greater understanding of the place of older people in communities, the centrality of water, and many other areas.

Finally, there is much theological work to be done. There are evangelical Christians who hold that there is 'one way' to salvation, through conscious allegiance to Jesus Christ. This conviction is often narrowed down even further to exclude forms of Christianity, particularly Roman Catholicism, which do not fit within the thought-forms of evangelical orthodoxy. However, this position also has its Roman Catholic equivalent which can at times exclude most other types of Christian. There is also an aggressive 'end of dialogue', militant and crusading stance, often dressed up in the language of postmodernity and even radicalism. However sophisticated it may seem, this position is at heart a regression to an earlier phase of Christian imperialism, 'a kind of exploitation, a new religious imperialism, a theological form of racial harassment' against which Hooker and Lamb warned in 1986.[47]

At the opposite pole there are Christians who have opted for an 'inclusive' approach, characterised by the idea that God leads people to truth by a variety of routes, an approach which sometimes avoids critique of alternative positions. One tendency has been to see different faiths as approaches to the same reality. It is perfectly true that 'God has many names', but it does not follow from this that all religions are equally valid paths, and this approach can be an excuse for intellectual laziness.[48]

Is there a *via media*? (I avoid the English version 'middle way', with all its strange modern associations!) Yes. It is a way of affirmation (*via positiva*) combined with a way of negation (*via negativa*), a combination central to the Christian mystical tradition and to Eastern Orthodox theology. It is important that we affirm our own experience of, and commitment to, the revelation of God in Christ, and share it, lovingly, passionately and humbly, with others. It is equally important to recognise that our ignorance of God is more central to our life than our knowledge of God. We forget this at our peril, for to forget this is to jeopardise our whole relationship with the God who is always beyond our reach and range. We need a rich, deeply rooted and humble approach to our faith tradition if we are to counter the intolerant and damaging tendencies of much in the contemporary Church.

David Tracy of the University of Chicago has called for the central place of conversation, and his account is important enough to print in full.

> Conversation is a game with some hard rules: say only what you mean; say it as accurately as you can; listen to and repeat what the other says, however different or other; be willing to correct or defend your opinions if challenged by the conversation partner; be willing to argue if necessary, to confront if demanded, to endure

necessary conflict, to change your mind if the evidence suggests it.[49]

As Tracy recognises, conversation will involve dispute and challenge, elements which can be forgotten in the use of the word 'dialogue'. But dialogue has its origins in the theme of argument. Thus Paul in the Ephesus synagogue both spoke out boldly and argued persuasively (*dialegomenos kai peithon*, Acts 19:8). The idea of dialogue is ancient and its practice is not without its conflictual edge. But it is always rooted in equality, respect and genuine conversation. It is not inherently confrontational and polemical, though these aspects are part of the dialogue.

Christian testimony within a context of plurality of faiths should be marked by reality, not fantasy; by humility, not aggressiveness and arrogance; fidelity, not embarrassment; and openness, not inflexibility. Our context is similar to that of the ancient world, the world out of which Christianity grew, but to which we cannot return as if the Constantinian/Christendom epoch had not occurred. We need to learn from the early Christians but also learn the lessons of Christendom. Neither epoch can be recreated.

In the East End we are looking to the future with hope and some anxiety. The East End of London has, for hundreds of years, been a place where people of many races, cultures and faiths have lived. This history has been marked by conflict, hatred and hostility, but it has also shown to the world examples of co-operation, tolerance, and the ability to live together in harmony. Many writers from the 1930s onwards have described this area as an object lesson in living for people everywhere. Today we are at a turning-point. All kinds of things are changing. The future of multi-faith and multi-cultural life and work is a matter of great urgency. The fact that there is, and has been for hundreds of years, a plurality of faiths and cultures here is no guarantee that life and practice will be based on a real understanding of, and commitment to, this fact. Plurality does not automatically lead to pluralism any more than diversity leads to equality. Those of us who value the diversity of faiths, and who also believe that progress lies neither in a vague tolerance nor in an attempt to ignore the facts, but in a positive commitment to work together towards a different, and as yet unclear, future, have a lot of hard work to do. The danger that both the majority community and the minorities will relapse into tribal politics and introverted faith traditions is obvious. How can it be avoided? How can negative and regressive trends be reversed? How can our work and networks begin a process away from this? And what are the other trends with which we need to link and co-operate? These are matters with which I and others will be concerned in the coming years.

Central to our concerns for the future must be the constant struggle against racism. It is impossible to discuss race and racism in the East End of London without locating it within the wider context: that of European legislation on racial discrimination and on the rights of minorities; of British immigration controls, not least as they affect refugees and asylum seekers; of inequities and distortions in the housing market; and of what is termed 'institutional racism'. While this book is concerned mainly with the East London context, these wider structural questions are vital.[50]

The East End has been called 'the heartland of British fascism',[51] and recent struggles against racism in East London have been linked with the rise of openly racist and fascist political movements, the National Front (NF) in the late 1960s and 1970s, and the British National Party (BNP) in the 1980s and 1990s. After the decline of the NF following the General Election of 1979 when their vote collapsed virtually everywhere, there was a fragmentation and regrouping within British fascism. The collapse of the NF vote was connected with a massive swing to the Conservatives in all the areas where they had been successful. The NF split into various groups, one of which, in April 1982, became the BNP, and it was the electoral victory of the BNP in a by-election in the Isle of Dogs in 1993 which led to a major crisis with repercussions way beyond East London.

The struggle against the BNP on the Isle of Dogs

The Isle of Dogs is an island community in the River Thames where, in September 1993, an openly fascist councillor was elected. There had been a build-up to the vote. Racial attacks had increased on the island where the Asian community was very small. In 1987–9, for example, there were 104 such attacks, although only 260 Bengali families lived there. Earlier, the NF had obtained 16 per cent of the vote in the local elections of May 1978 though at that time their main activity was in Bethnal Green where they got 23 per cent in St

Peter's Ward. But there was concern about housing. In 1988 sixty-three people on the island signed a petition, and announced to their fellow residents: 'If you sign this, you are objecting to Tower Hamlets letting our houses to Pakistani [sic] families when our own young couples are being denied the right to be housed in this [sic] properties.' In the six months before the BNP councillor was elected, 24 out of 135 council house lettings on the Isle of Dogs were to Asian people.

Derek Beackon, the BNP councillor who was elected in the Millwall Ward in 1993, was well known in local racist circles. His views were crude and unintelligent. 'If we don't have this multi-racial society anywhere, there wouldn't be any problem.' 'Only a white man belongs in this country.' When asked about rubbish in the streets, his comment was: 'The Asians are the rubbish, and that is what we are going to clear from the streets.'[52]

The struggle against the BNP in the Millwall Ward of the Isle of Dogs is an important example of local churches working in collaboration with other faith communities and people of good will to defeat a particular manifestation of evil. It is worth identifying some of the key elements in that conflict, not least because other people in places far from Millwall face the same issues that confronted the people there between September 1993 and May 1994.[53]

In the run-up to the 1993 by-election, Labour, worried by their loss of support to the Liberal Democrats, are said to have leaked a false canvas return, showing that the BNP were now their main rivals. This shock was intended to win back Labour voters. Instead it gave credibility to the BNP, and the concentrated attention of the media ensured a self-fulfilling prophecy. Nic Holtam, parish priest at the time, wrote:

> On the following Sunday, the congregation at the Anglican parish church, Christ Church, were asked to write how they felt on a sheet of paper. 'Angry', 'Tearful', 'Ashamed', 'Frightened', and 'Pissed off' were among the feelings. One elderly man, a member of the British Legion, left the church in tears. 'I spent four years of my life fighting Nazis, and now we've voted them in.' The congregations were also asked to write up their suggestions for what we could do. Dozens of ideas were put up. The Anglican ministers shared these with their ecumenical colleagues at our weekly prayers. We

decided to call a meeting of people from all the churches to see if we could work on a constructive agenda.

The churches identified five areas of work to focus on: truth telling; building bridges; housing; strengthening the local democratic political parties; and increasing the size of the electoral turnout. They also decided to employ Sue Mayo as a project worker. A link was made with the Joseph Rowntree Charitable Trust, whose trustees kept asking questions. As a charitable trust, they could not give a grant for political purposes, and the grant they eventually gave was thought to be the first charitable grant ever given in Britain for the purposes of Voter Education, encouraging people to exercise their civic right to vote. Of much greater concern to Rowntree was whether or not the Church had clearly thought out what they were trying to do. One of their trustees said it all sounded well intentioned but woolly. What difference would it really make? Nic Holtam wrote:

> At the time Rowntree were a thorough nuisance. We wanted to get on with the work, and they held us back, justifying why we should get a grant. Looking back, however, this was a critical period. Rowntree's tough questioning probably made all the difference in making us effective.

Sue Mayo's background was in theatre, and she had worked with young people in community settings, including drama projects around bullying and racism. She worked in two schools, and this work with children led to an important publication *Stories from the Island*. But it was the 'rainbow ribbon' idea which really caught on. At an early meeting, two women, Rosalind Williams and Helen Holtam, formed a 'Peace Group', and out of this came the idea that people who were not going to vote for the BNP should wear a rainbow ribbon. One hundred metres of ribbon were ordered from a theatrical costumer, but within a day a further three hundred metres had to be ordered, and within a week over a mile! Linked with the ribbon was the slogan 'Celebrate the Difference'. The ribbons raised people's spirits and imagination, and people realised that it was possible that the BNP would be defeated. The ribbons created a non-verbal bit of language. Some people said they began to feel safer as they saw more and more individuals wearing them.

They needed courage for at the by-election there had been intimidation, and it still lay just below the surface.

Truth telling was important because the BNP had thrived on false
information. Many white people assumed that Bangladeshis got
preferential treatment in every area of life, and it was important to
communicate accurate information. Caroline Adams, a former youth
and community worker in the area, was employed by Docklands
Forum to produce a pamphlet *Once Upon A Time in Docklands*, published in April 1994, and launched at Tower Hamlets College in
Poplar. The simple telling of truth was valuable, for, as Sivanandan
had observed in 1986, 'there is a politics in stories truthfully told'.[54]

One church member said that she didn't know any Bengalis –
'and they don't want to know us'. So the parish put much effort
into building bridges. People watched a video about 'Building
Bridges' between different faith communities in Bradford. They
decided to plan a New Year's Party for Christians and Muslims.
Seventy people came to Island House, a United Reformed church
and community centre, on a Sunday afternoon. They played games,
sang a song, and shared food and stories. Throughout people could
learn to make paper flowers and, at the end, everyone gave a flower
to someone they had met for the first time. About thirty Bangladeshis
came, mostly men and children. At least one white person asked,
'Where are their women?' As they left, two Bangladeshi men confided
that they weren't sure the party was going to be safe, and that they
were very pleased to have had such a good time. They said that, if
the church ever planned anything similar, they would ensure a much
better attendance. In the midst of it all were a number of conversations about what people needed to do together to prepare for
the next elections. This party was extremely important, and
showed the political value of what may seem trivial activity. The
parish priest stressed that 'the work we were able to do collaboratively
with Bangladeshi community groups at a later stage depended on
the relationships established at this party.'

Housing was the key issue, both the shortage of social housing
and the allocations policy, so the churches focused on trying to get
more social housing built. A lay Roman Catholic, Mike Barraclough,
began work with a housing association for a scheme on some vacant
land, incorporating the idea of 'pre-lets' which would allow potential
tenants to be involved in the design of their homes. Of course, they

soon discovered that things were much more complicated than they had expected, but the churches had got all the main players talking – the local authority, the LDDC, the Commission for Racial Equality, and housing associations. Church leaders met government ministers. Yet there was very little progress between October 1993 and May 1994 beyond establishing a willingness to develop a scheme for people already living on the island which might address the problems of this community without colluding with racism. Both the Labour and Liberal Democrat Parties locally had colluded with racism in the run-up to the by-election on 16 September 1993. The Liberal Democrat Party held a national inquiry which resulted in a critical report seeking the expulsion of three prominent members. The Labour Party had an internal inquiry which resulted in the resignation of the ward chair and secretary.

On 16 September 1993, 1,480 people had voted for the BNP, about one-third of a 42 per cent turn-out. The churches identified that the BNP would not be able to get many more votes, and guessed that their ceiling would be around 2,000 votes. A bigger turn-out would reduce the significance of the BNP's support. So the churches set about planning how this could be achieved. It became clear that opposition to the BNP must be united. The Bethnal Green based Institute of Community Studies, under the direction of Lord Young of Dartington (Michael Young, the sociologist) commissioned an Opinion Poll just before the May elections, showing that the BNP's support was still very strong, but that Labour was well ahead of the Liberals, and probably had just enough support to beat the BNP. The message was clear: if you wanted to be sure of defeating the BNP, you should vote Labour.

A meeting between representatives of the churches, Bangladeshi community groups, and the Labour and Liberals got an agreement from the political parties to translate all their main election material. They also agreed to ask the Returning Officer to establish a limit of three tellers from each party at the gate of each polling station. The police were asked to recommend this because of the extreme intimidation experienced from the BNP at the by-election. In the event, the agreed limit was four, but the police presence was much stronger and there were also independent observers from Liberty. It was the first time that independent observers had been used at a British election.

The Island Neighbourhood Project put an enormous amount of work into translating information about how to vote and into providing transport for voters on election day. The churches helped register the housebound for postal votes, organised election day vigils, and advertised that those who wished could gather at the churches, and either go to vote in a group or be escorted to the polling station. Fewer than 100 individuals made use of these offers, but they were significant in establishing a climate in which people felt it was safe to vote. Although the BNP presence was intimidating, their effectiveness was minimised by this very careful and well co-ordinated planning and activity. People were determined to vote this time. The turn-out was over 67 per cent, remarkably high for a local election.

The churches' group met monthly. Numbers attending Christ Church (which had grown steadily over the preceding four years) began to decline slightly. But one member said, 'I think the leadership offered by the churches to this community has been streets ahead of that offered by any of the political parties. I am really proud to be a member of this church.'

At the by-election and afterwards the *East London Advertiser* had given the impression of being sympathetic to the BNP, maybe feeling that they were reflecting the views of their mainly white readership. To others it looked as though they were helping to create a climate of support for the BNP. The churches sought to persuade the *Advertiser* to be less positive about the BNP. Probably Lord Young deserves the credit for any success here. He spent time with the editor just a week before the election, talking about the seriousness of the circumstances in a personal, factual and non-hectoring way. On election day the *Advertiser* gave its front page to an article saying that the BNP was a serious threat to our society. To vote for them once at a by-election could be viewed as a protest: to do it twice and at the main council elections was a folly.

It is clear that the election of Derek Beackon was experienced as a real crisis, but, like most crises, this represented both danger and opportunity. Once he had been elected, issues which had been simmering were thrown into a sharper focus. Sue Mayo observed that 'it became more possible to name the conflicts which surrounded issues of housing, employment and education'. Doors were opened which had proved closed before, because so many people were concerned at the BNP's first foothold in legitimate government. One of the dangers was that people were overfocused on the election, ignoring the fact that the reasons for which many people had voted BNP would not go away were Beackon defeated. At the same time, encouraging more people to vote seemed an essential part of the strategy. The issue was, therefore, not only about getting a good turn-out for this election, but encouraging people to believe that their vote could make a difference.

In the application to the Rowntree Trust the church talked about 'changing the climate'. They were aware that a number of factors had led to the vote for the BNP, and that there were real issues to be addressed – housing, work opportunities on the island, and the tremendous change that had been brought to the island by the building of Canary Wharf. There was still a lot of resentment at the stresses which the building programme had placed on people's lives, and the disappointment that there had been fewer benefits than hoped for in terms of jobs. There was no single approach that would change the climate. On any one day there might be a meeting with a Minister at the House of Commons, an informal cup of tea with a local Bangladeshi family, a meeting with the TUC to plan a march through the East End, and a phone call to the Chief Executive of Canary Wharf. It was essential that work took place on many levels.

Some of the work was based around events such as the New Year party, meetings with agents of the political parties, or the TUC march. Other work was slow, dogged and delicate. Some people in the Bangladeshi community already felt at ease with the church. For others, their experiences had led them to be distrustful, and unsure of communicating outside their immediate community. Building up trust could take many meetings, many invitations, and good experiences which can help to heal bad ones. There was equally careful work to be done with churchgoers who felt that far too much attention was being paid to this issue, or who had many sympathies with the BNP, or who were baffled by their Bangladeshi or Somali neighbours. As the election drew near, the churches organised a party with two plans. Plan A would be a victory celebration. Plan B would be an occasion for gathering, talking, regrouping, and planning further action. In the event, the BNP were defeated.

This episode helped people to see that combating racism is not just a matter of dramatic demonstrations. Indeed, it was the local churches' recognition of this fact, their refusal to be content with a 'Fascists Out' approach, their combination of short-term and long-term strategies, and their commitment to the need for grass roots activity, learning from the local community-based work of the NF and BNP, which led to the defeat of the fascists. Sue Mayo noted:

> The story which sticks most vividly in my mind is that of a Bangladeshi shopkeeper who said, ' "Smash the Pakis!" and "Smash the Nazis!" sound pretty much the same when it is being shouted down your street. Whoever it is, I pull down the shutters.'

She went on to stress the importance of boring humdrum work including the sustaining of hope.

> Some of the friends in high places whom we had acquired melted away now that the 'crisis' was over, and it was back to the long, slow, painstaking, and sometimes unrewarding task of building bridges in a divided community. Many people were exhausted after the intensity of the past six months. And yet the work had to go on. It can be very hard to remain hopeful, and it is useful to remember sometimes that hope is a piece of work, and not just a feeling.

Reflection on this struggle was also important. The vote for Beackon had been described by a Jewish historian as 'more an assertion of community spirit than a protest against immigration'.[55] Certainly research had shown a link between the vote for the BNP and length of residence on the Isle of Dogs. Those who voted for the BNP were mainly long-term residents. Sixty per cent of them had lived on the Isle of Dogs for over twenty-one years. It was vital to take this 'community spirit' seriously.

Theology and racism

It has taken many years for the Churches in Britain to take racism with any kind of practical seriousness. In the early 1970s the Advisory Council for the Church's Ministry produced a textbook on *Teaching Christian Ethics* for use in theological colleges. The final draft dealt with the whole area of race in eight lines which included, as its only item of recommended reading, Anthony Richmond's *The*

Colour Problem, published by Penguin in 1955! While the published version made some minor changes, mainly in the bibliography, it included no attention to racism as such. This was the main academic text used in teaching ethics to those preparing for ordained ministry.[56] A study of Roman Catholic seminaries in England and Wales showed that there was less multicultural material in the seminaries than in most primary and secondary schools. In most cases, the single issue of marriage was given more attention than the entire area of justice. There was no attention to racism. The report concluded: 'In none of the seminaries did we find a clear and explicit commitment to preparing future priests to exercise their ministry in a racially mixed and culturally diverse society.'[57] When the East London Pastoral Assembly of the Archdiocese of Westminster, meeting in 1981, came to discuss race, they 'found it difficult to identify the problem, and so there was very little perception that anything needed to be done'.[58]

There is no doubt that there have been major shifts in Christian anti-racist practice since the early 1980s. Thus there has been a remarkable change in the seriousness with which church organisations and church leaders have taken such issues as racial attacks, deaths in police custody, and so on. For example, the East End of London is said to account for one quarter of all racial attacks in the country, and, while we have seen a decline in some parts of the area, this has been the result of constant vigilance and activity over many years. The record of the local churches in combating the rise of racial violence and of Nazi groupings is better than that of most organisations, not least because the churches, unlike some of the national anti-racist groups, realised the need to work with the local communities at a grass roots and highly contextual level.

Not surprisingly, the areas in which least progress has been made in the 'mainstream' churches have been those of class and power. It is probably still broadly true that most British Christians find it easier to approach race issues from the perspective of personal change. Approaches such as 'race awareness' strike an obvious chord in Christian hearts and find a good reception at retreat and conference centres where heightened consciousness, personal awareness, Myers-Briggs, and spiritual formation are high priorities. If racism can be seen, in Amrit Wilson's phrase, as 'a temporarily disfiguring individual disease',[59] then the appropriate response is education, therapy, perhaps even Sivanandan's famous 'deodorant stick'.[60] In fact, theological activity has continued to be more concerned with cerebral activity, or with the 'experiential' area, than it has with the conflicts of class, power and structure. Somehow education and therapy are seen as occurring outside of such realities, as if ideological and class interests did not exist. Yet, as two church activists wrote in 1980: 'Church circles sometimes seem to imply that if only we communicated more professionally, and expressed ourselves in better English, then everyone would automatically agree. But the problem may be not that people don't understand but that they do.'[61]

The liberation theologian Leonardo Boff wrote in 1985:

> In terms of power, the Church fears all transformations that jeopardise the security of its acquired power . . . And power itself will never abdicate. It is only shared when it is in jeopardy.
>
> We must . . . do away with the idealist temptation that is satisfied with raising people's consciousness in order to change the structures of the Church. It is not new ideas but new and different practices (supported by theory) that will modify ecclesial reality.[62]

On the idealist approach, Boff pointed out, we end up with good individuals with pure intentions who are uncritical towards the institution. As Pascal had observed, evil is never done so perfectly as when it is done with good will and purity of heart.

9
God on the edge:
theology and 'social inclusion'

The society of the Christian church has seldom been open to all, despite its founder's explicit teachings. The doors often have to be broken down before the outsiders are permitted in.

KENNETH ARNOLD[1]

There is no more hopeful sign in the Christian church today than the increasing attention which is being given by it to the poor and outcast classes of society.

The Bitter Cry of Outcast London 1 (1883)[2]

The renewal of Christianity today is coming not from the centre but from the bottom and from the edges.

HARVEY COX, 1986[3]

In this chapter I want to attempt to examine the current rhetoric of 'social exclusion' and 'social inclusion', which has, in Britain under the Blair government, to a certain extent replaced other ways of speaking about those on the margins of society; to examine responses of Christian groups to work with some of these 'excluded' groups; and to try to outline a general shape for a theological approach to exclusion and marginality. I will reflect, mainly, but not exclusively, from the background of my experience in London, and will concentrate on those areas with which I have some personal experience – homelessness, drug misuse, prostitution, and mental health – though I will draw on the work of others with greater experience in these and other fields. I will raise questions and insights, both from and for theology, and consider some practical consequences for the future of the Church and the kind of ministry needed in the future.

I have argued earlier that theology is, among other things, a reflective discipline which arises from, and is nourished and stimulated by, practical involvement with particular issues and particular communities. This chapter looks at the questions raised by marginality and exclusion, by the experience of groups and individuals who are in some way 'on the edge'. What is the theological task here?

I suggest that it is at least threefold. First, to make connections between specific developments in a given place, and the Christian tradition in its understanding of the created world and of humanity. This is a task which calls both for active involvement in a place, and for the discipline of reflection beyond the immediate context. Second, to critique processes and structures in the light of that tradition. This will bring the theologians and the theological community into direct conflict with the 'principalities and powers' who are operative in the situation. Third, to test, constantly and carefully, this theological work against the experience of groups and individuals who are casualties of, and who, by their very existence and predicament, reveal the weaknesses and distortions of the wider society. This will involve a process of continuous unlearning and relearning. The experience of many of us is that much can be learnt, and perhaps can only be learnt, from people who are in various ways marginalised. Marginality is often a place of creativity, and many have seen it as a key to theology.[4]

In this work, the question of theological posture is crucial. The theologian, like the anthropologist or social scientist, cannot be neutral or detached, cannot be other than a 'vulnerable observer', prepared for her or his heart to be broken.[5] Like the anthropologist, the contextual theologian will spend much of her or his time loitering, hanging around, getting the sense, the atmosphere, the feel, the smell, of a place. There is no way of short-circuiting this essentially contemplative work. *The Shorter Oxford English Dictionary* has a fascinating definition of 'loiter': 'to linger indolently on one's way; to hang idly about a place; to dawdle over a task. To travel indolently and with frequent pauses'. It then adds that the word was 'possibly introduced into English by vagrants from the Low Countries'.

In my experience, out of the work of theological reflection, certain practical tasks are likely to arise. For example, it is important for the theologian to build on the existing strengths, rooted in committed physical presence, of the Christian community, and to mediate that experience beyond the local churches. It is important, since theology is about truth, to practise truth telling and discernment, exposing and calling into question stereotyped and shoddy thinking. But, since theology is not a purely cerebral activity, it is important to try to live out a practical theology of inclusion which is not idealist but rooted in specific struggles, engagements and alliances.

There is no doubt, however many differences of interpretation there may be, that concern for 'the poor' is a central theme in the Jewish and Christian Scriptures. That God cares for those who are poor and oppressed, downtrodden, neglected, is clear from the texts of ancient Israel. God is seen as the defender of the poor and needy, the alien, the orphan and the widow, the judge who puts down the oppressors. Indeed this belief is much clearer biblically than are most of the issues over which churches have divided! The destruction of the ancient city of Sodom was attributed in part to its neglect of poor people (Ezek. 16:49-50). In the Synoptic Gospels, one in ten verses is about the rich and the poor, while it is one in seven in Luke, and one in five in the Epistle of James. The idea is common too in early Christian writers. Thus St John Chrysostom says that a poor person is an altar more venerable than one of stone.[6] St Lawrence, when confronted by robbers who demanded that he bring out the church's treasures, brought out dozens of poor people – dossers, ragged orphans, and demented old widows. These, he said, were the church's treasures. So far, so good.

But there is also a long, and deeply embedded, tradition in Christian churches which views 'the poor', 'the outcasts', 'the unemployed', 'the homeless' and so on, as categories of people who are not present within the Christian community but are the objects of its benevolence and care – to be discussed, talked about, and prayed for in their absence. My sense is that, as churches become smaller and more 'gathered' than neighbourhood-based, the tendency to exclude poor people, while promoting 'inclusiveness' among the respectable, will increase. At the same time, as the British research unit Demos has pointed out, 'much of the best innovation in the provision of local health, homelessness, community regeneration, and drug-related services is now being shaped by people with strong religious beliefs'.[7]

In fact, in practice, the witness of the Church is highly ambivalent. The nineteenth-century Archbishop of Dublin, Richard Whately, said that paupers should be tattooed on the foot to prevent them from begging, and that women receiving relief should have their hair cut off.[8] (While we may be shocked at Whately's proposals, some of the sentiments expressed by contemporary politicians, allowing for cultural changes, are not all that different.) And even where attitudes were not so hostile, much Christian rhetoric has been patronising and condescending.

But also in the nineteenth century the theologian F.D. Maurice said that Christ, through his incarnation, had 'entered into the state of the lowest beggar, of the poorest, stupidest, wickedest wretch whom that Philosopher or that Pharisee can trample upon.' The purpose of this entry was to 'redeem the humanity which philosophers, Pharisees, beggars and harlots share together'.[9] Later William Temple asked:

> Of what avail is it that I glorify [Christ] in his sanctuary or adore him in the Blessed Sacrament if, when I meet him in the street, I turn away from him, or if I leave him to languish in the prison? . . . It is Christ who pines when the poor are hungry, Christ who is repulsed when strangers are not welcome.[10]

However, a commitment to value, respect and serve poor people has not always gone hand in hand with a commitment to change the conditions, or to work to end poverty.

Today the state of marginality is one which affects a large number of people, and it is manifested in many different ways. For some, it is a chosen way of life. Exclusion is a concept to which I shall return, but I take it to mean a situation in which an individual or group is deprived of the benefits of the mainstream society. The process of exclusion may be quite deliberate and conscious, as in the case of asylum seekers or people under deportation orders, or it may be a process of gathering prejudice and hostility, as in the case of vagrant alcoholics. Exclusion may differ from one place to another, and from time to time. And, of course, people may exclude themselves. One common way of identifying the excluded is to say that they are people with 'no stake in society'.[11] Abandonment represents the most extreme form of social exclusion. It means the writing off of individuals or groups as beyond the pale, beyond redemption, beyond hope.

We need to be very careful, however, not to confuse poverty and deprivation with marginality and what is increasingly termed 'social exclusion'. The concept of marginality did not figure in social policy thinking until the end of the 1980s. An equally problematic term is 'the underclass', the descendant of the nineteenth-century term 'residuum'. But poverty and deprivation are far more widespread in the very heart of our society, and not on its margins. For many people and many communities, they are the norm and not the exception.

There is some evidence that the nineteenth-century idea of the 'residuum', and its subsequent development into what we now see as 'underclass', was in part shaped by the East End experience. Certainly the notion of 'outcast London' and of East Enders as 'people of the abyss' helped to shape such ideas, and there are certainly antecedents of underclass rhetoric in the accounts of poor Irish people in the last century. Locations such as Christ Church Gardens in Spitalfields, St Mary's Gardens in Whitechapel (both of them referred to at various times as 'Itchy Park'), and parts of the Cable Street area became centres for vagrant alcoholics and methylated spirit drinkers in particular, and helped to strengthen notions of 'skid row', a term derived from North American cities.[12] Later the language of 'underclass' was developed.[13]

The existence, persistence and return of poverty is not the same as the emergence of groups who may be classified as 'outcast', 'residuum' or 'underclass', but the two are directly related. Poverty is far more widely distributed, far more diverse, far commoner, than most people – including many poor people – realise. For example, children are more likely to be born in poverty in Britain than elsewhere in Europe. Almost one-third of British children live below the official breadline. Between 1980 and 2000 the number of children in poverty grew from 1.4 to over 3 million. According to UNICEF, the British record is worse than those of Turkey, Poland and Hungary.[14] Disparities of wealth and access to influence have become more marked. Take, for example, access to the Internet. Recent data from the Office of National Statistics show that, while 48 per cent of affluent households have access, the figure for poor households is 3 per cent.[15]

Social exclusion

Since the coming to power of Tony Blair and 'New Labour', the fashionable term is 'social exclusion'. A Social Exclusion Unit (SEU) has been established, and this concept plays a key role in government social policy. It has replaced earlier terms such as deprivation, marginality, discrimination, and disadvantage. It is in danger of becoming a catch phrase, a term used without careful thought or analysis. Thus a government minister, Paul Boateng, has said that socialism is 'about caring, about being inclusive'.[16] This is all very well and few would dissent from it but as a definition of a socialist agenda it is simplistic, naive and verges on the sentimental. This language needs to be examined before it becomes yet another part of uncritically accepted rhetoric. The positive side of it is that clearly persons and communities have been excluded, and its use recognises that this is a more helpful and more accurate approach than that which portrayed such people as an underclass.

Yet it is easy to focus on well-publicised groups and ignore others. For example, data suggest that the most marginalised group within the workforce is not the 18–25 age group but the older male manual workers. However, there are some weaknesses in the concept of exclusion which need to be considered.

(i) It tends to ignore the nature of 'society' and of the 'social'. We cannot speak meaningfully of social exclusion without an understanding of what it is to be part of society and of the nature of the social. Worse, social exclusion seems to have replaced the idea of equality. Indeed, Will Hutton admits this, claiming that the objective for 'the left' should be inclusion *'rather than equality'.*[17]

(ii) It tends to forget that exclusion is the result of some agency. It does not simply happen by accident. Someone, or some cluster of agents, perform the exclusion. Wilkinson's work on health inequality shows that processes of social differentiation create social exclusion.[18] So who does the excluding? What forces are at work? It is obvious, for example, that some outer city estates were designed specifically with exclusion in mind.[19] There is no doubt that the London Docklands Development Corporation quite consciously excluded not only individuals but whole communities, since the entire project of 'regeneration' was based upon the systematic exclusion of those who were in the way of the developers.

The role of the media is important here too. In Britain we have a dreadful newspaper called the *News of the World* which specialises in 'scandals' and what is usually referred to as 'dirt'. As a result of their uncovering and 'shaming' people whom they described as 'paedophiles', giving their alleged addresses and producing photographs, numerous innocent people were attacked, and a climate of hatred and mass panic was built up. While the newspaper has been criticised, no action has been taken against it, and there has been no apology for this behaviour. This too is an example of social exclusion.

Again, asylum seekers are excluded by design, but the Social Exclusion Unit is not involved in asylum issues, in spite of the Audit Commission's recommendation that it should be.[20] More generally, as the Latin American Bishops' meeting at Puebla in 1978 stressed, structural poverty is not a chance stage but the product of definite economic, social and political situations and structures.

(iii) It bypasses issues of power, income and wealth, and access to resources, and tends to see inclusion in terms of moral and educational improvement. In this it is similar to the old – and now largely abandoned – approach to race relations in the 1960s which was dominated by the ideas of host society and assimilation. It blurs social divisions, seeing them as abnormal, and stresses social cohesion.

(iv) There is also a tendency to see exclusion as a property of populations or of places rather than as a dynamic process. If this is so, the answer lies in the labour market or the educational system. In fact, exclusion is 'a process, not a condition'. Castells warns that the 'information age' is likely to be one of 'stepped up inequality, polarisation and social exclusion', and speaks of a Fourth World of Exclusion which is 'made up not only of most of Africa and rural Asia, and of Latin American shanties, but also of the South Bronx, Le Courneuve, Kamagasaki or Tower Hamlets of this world'.[21]

Linked with this is a concern with control – of rough sleepers, homeless people, and so on. In much of the rhetoric, exclusion is contrasted, not with inclusion, but with integration, often narrowly conceived as integration into the labour market. This can be seen in current official attitudes to homelessness.

'The time of the end is the time of no room' (Thomas Merton): reflections on homelessness

I have been involved with homeless people since the 1960s when we heard a great deal about the 'new social drop out'. Homelessness, it was then claimed, was now connected less to economic distress and more to 'social nonconformity'.[22] This was not correct then, and it is not correct now. In fact, the causes of homelessness, while diverse, show more continuity than dramatic change over the decades. The main changes have been in the ratio of young people who are homeless, and in the role of government in making the position worse.

The 'reforms' in Social Security since 1986, which included cutting income support for 16–17 year olds, created a new generation of homeless people. The Housing Act 1996 removed homeless people's rights to permanent accommodation and led to a spiral of insecurity and a kind of imprisonment within temporary accommodation.

In 1988 Centrepoint estimated that there were at least 50,000 young homeless people in London,[23] while studies over the years suggest that there are more rough sleepers than official figures recognise (though there have been government campaigns recently to 'reduce' the numbers under threat of withdrawal of funding from agencies). In 1999, for example, although official data recognised only eleven rough sleepers in Newham, the Department of the Environment was funding an outreach worker who was expected to contact 200 rough sleepers each year. Debates about the numbers of rough sleepers will no doubt continue, though today the debates have more explicit political aspects.

The changing character of homeless people has been worrying. One in ten young homeless people in London are graduates, and day centres are seeing more young people who have jobs but can find no point of entry into the housing market. There has been an increase in the numbers of people whose homes have been repossessed, a phenomenon unknown in Britain before the late 1980s. By 1997, however, there were 1,000 cases per year. There has also been an increase in the numbers of runaways. In a study of 200 homeless drug users in Manchester, aged eleven to twenty-five, 68 per cent were runaways.[24] The numbers of people who die in the street has been a matter of concern, and in November each year the names are read out at St Martin's in the Fields. At a recent liturgy around 200 names were read.[25]

The seriousness with which the Blair government takes homelessness as a symbol of social exclusion is seen both in the establishment of its Social Exclusion Unit and in the attention it has given to rough sleeping. The Social Exclusion Unit report *Coming in from the Cold* laid down the lines of the government's strategy to reduce rough sleeping, and led to the establishment of Contact and Assessment Teams (CATs). (St Botolph's Project became the CAT for East London. Interestingly, London was divided by the SEU into 'central' and 'outer' – the notion of 'inner' has disappeared – and so the East End is now, officially, part of 'outer' London!)[26]

It is worrying that, as in the past, much of the rhetoric is not about the plight and needs of homeless people as such but about the damaging effects of their presence on tourism. As Tony Blair wrote in 1999, 'rough sleeping can blight areas, *and damage business and tourism*'.[27] Much government rhetoric about homelessness in recent years has been about the visibility of homeless people, rather than about their existence. Bernard Ingham, one of Margaret Thatcher's colleagues, talked about homeless people as a 'blot on the landscape'.[28] Recently, there has been a government-funded campaign to discourage people from giving money to beggars. One is bound to wonder in whose interests is all this effort.[29]

We are confronted, much of the time, with action without consciousness. A great deal of recent publicity is alarmingly simplistic, and shows little real understanding of the causes of homelessness. Nor does there seem to be much understanding within some of the 'caring professions'. There is considerable evidence, for example, that nurses and medical students have low levels of understanding of the problems of homeless people.[30]

Churches in Britain have been involved with homelessness for a long time. The developing Franciscan movement in the Church of England played an important role in the formation of the Vagrancy Reform Society, founded in 1928 at the Home of St Francis, Cerne Abbas. It led to the reform of casual wards, the creation of lodging houses, and, after the election of the Labour Government in 1929, to the Public Assistance (Casual Poor) Order 1929. It was the Franciscan vision too which led to the founding of the Simon Community in 1963. Simon certainly made 'the major philosophical impact on the residential field' and helped undermine the 'we–them' syndrome in social care.[31] There seems little doubt that the activity of the Simon Community led directly to the report *Homeless Single Persons* (1966).[32]

On 16 December 1969 a group of us started a little project called Centrepoint. The immediate context was turbulent. The London Street Commune had occupied a mansion at 144 Piccadilly. There had been a massive increase in the numbers of young homeless in central London. Many of us had been working for several years with the large communities of street people, addicts, 'young drifters' (as the current youth work jargon called them), and other subcultural groups. But we were neglecting the largest group of all – the increasing numbers of young people, new arrivals to London, who were outside of all these groups and were simply homeless. They had come to London in search of work and found themselves on the street.

So on that night in December 1969 we opened up the basement of St Anne's House in Dean Street as an emergency night shelter. The story of the building goes back to the 1940s when the Diocese of London's Reorganisation Committee decided that there was no need for a parish house in Soho, and that they would sell it for a large amount of money. However, they reckoned without the formidable churchwarden, one Dorothy L. Sayers. It seems that the diocesan bureaucrats were terrified of Dorothy Sayers and, as a result, the plan was abandoned. St Anne's House stands to this day.

It was there that Centrepoint night shelter began. We chose the name 'Centrepoint' for two reasons. It was more or less the 'centre point' of the Soho district. But we also had in mind the existence of another building called 'Centrepoint', a tower block at Tottenham Court Road, kept empty for years in order to increase the value of the property. We wanted to draw attention to the outrage and scandal of what Professor Ruth Glass termed 'that insolent building'. Ruth Glass was quite important in inspiring and guiding us in terms of a wider context of social philosophy. She pointed out, a few weeks after Centrepoint opened its doors, that 'the very people who are wanted on the labour market are regarded as expendable on the housing market'.[33]

Since those early days I have continued to maintain contacts with homeless people in London and elsewhere, though I have realised that over time the focus and approach of a person's work often needs to change direction. Having been heavily involved with street work and running an all-night emergency centre in the 1960s, I tend now to focus more on helping and supporting other people's work in that area, and on trying to understand and develop what an incarnational Christian community can do in this field of work. In the early 1990s I became involved with Mary Beasley and the Mission on the Margins project. Mary, a disabled woman and former social worker, works with homeless 'street people' in Birmingham. I sit on her Support Group and wrote the preface to her book *Mission on the Margins*, published in 1997. Out of Mary's work has grown a network called Mission on the Margins which seeks to help and support people involved in marginal areas of ministry. Among the inspirations for Mission on the Margins is the work of Claude Marie Barbour in Chicago who popularised the term 'mission in reverse'.[34]

I have also maintained links with projects in the USA. In 1999 I went to Asheville, North Carolina, and was involved with the Street Ministry Program led by Judith Whelchell at the Church of the Advocate, a church consisting almost entirely of homeless people. A weekly Eucharist and lunch brought together about 120 people, most of whom were homeless. Some prostitutes and other local 'street people' wandered in and out. The Eucharist was entirely voluntary and I suppose about thirty people attended the whole, while a larger and changing group drank coffee in the rest of the hall. Communion was offered to all, and was taken around beyond the circle of 'worshippers'. Many received, but there was a strong sense of freedom, a lack of pressure, and tremendous reverence. The sermon was replaced by an open discussion of gospel themes and their relevance to issues facing the people, on the lines of the 'base communities' in the liberation tradition. I was asked to preside, which was a great privilege and joy. Many of the people could not read, a few were drunk or high, quite a lot were mentally ill, and so the rite was very informal and flexible. I made up a eucharistic prayer using the basic structure of the western canon. I was very moved by the sense of equality and openness to all – no sense of 'congregation' and 'clients' – at the Church of the Advocate, something we have never fully achieved at St Botolph's after forty years.[35]

I also spent time with the Open Door Community in Atlanta, a Protestant house of hospitality, run on Catholic Worker lines, and heavily involved in political action around homelessness, medical care, and other local issues. According to the Atlanta Task Force for the Homeless, on any one night, around 11,500 to 16,000 people in the city are homeless. The Open Door provides breakfast six days a week, and around 65,000 breakfasts a year. The close connection between care and political commitment seemed a contrast with the caution and lack of much (if any) radical edge which I find in a lot of the London work. I have always felt that the Dorothy Day/Peter Maurin approach had a lot to teach us. (Quite a few of the early volunteers at St Botolph's Crypt in the early 1960s were Day–Maurin types.)[36]

Recently, a group of eight-year-old children at Kobi Nazrul Primary School became very concerned about the homeless people who had squatted in the derelict Tower House in Fieldgate Street, close to the school and to their homes. (Tower House was a former hostel, one of whose more famous residents was Stalin!) As a result of the expression of their concerns to their imaginative teacher Sindee Bass, they went on to study the history of homelessness in the district where they lived, and to reflect on what it all meant. Lukas Veritas wrote:

> I wish I had a home but I haven't,
> I wish I had a job but I haven't.
>
> I wish I had a car but I haven't.
> I wish I was rich but I'm not.
> All I have is a heart and a hard life.

Sadia Sattar wrote:

> It feels good to be home . . .
> It's great to have some shelter.
> I wonder if homeless people have
> Enough to eat and drink . . .
> I wonder how hungry homeless people
> Must be?

Steven Alehandro imagined that he was a homeless eleven-year-old whose father had kept beating him up.

The children were not content with their personal and poetic reflections. When the local council sold the property, they found out who the new owners were, and wrote to them. (I should add that, having written twice to the Acting Director of Housing, and received no reply, the children put me to shame in terms of political strategy.)

Drugs, prostitution and drifting youth

I have written extensively about drugs and pastoral care over the last thirty-five years. Here I want to concentrate on the role of the Christian community in terms of action, prayer and theological reflection. I believe there are a number of levels of action which are vital. The first task of the Christian community is to witness to the truth. As I said earlier in relation to racism, it is impossible to minister to individuals with problems and ignore the wider political and economic dimensions which are global as well as national. One expert and former official of the World Health Organisation has referred to 'the complete failure of national and international drugs policies',[37] and this is clear to many of the Christian groups in the field. They are in a strong position to say so loudly and clearly, and they must do so.

It is obvious that churches need to function within the specific context in which they are set, and they can only effectively do so if they are aware of what is happening in their area. Yet this is not always so. A study of the role of faith communities in Croydon commented on the local religious leaders: 'The leaders of all the religious communities were aware that drug abuse existed in Croydon although none of them had any personal experience or knew of anyone who was affected . . . None of the leaders had any real knowledge.'[38] It is of vital importance, if churches are to become more involved in pastoral care of drug users, that they are well informed and aware of what is going on, including what is going on among their own members. A study of 7,666 young people by the Evangelical Coalition on Drugs at the Spring Harvest festival in 1995 suggested that there was almost as much drug use among young people within churches as among non-churchgoers.

Often responses to drugs are more harmful than the drugs themselves. Public responses and policies can hinder and impede as well
as aid and strengthen pastoral work. R.H. Tawney, the economic
historian, made the point powerfully many years ago.

> One whole wing of social reformers has gone, it seems to me,
> altogether astray. They are preoccupied with relieving distress,
> patching up failures, reclaiming the broken down. All this is good
> and necessary. But it is not the social problem . . . It is no use giving
> opiates or stimulants to men whose daily regimen is unhealthy. It
> is no use devising relief schemes for a community where the
> normal relationships are felt to be unjust.[39]

Until the damage due to policy is recognised, there will be no
substantial improvement. There is therefore a need for churches to
engage in policy issues on drugs as they have in other areas. In the
USA, the Religious Coalition for a Moral Drugs Policy has brought
together people from many faith traditions, and similar work is being
done in Britain by the Drug Policy Review Group.

I was a founder member of this group which is concerned with
reform of drug policy. The other founders were the late H.B. Spear,
for many years Chief Inspector of the Home Office Drugs Branch,
and Dr John Marks, a consultant psychiatrist in Merseyside. It
includes doctors, economists, psychologists, and others, and is united
by the belief that current drugs policies are counter-productive, and
that alternative approaches must be sought and studied. We have
submitted evidence to the European Parliament and recently to the
Independent Inquiry on the Misuse of Drugs Act initiated by
the Police Foundation – a report totally ignored by the government.

A second area is that of crisis work, including street contact, crisis
intervention, and harm reduction. From its early involvement with
preventive work and drugs education, the Maze Project, based in
the East End, became involved with the increasing numbers of
commercial sex workers in the Commercial Street and Old Montague
Street districts of Whitechapel. It has been shown in earlier chapters
that Whitechapel had been a centre for prostitution for several
hundred years, and for juvenile prostitution in particular since the
1940s. As a result of the street work, relationships have been
developed with the young women which has led to many positive

results. There is no way that this kind of crisis work can be bypassed, but it is messy, imperfect, frustrating, and yet increasingly necessary.

Drugs work now necessitates involvement with gangs, fighting for territory. A Bengali group called Asha (hope), initiated by Abdul Khayar Ali, helped to negotiate a truce between a number of rival gangs in the East End. But experience shows that the work of reconciliation has to be continuous, and the decisive intervention cannot stand alone without the day-by-day routine, boring work of building bridges and building confidence.

In some places, street work has led to changes in theological education. In Chicago, for example, the work with prostitutes, pioneered in the early 1980s by Edwina Gateley and Fr Depaul Genska OFM has led not only to the establishment of Genesis House (1984), which has so far housed over four thousand women seeking an alternative life, but to new developments in seminary training. At the Catholic Theological Union, the major Roman Catholic seminary, students have been encouraged to familiarise themselves with the world of prostitution, and to establish friendships with women in prostitution, on the basis of genuine human respect and equality. Fr Depaul's study guide on the film *Pretty Woman*, with its study of a relationship between a prostitute and a customer, has been valuable in helping to clarify and deepen fundamental theological themes about human dignity and care in relation to those whom mainstream society has tended to cast off.[40]

Thirdly, Christians have been playing an important role for many years in after-care and in the rebuilding of damaged lives. Twelve-Step programmes claim a 70 per cent success rate, and their work is of great relevance. However, my experience is that most official drugs services, and many voluntary ones, do not reach minority groups.[41]

Ministry on the margins

Much of the experience of work with drug users is applicable over a wider area of marginalisation. People with mental health problems are not included within the British government's concept of social exclusion, though there has been some important work from government sources, and the Health Education Authority produced *Mental Health Promotion and the Christian Church* in 1999. While churches have been active at a local pastoral level, Pattison is right to say that 'institutionally the churches have shown relatively little interest in fundamentally changing the injustices of society or in the situations of mentally ill people'.[42] As I write, we are in the midst of adverse, or at least ineffectual, government responses to mental health, including very ill-informed plans for the compulsory treatment of some mentally ill offenders. Meanwhile crude stereotypes often take over from, and damage, local-based networks of care. One of the factors which often crops up in local inquiries is the breakdown of informal networks of care. In Newham, for example, only 11 per cent of those interviewed thought that the community was friendly, and only 50 per cent felt that they could ask their neighbours or friends for help.[43]

As in the drugs field, many Christian communities are heavily involved at a street level in work with people with mental health problems. In Atlanta, the Church of the Holy Comforter stands in a district which contains a concentration of 'group homes', houses provided for former inmates of psychiatric hospitals with a range of needs from learning difficulties to schizophrenia. It is this community who form the bulk of Holy Comforter's congregation, and the parish priest, Mark Baker, has played an important role in developing mental health provision in the city. As in other places, mental health and poverty are closely linked. At the group homes, individuals receive $480 per month and pay $420 in rent, leaving $15 per week for all other needs.

One of the congregation, Laura, wrote her reflections as a poem:

> I hate everything that's happening
> And I can't change a thing,
> and social services are anything but social.
> They took my beautiful granddaughter and I
> I have no idea what to do.
> How do you get out of this?

Peggy, however, said that people at Holy Comforter 'put a glow in my heart and a smile on my face', for here she had found good friends.

> I give them my good words when they're blue.
> Let's make them cheerful and not alone any more.

'Holy Comforter is the place to go,' wrote Peggy. Liz Ellis, former art tutor at St Botolph's, and I have been privileged to work at Holy Comforter, and it has been a profound insight into how a local Christian community works, practically, spiritually and theologically, with people on the edge.

Another area of marginality is homosexuality. St Botolph's has been consciously involved with gay and lesbian people for almost thirty years, and it is important that some of this experience is written down for the benefit of the wider Church. I am not competent to do this, having only been involved peripherally with this area of the ministry here. So I want to examine it, not in abstract theoretical terms, but by reflecting on the ministry of a former colleague, David Randall, who died of AIDS in 1996.

By any standards other than physical size, David Randall was a larger than life character. He once described himself as the smallest priest in the Church of England, but he was one of the most flamboyant, most colourful, most entertaining, and, at his best, most pastoral and prayerful priests of his generation. Born in Ashtead, Surrey, David fell in love with the East End as a student where he was influenced by John Groser and Joe Williamson, whom I discussed in Part One. (See also Chapter 11 on Groser.) In many respects he modelled himself on them, possessing Williamson's dramatic, histrionic streak, style of preaching, and singleness of vision, though lacking Groser's political analysis and personal stability. After a turbulent first curacy at All Saints, Poplar, where he was a key figure in founding the Teviot Festival, chaired Tower Hamlets Youth Workers Forum, and helped create the rock group Iron Maiden, he moved to be unattached youth chaplain at St Botolph's in the mid-1970s. Here he exercised a remarkable street ministry, and spent much of his time in clubs and sleazy bars. These were the days of real creative work at St Botolph's. One of the first Bengali youth clubs was set up here, and David and Josie Harriot began the Kipper Disco at St Botolph's which ran from 11.00 p.m. every Friday to 2.30 a.m. every Saturday!

It was during this period that the then Bishop of London, Gerald Ellison, asked to see his work, insisting on coming in 'mufti' in spite of David's attempts to persuade him to dress as a bishop (as East Enders would expect). When Ellison arrived in an expensive Moss Brothers suit with Oxford college tie (in order not to be conspicuous!), he said, 'David, my boy, you mustn't say I am the bishop. Say I am your friend Gerald.' In one gay bar in Whitechapel, David introduced his friend, at which Ellison held out his hand and said loudly, 'How do you do?'

At St Botolph's, where he worked with Malcolm Johnson, David helped to create the Kipper Project to work with homeless young people. He was a founder member of the Jubilee Group. Like many politically radical Christians, he had a very traditional theology with a strong emphasis on the daily office, prayer and eucharistic adoration. His Catholic socialism was the theological and political basis of all his pastoral work.

David was one of the first priests to be public about his homosexuality, and later about the fact that he had AIDS, speaking about it on TV and in various publications. His involvement with HIV and AIDS began in Notting Dale where he had gone in 1978 as Vicar of St Clement's. During these years, he led the most colourful and inspiring worship of any church in London. The highlights of the year were Holy Week and Easter (with the Way of the Cross dramatised through the streets and attended by thousands of people, and the Easter Vigil at 5.00 a.m.), the Notting Hill Carnival Mass with steel band and fantastic costumes, and the Feast of Christ the King in November. The liturgy at St Clement's combined the best of Anglo-Catholic splendour with a warmth and a crazy informality rarely seen in Anglicanism. David had an intense devotion to the Virgin Mary, and St Clement's was probably the only church in the world to have a shrine for racial justice focused on a statue of Our Lady of Fatima, beneath which was printed the Litany of Our Lady of the Freedom Fighters, composed by some Catholic Worker activists in prison in Alabama during the Civil Rights Movement.

In the mid-1980s David nursed Richard who had AIDS. Richard lived at St Clement's from 1985 to the end of 1986 when he died. He had been a member of St Clement's parish, and his funeral was attended by members of the congregation, the school choir, the local dustmen, and many members of the local community. David wrote:

> Richard changed our lives and opened the way for the community to support him without in any way creating him as a victim. The combination of a personally afflicted person, the local community,

and professionals proved a powerful one, and unlocked resources of which we never dreamed.[44]

The positive, supportive and loving acceptance of Richard by the congregation of St Clement's was a major factor in David's own decision to devote the rest of his ministry to work in the field of HIV and AIDS. Soon afterwards he resigned from the parish and went to work as a nursing auxiliary on the AIDS ward at San Francisco General Hospital. On his return he founded CARA (Care and Resources for People with Aids) which is now, appropriately, based in the old vicarage of St Clement's. He was involved in the creation of the London Lighthouse, the hospice for people with AIDS, where he finally died. He was the founder of the International Christian Aids Network (ICAN), and spent much of the last few years running training courses and lecturing on AIDS throughout Britain and beyond.

David was a warm, passionate, outrageous, infuriating, at times utterly indiscreet and irresponsible person. Highly emotional and prone to tantrums, he could also be incredibly sensitive and loving, practical in a crisis, disciplined and God-centred. He did much good and some harm to people in his care. All his public events were done with high drama and finesse, and he would throw extravagant parties for any and no reason. But there was also a very compassionate, deeply caring, priestly heart. Marybel Moore, former churchwarden of St Botolph's and a close friend of David, said that 'his great gift was of holding the incarnational and transcendental within himself and consequently in his words and actions both as a priest and as a human being'.

The experience with AIDS led to a sadder, more reflective, broken person. In a moving passage in 1988, written in San Francisco, he reflected:

> After seventeen years as a London parish priest where my ministry has been built upon the ongoing building up of relationships, and community development centred on the eucharistic community, I have found it especially hard adjusting to the ministry on the AIDS unit ... I have always been a great fixer, both as social activist seeking to change the world, and as priest-actor-manager offering a sacramental merry go round of exciting worship and meaningful spiritual comfort. Only now am I slowly, falteringly

and fearfully facing the challenge of staying where the suffering really is, of not knowing the answers, and being honest about this, of allowing others to set the agenda for ministry, and even admitting that I receive from them as much as I can ever give.[45]

The paragraph captures something of this ambiguous, complex, loving, strange, joyful and in some ways deeply tragic life, a life symbolised equally by the Notting Hill Carnival and by the long loneliness of AIDS. In 1990 he wrote: 'There are three things I want to bring to the church. Two of them have always been there: my priesthood and my sexuality. And now I want to bring the virus to the church.'

In tape recordings made by David's cousin, Ruth Silvestre, shortly before his death, David conveyed something of his pastoral vision, in an incoherent, jumbled and yet profound way. These are some examples.

It's getting a cross section of people together – you have to take a risk. But I don't think it's ever failed. I don't know what the ingredients are, but I think it is the risk taking . . . You've got to get out into people's homes . . . Often clergy I know sit behind computers the whole bloody day, producing more and more paperwork. That I think is very sad, because when they're doing that, they're not with the people . . . So the kind of job that I was ordained into, for instance, the focus is the parish, whether they were church members or not. I've always made that my focus in ministry . . . that's where the whole thing's breaking down. You're not running a company, you're creating homes and hearts where God's love can be released and energised, in often very fragile, broken, vulnerable people. I regard that as a great, great pleasure, to be called to that ministry – I don't like social workers.

In an earlier book I wrote about St Clement's in David's time:

These are the kind of churches which have nourished me and kept me in (albeit on the edge of) the Church of England. But I fear that such places may be diminishing as 'middle Anglicanism', the religion of the dull, nondescript, middle class, boring, safe, clerical elites, takes over. I hope desperately that I am wrong. But I am sure that Anglicans need to lose most of their respectability, restraint, and control which marks their worship and culture if they are to make a genuine contribution to the worship of the coming church.[46]

It is a theme to which I shall return later in this chapter.

I learnt a great deal from working closely with David about priesthood, sexuality, humanity, prayer, weakness and pastoral care. Indeed, there is a whole agenda of unfinished spiritual business here with which at present many Christians are seeking to grapple. While gay and lesbian people are increasingly accepted as equals within many Christian communities, the amount of dishonesty, doublespeak and refusal to engage with the issues remains a serious problem, not least in relation to many of our bishops. So, while it is well known that the Church of England has been ordaining 'practising' homo-sexuals for many years, and that they have exercised valuable ministries as parish priests, members of the staff of what is now called the Division of Ministry (formerly CACTM, ACCM and ABM), bishops' chaplains, and so on, bishops continue to speak as if this were not so. Unlike the Episcopal Church in the USA, few bishops have helped parishes to respond to the demands for blessing of same-sex unions, or given much pastoral guidance as to how to respond to the expressed pastoral needs of gay and lesbian people. (In recent visits to the USA I was struck by the seriousness and positive pastoral approach with which all the American dioceses and their bishops which I visited (especially in Vermont, Arkansas and Oklahoma) were taking the difficult question of the blessing of same-sex unions.) I don't find the same here where the culture of dishonesty and evasion is still dominant.

So we have created two worlds, two levels of communication, and a culture of falsehood which is not conducive either to personal honesty, spiritual integrity or pastoral care. It is a profoundly unhealthy situation which calls for more work. Meanwhile gay and lesbian people leave the churches and seek God elsewhere.

Of course, that is only part of the story. Since the 1970s the ministry at St Botolph's has tried to build on the pastoral foundations laid by Malcolm Johnson, David Randall and others. We have been involved with work with people with HIV and AIDS, and with theological and pastoral reflection on the issues. Several years ago, one of our two vocational deacons, Pat Wright, a nurse who had been in charge of the AIDS ward in a major London hospital, was asked to develop an AIDS clinic in Swaziland. She is still there, and we see her work as an extension of our ministry here.[47]

Work in the HIV and AIDS field has been one of the most significant growth areas for contextual theological reflection, and people with more involvement in it, and more competence than I have, are, hopefully, writing up some of this experience from the British perspective. In the USA, it is clear that to many churches it has brought a new and powerful understanding of what it is to be a 'community of the resurrection'. The Metropolitan Community Church in San Francisco sees itself as 'a community of the resurrection, living in the very epicentre of AIDS-related death . . . an eschatological community . . . a community of joy in the midst of tears . . . a community that can sing songs about heaven with integrity because it is singing from the cross.'[48]

It has brought too a deeper understanding of solidarity and of the meaning of being 'the body of Christ', a body which bears wounds. If one part of the Church has AIDS, we all have AIDS. As one hymn puts it:

We are the church alive,
The body must be healed.
Where strife has bruised and battered us
God's wholeness is revealed.[49]

This experience has also emphasised and focused the real hopelessness and helplessness which pastoral workers encounter, an experience which extends well beyond the specific area of incurable illness. All over the country and the world, pastoral care takes place in environments where there seems little or no hope, no future, no jobs, no likelihood that things will improve. How do we sustain hope in such places? It is significant that a number of Christians, reflecting on the experience of AIDS, focus specifically on the question of nurturing a 'praxis of hope'.[50]

But we are confronted by a deeper and wider problem – the problem of contempt. While the specific issue on which it is focused changes, the reality of contempt remains. Take that revered figure of English socialism, George Orwell, who showed a deep contempt for ordinary people. 'You can have an affection for a murderer or a

Sodomite, but you cannot have an affection for a man whose breath stinks'.[51]

I wrote in Part One about the communities of methylated spirit drinkers in our area, and I often recall and reread the words of Norman Ingram Smith, a distinguished social worker and former colleague, given in evidence to a London County Council report on crude spirit drinkers in 1964.

> Unwashed, evil smelling, incapable of work, occasionally emerging from his psychotic drunken state when restrained by the law or on an observation ward, he fights his bosom pal, he risks death by burning in disused houses. He is repulsive not only to others but to himself. Largely due to the aroma of his urine, he is unacceptable both in lodging houses and indeed in police cells. During the winter this kind of man spends his time in bombed out houses, under railway arches, in disused cars, and is frequently the victim of malnutrition, bronchitis and other diseases of deprivation and exposure. His condition gives rise to contempt even amongst the worst of the alcoholics who only drink recognised alcoholic beverages. When asked if they have drunk surgical spirits or meths, the average alcoholic will say 'Thank God, I have never sunk to that yet.'[52]

In seeking liberation from contempt and struggling towards equality and dignity, I am sure that we are following the ministry of Jesus. Jesus attracts and draws people from the periphery, but he does not draw them towards the centre. The New Testament has been described as 'an archive of the dispossessed ... the record of a counter-Establishment community of the dispossessed'.[53] It is certainly clear that Jesus cut at the heart of the classification of people into righteous and sinners, and we must follow his example.

Theology at the edge of chaos

In much of the discussion about people on the margins, the term 'chaotic' appears frequently. We are, it is said, working with people who have 'chaotic lifestyles'. Pastoral care is about order and structure, about the avoidance of the threat of chaos. I want therefore to introduce at this point the question of chaos. The relationship between chaos and order seems to be central to my life. I want to raise some questions which have been sparked off by three coincident moments: my promise to David Randall, shortly before his death, that I would try to write up the main aspects of his ministry; the publication of my *Drugs and Pastoral Care* in 1998;[54] and my ongoing thinking around issues of pastoral ministry in the East End, including the review of my work, my own self-scrutiny, and the criticisms of others.

As I went through David's papers and tapes, there is a consistent thread of frustration about, and hostility to, the growing 'professionalisation' and bureaucratisation of much pastoral ministry. He believed, as I do, that many models of ministry today are derived more from secular managerial models, influenced by social work and office-based professionalism, rather than from classical theology or more radical and politically conscious modern movements such as youth and community work, Freirian pedagogy, or Marxist analysis. Hence the tendency to retreat into offices, to lose contact with people and communities, and to collude with modern (not even postmodern) categories, jargon and assumptions.

Writing the drugs book, I kept going back to the situation in 1969 when I produced an earlier work on which it was based, a situation when the core of pastoral theology was one of moving beyond the limitations and cultural boundaries of the established Church into uncharted territory, with all the risks, uncertainties and challenges that this involved. I contrasted it with the situation today which seems to be more secure, remote, conservative, and theologically unreflective. Perhaps I am cynical or just getting old. But I don't think so: there are abiding and really important matters here.

As I reflect on my own work today I find that I am moving all the time in a direction contrary to, and incompatible with, those pursued by the conventional structures – social work, health authority, corporate management, service-providers, and so on. I find that I am utterly unsympathetic to, and alienated by, the rhetoric (if it deserves such a noble word – jargon is better) of the established agencies, and am finding that my own ministry can only be exercised by a sustained disaffiliation from them in the way that Ivan Illich suggested in his *Disabling Professions.*[55] When I say 'established agencies' I include the Church in its institutional form as one of the 'principalities and powers'. Such a disaffiliation was once part of the Christian tradition at its best: part of the work of what is now called 'deconstruction', once known in Christian terms as *metanoia*, involved the questioning, demystifying, subversion of conventional stereotypes and pretensions. But now, it seems to me, the Church is more and more succumbing to what Stephen Pattison calls 'the faith of the managers'.[56] This also is something to which I will return.

Complexity theory, of which chaos theory is a part, is of crucial importance. It shows that order emerges out of chaos without any outside intervention or direct internal control. The key moment is what is called 'the edge of chaos'. Chaos is no longer seen as entirely destructive but as a crucial link, a precondition for, and stimulant towards, the activation of latent creativity.

One of the most interesting accounts of the relevance of complexity theory to the human sciences is in the field of community development, and specifically in the work of Alison Gilchrist who works for the Community Development Foundation in Bristol. Gilchrist's work has important implications for pastoral theology, and provides, albeit not intentionally, a bridge between pure science and pastoral care. Gilchrist sees networking as a way of handling uncertainty and ambiguity, and even defines community as a complex system at the edge of chaos.

> Community development cannot be realised through business plans or the fulfilment of specific performative criteria. Rather it is about helping disadvantaged populations move towards the 'edge of chaos' by sowing and nurturing dynamic, integrated and socially diverse networks, which are neither utterly confusing nor frozen rigid. It is human horticulture rather than social engineering.[57]

It seems to me that 'the edge of chaos' is where we are in theology and pastoral care.[58] Yet much of our pastoral work has been shaped within a framework of a culture of order, and of a Church obsessed with tidiness. In a perceptive study of congregational leadership in postmodernity, Sandra Schneiders writes: 'The organism is always off balance. Local chaos is the normal condition out of which global order is continuously being both threatened and resourced.'[59]

Church of the centre or of the margins?

The word 'parish' derives from *paroikia* which is used in the New Testament with undertones of exile. In 1 Peter 1:17, for example, the word is translated 'exile' (RSV), 'on earth' (NEB), 'living away from home' (Jerusalem Bible), and 'strangers' (New International Version). However, in popular usage, 'parish' has come to mean ministry based on a locality. Is the parish concept obsolete?

In Britain it was certainly seen as 'inadequate' for ministry to marginalised groups as long ago as 1889.[60] It was some thirty years earlier that the word 'parochial' had come to be used as a synonym for narrow, limited, small-minded. In France in 1949 the Abbé Michonneau spoke of the parish as 'like a mother cell, the source of all apostolic work . . . it is in the parish that all new cells must be joined in a common life'.[61] Today many see it as a relic of Christendom. Yet it is fascinating to see how in the USA and Canada many churches are moving back towards the parish model.[62]

I was recently in Halifax, Nova Scotia for the 200th anniversary of St George's Church, the Anglican parish in the inner city. Here was a very concentrated district, mainly focused on Gottingen and Gerrish Streets, a kind of mini-East End crushed into a square mile. Most things happen here. I arrived at midnight on Monday. By 12 noon on Tuesday I had said Morning Prayer, attended Mass, visited a night shelter for homeless people, called at the public library to discuss child literacy, visited a Homeless Support day centre, met with Shining Lights (a choir of homeless people), called at Stepping Stones (for women trying to get out of prostitution), visited Turning Point, the Society of St Vincent de Paul, and the Mainline Needle Exchange, and had lunch at Connections Clubhouse for ex-psychiatric patients. (It was interesting to see how the whole community revolved around the library at its heart. Ironically, I came back to find that my local council is planning to close Whitechapel Library!)

Within an intensely packed week of observation, I taught a seminar at the Maritime School of Social Work at nearby Dalhousie University. In the evening, a group of us held a symposium on 'Race, poverty and the inner city', again in the public library, and 150 came. The following morning at the Methodist Church I spoke to a breakfast meeting of programme managers, local government and voluntary sector workers, and then met with YouthNet, a project of the local parish. I gave an address to the local Christian communities on 'Catholic Worship and Community Activism'. On Saturday I visited three halfway houses for ex-prisoners, the local soup kitchen, and a meeting on criminal justice addressed by a man doing life for murder who is on parole and working with the correctional services. This was part of a day in which I looked at Canadian penal policies, including the programme 'Circles of Support and Accountability' which works with sex offenders. On Sunday I preached at Mass, and addressed a community meeting with the Shining Lights choir and a black Revival Choir.

The work of the neighbourhood parish was really impressive, and it made me sad to see how much the Church of England has moved away from it in its current managerial culture. The ministry of St George's, Halifax seemed to me a splendid example of parish ministry at its best. Much of the activity and reflection took place in the church building, and in Bob and Lori's Emporium in Gottingen Street, a cafe set up by two people who had been influenced by John Wimber and the Vineyard movement.

However, as mobility increases, and as people's relationships are more and more formed beyond the context of residential neighbour-hoods, the old notion of the residential parish must become questionable. Most of the language of pastoral ministry used in England assumes the parish model. In many places it is still valid, but we need to move beyond it.

Yet, whether we are thinking of the residential parish or some other model of ministry, a key question is: Does the Church really want marginal people? William Booth, founder of the Salvation Army, greatly outraged the Wesleyans of Nottingham by taking young roughs from the streets and placing them in the key pews of the chapel. Booth accepted them, but the Church rejected them, and it was this rejection which was a major factor in the founding of the Salvation Army.[63] My sense is that we have not made too much progress since then.

Of course, churches care for 'the poor', but, on the whole, they have perpetuated a 'soup kitchen' approach. I have no wish to 'knock' the corporal works of mercy, of which feeding the hungry is an integral part. There are some remarkable examples of feeding min-istry. At Holy Apostles' Church in New York City a few years ago, an observer counted 832 meals served on one morning between 10.45 a.m. and 1.00 p.m. – and this was not a very busy day! But the soup kitchen approach can easily turn into what Stanley Evans termed 'the Church Condescending'. We need a Church with a firm commitment to equality and to respect for the dignity of all. We do not need a Church which simply serves 'the poor' from a distance. Evans described the clergy in East London in the nineteenth century as 'the executive officers of the Church Condescending', and went on: 'An intelligent man could have prophesied the reaction of those whose fate was to be done good to.'[64]

This approach tends to assume that there are fixed positions – Church active, homeless people passive. So the active Church becomes an agency which does things to and for the passive homeless. (I recall a church in one American city which advertises 'lunch for the poor – once a month'.) In fact, positions are not fixed, but are constantly shifting. Church action can also resign itself to alleviation or rescue, and ignore structural issues of wealth, power and resources. A major consequence of this is that the Church becomes a Church for 'the poor', rather than a Church of 'the poor'.

The 'Church Condescending' and its course can be illustrated from a study of the history of responses to homelessness from church-based groups. The church is motivated by an attitude of care, concern and genuine desire to help, manifested in real commitment, often over many years. Yet there remains a clear distinction between the active helpers and the 'clients' – passive, 'done good to', the recipients of benevolence. Linked with this very often is a distinction, manifested in physical space, between the worshipping community and the 'cared for' community. The physical distinction is often, in fact, one of 'upstairs/downstairs'. There will be moments, and special enclaves – back seats, zones separated off from the main body, and so on – when the latter group may impinge or intrude upon the former. But mostly there is separation, and often considerable care that this separation is maintained in the interests of order, safety and the security of the dominant group. What would happen if members of the 'cared for' group reject their inferior role and demand membership, involving equality, within the worshipping community?

One member of St Botolph's resigned recently, claiming – rightly in my view – that the church had lost its radical edge. She raised various questions to the congregation, including:

> What would happen if numbers of users of the Project, say six from the Day Centre and two or three from the Lodges, hardly an enormous proportion, started to attend Sunday Mass on a

regular basis? Project staff and volunteers are supposed to observe 'boundaries' with their 'clients', for example, they mustn't socialise with them, go for a drink, or a meal. They are not allowed to exchange addresses or phone numbers, or be too friendly or too 'physical'. What then would be the relationship of the Project to the church and vice versa given that such boundaries cannot be maintained between equal members of a congregation?

An American Jubilee Group comrade, Ted Mellor, has made the same point in a recent letter, pointing out that in the early Church the people who prayed were mainly poor people and those who stood in solidarity with them. Clement of Alexandria even had to argue for the full inclusion of the well-to-do in the church! The poor were present, active participants in the assembly. They *were* the church. But often today the assumption is that the praying 'we' are, mainly, the well off, the respectable, and that poor people are in fact outside the praying assembly. Ted continued:

> A hymn which was sung one Sunday when I had no job, no money, hadn't eaten for several days and was about to be evicted . . . asked 'that we may feed the poor aright'. A noble sentiment, no doubt, but it made clear who the 'we' are – and the 'we' didn't include me or people like me. Is it any surprise that the poor stay away from our churches in droves? They are simply not expected to be there in the first place.

At a certain stage in the history of many such church-based projects, the worshipping church and the servant church go their separate ways, or, more accurately, the latter dissolves itself out of existence. The church hands over its servant role to an organisation which employs trained workers, and which gradually becomes a social service agency with less and less contact with the church. The church, of course, claims the credit for this, and is proud of its offspring, but is also rather relieved that it can now wash its hands of the 'cared for' – though it often continues to glory in the work done by the paid professionals. Meanwhile the professional agency becomes increasingly organised according to the prevailing ideology of professional social work, and the theological and political dimensions fade into the background. If the agency by this point has become the recipient of government funding, as it very likely will in the present climate, the critical, prophetic role may vanish altogether.

It is argued by many that the Church of the future will have the character of a 'remnant Church' more than that of a 'national Church'. This is not only likely, but almost inevitable, for the 'national Church' idea is mostly mystification for which the establishment provides a form of disguise. There is much about a remnant Church which is very attractive, and theologically powerful. As long ago as 1956 Martin Thornton was arguing that nine-tenths of the pastoral work of the clergy should be in the 'direction of the remnant', and his approach to pastoral theology was rooted in the notion of the remnant.[65] The danger, however, is that a remnant Church will be more concerned with purity than with outreach. If we are to be a remnant Church, a disciplined minority, we need also what Schreiter and Volf and others have called a 'new catholicity', a new understanding of what catholic consciousness means in a globalised world.[66] Catholicity is intrinsic to the Church's being, and without a strong sense of catholicity, local churches can become inward-looking sects or clubs. We do need a church, not just the idea of a church, an actual 'section of humanity in which Christ has really taken form', 'a new sociological principle', the body of Christ.[67] This raises a critical theological question about the church, for it is the body of Christ crucified, an extension of the passion. Only a church which is in solidarity with the suffering Christ and which seeks to live with a 'crucified mind' can be of the slightest use in work with marginalised people.

I ask again the troubling question: does the Church today really want to be 'inclusive' with all the ramifications of this over-used word? There is evidence that some sections of the Church are less sensitive to poor and marginal people than in the past: their primary concern is to grow numerically. It is also not uncommon to find churches which are passionate in their commitment to 'inclusiveness' but which are highly selective in who are in fact included. So they become friendly clubs of people who have been marginalised elsewhere, not churches reaching out lovingly to all people.

But we are faced now with a serious structural threat to innovative ministry in the form of the increasing dominance of the centralised executive church model. A major critic of this model is Professor Richard Roberts who has expressed one of his fears: 'My fear is that all marginal ministry will be disallowed in favour of ministry that is in conformity with centrally dictated "vision" statements and subject to de-skilling managerial enforcement . . . There will be no place for non-conforming figures in a rationally managed church driven from the centre by executive power.'[68] His warning, repeated in several papers, raises serious issues about the dominant trends in the contemporary Church which seem to owe less to theology than to dated managerial and bureaucratic notions about viability and efficiency. Roberts has referred to the regime of Archbishop Carey as one of 'an ecclesiastical "neo-Fordism" ', and sees it as part of the Anglican appropriation of elements from the Thatcherite period. He speaks of ecclesiastical managerialism, a view which sees the Church of England as an executive-led, highly unified organisation, based on the model of the business corporation. Stephen Pattison has also warned of the danger of 'a kind of "McDonaldised" pastoral care in which the creative, the unpredictable, and the symbolic is dominated in the interests of normativity'.[69]

Today the Church of England is run by an Archbishops' Council. This came about as a result of the Turnbull Report which claimed that it was using 'radical ideas' and was 'willing to be very radical'.[70] What has happened is a centralisation of power, and the increasing tendency to identify the central bureaucracy with the Church itself. One subtle shift, with major theological implications, is the way in which the telephone is now answered at Church House, Westminster. Until recently the receptionist simply said 'Church House' – indicating that this was a building within which various people worked. Today he or she says 'The Church of England'. I had always thought that the Church of England was dispersed throughout the country, and that I was as much a part of it as anyone. But now it is a company, an organisation. Anyone who has ever visited the Church Commissioners, the body which controls – and from time to time disperses – the finances of the Church of England, knows that one has to sign a sheet on arrival with one's name *and company.* The fact that anyone might exist without being part of, or owning, a company seems not to have occurred to the Church Commissioners. When I asked the security officer whether the Church of England was itself a company, he said that he didn't know and advised me to leave the space blank!

What has occurred is a co-option into an already damaged social structure. (I understand that one of the consultants to the Arch-bishops' Council was previously involved with Fairy Liquid and Kleenex Tissues.)

A major problem with this kind of development is that the growth and financial stability of the company tends to become the central concern, and work, or thinking, which threatens growth and stability is not encouraged. In 1975, Peter Selby, now Bishop of Worcester, was the Director of Lay Training in the Diocese of Southwark, whose bishop was Mervyn Stockwood. Selby gave a paper on 'lay training as a point of growth' in which he raised the question of what churches were for, and what they were doing, and the conflict which often arose between the two. He commented:

> The truth is . . . that it is the privilege of a congregation to exist only for the purpose of supporting and enabling the divine purpose for the salvation of humanity. If a congregation fails to exist for this purpose, it might be important to prevent it from extending its membership and so absorbing the energies of more and more people in activities that are not only useless but have the added disadvantage of claiming to be immensely important.[71]

His words, not popular at the time, are even more relevant in the world of the McDonaldisation, packaging and marketing of the Church.

I have been critical in much of my writing of the 'professional model' which has become increasingly dominant both in Christian ministry and elsewhere in society, and it is good that there is now growing criticism of this model. It is important, however, that the nature of this critique is clear. I am entirely in favour of efficiency, the use of technology (combined with an awareness of its addictive potential), the acquiring of knowledge and wisdom (which are dif-ferent from 'information', that increasingly jargonised word), and a high degree of pastoral competence. I am not even against 'bound-aries' though I believe that the deliberate transgression of them is often central to Christian ministry, as it certainly was to the earthly ministry of Jesus. My concern is rather with power, control, the culture of management, and the threat of this culture to much that is really at the core of being a Christian. My concern is that theology has been co-opted by certain forces within late capitalism.

Professionals have power to define a person and to determine what are that person's needs.[72] A central feature of professionalism is a concern with 'boundaries', a relatively modern concept, often related to time. Professionals appear in a place at a certain time and leave it at another. They do not belong there, they simply work there. Their personal involvement is clearly controlled, confined within clearly defined limits. In relation to Christian ministry, this has been called 'rigid boundary fundamentalism'.[73] It is recognised more and more how gendered this concern is, based on a very male notion of the strongly bounded self, and it has come under fire from feminist writers on social care and from workers in the health service.[74]

The dominance of the professional model is more serious than many realise, for it is not only a question of political ideology. That would be serious enough, for ideological assumptions shape practice to a high degree. But what is involved here is the whole under-standing of what it is to be human, to be a person. Moreover, it is, like most such forms of oppression, largely unconscious and therefore unexamined. But 'pastoral care constructed according to unexamined axioms of personhood may effectively reproduce oppressive norms'.[75]

Much of this chapter has been related to work on the margins, and such work can only flourish if there are people involved who do not conform, who transgress boundaries, who are unreasonable and innovative. Most of the people mentioned in this book who have influenced me are such individuals. But the truth is that the Church of England has, for some decades, been losing many of its most creative people. It simply does not know what to do with them for they do not fit into the new tidy systems. I received a letter recently from a priest who has been a key figure in creative outreach ministries in East London over twenty-five years. He wrote sadly, 'I have little wish to help the Church of England any more'.[76]

It goes without saying that, once the above trends have become dominant, the prophetic dimension in marginal work disappears. The Canadian theologian Douglas John Hall has said that 'ours is a time for prophetic ministry, not for pastoral directors',[77] but he is speaking against the controlling models. Most people, including most of those in authority in the Church, prefer the chaplaincy model to the prophetic model of Christian action. If the role of the prophet is to be a destabilising presence and offer an alternative reality to the dominant one, then clearly such a tradition will always be marginal. I worry today that some of the prophetic figures of the past are not simply marginal but extinct.[78] I worry that much current Anglicanism lacks the prophetic edge and the 'principle of surprise' that marked some of the great figures of the past, that we are colluding with the contemporary pressure to produce mass men and women as well as what Sorokin called 'fads and foibles' instead of serious thought and commitment. We need to recall, more than ever today, that

> it is not just a question, as all too many think, of the church "modernising itself". Young people may prefer snappier music, but they will not for long be fooled by it. Not snappier music nor shorter psalms nor basic Bibles; not cushioned pews nor rocking parsons nor jiving in the aisles. Nothing but sincerity and truth will do.[79]

It is encouraging to read similar concerns from American Christians. Kip Tiernan founded Rosie's Place, the first drop-in centre and emergency shelter for women in the USA, in 1974. Eighteen years later, he wrote:

> I have discovered that the alternative I created became institutionalised: that I not only did not stop homelessness and hunger, but that there were more people than ever in desperate need almost 18 years later and in all of this we had developed an ethic to fit these new needs, rather than acknowledging the need for a new ethic.[80]

He identifies the choice before us all, the choice between the language of accommodation and that of confrontation.

One aspect of ministry which has continued to be popular in recent years is that of 'servant ministry' or 'servant leadership'. Again, it is important to be clear about the nature of the critique here. I am not denying that the concept of the diaconal character of ministry is important, nor even that it can be helpful to speak of 'the servant church' (though it is not as clear from the New Testament as some have claimed). I believe that the growth of servant leadership programmes, 'Stephen Ministries', and so on, has been of very great benefit, and such programmes have been among the features which have helped churches to recover the meaning of 'total ministry' and the ministry of all the baptised, most dramatically in such places as the poor, largely rural diocese of Northern Michigan. Out of this work has come the Living Stones Network which tries to help churches to recover the ministry of the whole body. All this is excellent. What concerns me is the danger that exclusive emphasis on the church as servant can obscure other important dimensions.[81]

The role of the deacon, according to the American Book of Common Prayer, is to 'interpret to the church the needs, concerns and hopes of the world'. (Significantly that book also defines the ministers of the Church as 'lay persons, bishops, priests and deacons'.) The definition has the advantage that it does not restrict itself to servanthood, but lays stress also on the prophetic role of interpretation. It may be that the Bishop of London had this concern with interpretation of the needs of the world when he suggested that many young people were ready to respond to a call to Christian ministry which had a 'more diaconal character'.[82]

Yet there are elements in the theology of priesthood which are equally essential to spiritual health as well as to understanding the nature of the church and its ministry, elements which we neglect at our peril. Both Urban Holmes and Bill Countryman have, in their writings, emphasised the essentially human character of priestly identity and priestly work. Holmes, disagreeing with Durkheim's view of the priest as a symbolic force for stability and the status quo, and of priesthood as the enemy of chaos, argues that priesthood is rooted in the receptive mode of being, that its roots 'lie firmly within the wilderness of the antistructure'.[83] The inadequacy of the servant model comes out in a paper from a theologian with a background in psychotherapy, who warns of the 'tendency to collapse this ministry into servanthood'.[84] It is all too easy, now as in the past, to adopt a 'Samaritan' model of the church and retreat into good works. Pastoral ministry cannot be based on the Good Samaritan – for whose 'goodness' there is in fact no biblical evidence – without a wider framework of vision.[85]

These ways of looking at ministry are very one-dimensional, functionalist and focused on doing more than being. Yet much of the symbolism of priesthood is about being, identity, brokenness and sacrifice. The language of sacrifice lies at the very core of priestly identity. Michael Lapsley, who had both his hands blown off by a parcel bomb in South Africa, once made the frightening but surely sanctified comment that he was a better priest without hands since brokenness and incompleteness were the norm, not the exception, within the human family.[86] In the understanding of the nature of priesthood we do need to recover the idea of priestly spirit, priestly heart, which was so central to the thought of writers such as R.C. Moberly.[87]

Of course, Christians have no monopoly on sacrificial love. In my experience, however, much of priestly ministry consists of standing by people in their pain in silence but with a rooted conviction in their central goodness and value. In this, Christian priests are not alone, and many others share in this work. Kay Redfield Jamison, in her courageous and helpful account of her own struggle with depression and suicide, speaks of a psychiatrist who stood by her in her time of anguish. What mattered most was his silence and his solidarity.

> What on earth can he say that will make me feel better or keep me alive? Well, there never was anything he could say, that's the funny thing. It was all the stupid, desperately optimistic, condescending things he *didn't* say that kept me alive; all the compassion and warmth I felt from him that could not have been said; all the intelligence, competence and time he put into it; and his granite belief that mine was a life worth living.[88]

Authentic diaconal and priestly ministry is rooted in such a posture of solidarity with people in their pain, and the practice issues from the inner rootedness in silence, solidarity and commitment. Edward Norman is surely right when, writing about responses to AIDS, he says that Christians

> should put themselves at the service of the victims as Christ gave himself unsparingly to the afflicted. He was accused of resorting to the company of outcasts – the ritually unclean, the lepers, the sinners. His contemporary representatives could follow his example.[89]

10

Agenda for an urban spirituality

For we do not keep vigil for ourselves alone but for the whole church, the light of our faith, steadfast against the darkness. We have to be the vigilant heart of the city.

A Carthusian[1]

The fact that this and the following chapter are the shortest chapters in the book does not mean that they are the least important, but rather that 'spirituality' and politics are done, practised. They are integral parts of our struggle and engagement. Too much writing about them can get in the way of this. I am also aware that there are no special compartments labelled 'spiritual' or 'political', and that most of what I want to say on these matters is dispersed, scattered, throughout the book. So I want here simply to emphasise certain aspects which have come to seem particularly important.

A sense of priority, and a commitment to clearing away the clutter which gets in its way, is a preliminary condition of prayer, attention and openness to the Spirit of God. In the Book of Nehemiah, which is concerned with the rebuilding of the wall of Jerusalem, the writer tells us that 'there is too much rubbish so that we are unable to work' (Neh. 4:10), and, a few verses later, comments that 'the work is great and widely spread out, and we are separated from one another' (4:19). In our situations, we must face the problem that accumulated rubbish in our lives, minds and hearts, brings. Being separated from one another too is not helpful to spiritual strengthening. It is easy to find ourselves 'divided and torn to pieces'[2] so that we are unable to concentrate on prayer or work effectively. So I want to stress the danger of accumulating too much rubbish, and of trying to 'go it alone'. The support of the body, and of specific persons within the body, is of critical importance. All spiritual life is social. As John Wesley said, there is 'no holiness but social holiness'.[3]

As in the wider area of social and political activism, there is a deeply embedded sense among many Christians that dependence on others for friendship and support is somehow a sign of weakness. Thus we often encounter the 'isolated Christian' – a contradiction in terms if ever there was one! – who exists and works in lonely individualistic activism. Sheila Rowbotham and her colleagues, deploring harmful trends within political activism at the end of the 1970s, identified the syndrome well.

> The individual militant appears as a lonely character without ties, bereft of domestic emotions, who is hard, erect, self-contained, controlled, without the time or ability to express loving passion, who cannot pause to nurture, and for whom friendship is a diversion . . . Left to carry the burden of a higher consciousness, members of this elect will tend to see the people around them as, at worst, bad, lazy, consumed with the desire for material accumulation and sundry diversionary passions; at best, ignorant, needing to be hauled to a higher level. In the hauling, the faint-hearted fall by the wayside, the cuddly retire into cosiness, and all the suspicions of the elect are confirmed. Being an elect, they can rely on no one, and being an elect means they have to do everything.[4]

Neglect of close friends and neglect of self seem to go together. Friendship and close emotional ties are seen as luxuries which impede commitment. This, of course, can be true. However, this neglect often leads to a real personal decline, and both political activists and pastors often become diminished human beings. No one saw this more clearly than the poet Denise Levertov, herself a political activist, but one who recognised the close connection between personal and social wholeness: 'The self will surely suffer if egotism leads a person away from the experience of the human community. And the commonweal as surely suffers if those who wish for its betterment are hollowed-out self-neglecters'.[5]

The New Testament speaks hardly at all about personal spiritual formation, but a great deal about the building up of the body and its movement towards fullness. It is important to remember that we are, by our nature, 'dependent rational animals'.[6] Part of this sense of solidarity, though only a part, is the need for spiritual direction. This is, primarily, a corporate theological requirement, not an individual therapeutic one. According to Martin Thornton, spiritual direction is simply 'the application of theology to the life of prayer'.[7] But what is more important, and what provides the essential framework for that ministry, is our need for an accountable discipleship.[8] We are in grave danger of 'not discerning the body'.

We need too to be wary of 'spirituality' in its currently fashionable sense.[9] Orthodox Christianity, at its best, has insisted on the unity of the spiritual and the material, and has stressed the involvement of God in the human story, not in some 'spiritual dimension'. As the Council of Chalcedon stressed, the divine and human are united, without separation (*anchoristos*). The implications of this statement for the practice of spirituality are immense. It is interesting that, ten years before the word became popular, the English theologian Eric Mascall was warning of the danger of 'false spirituality', pointing out that 'the New Testament has no confidence in spirituality as such' and that 'Christianity is not a purely spiritual religion'.[10]

The currently growing tendency to distinguish between spirituality and religion, with religion often being identified with rule, conformity and outward performance, is not only unhelpful and misleading but can be harmful.[11] It can lead to a view of spirituality which is undisciplined, narcissistic, individualistic, excessively interior, and lacking in social consciousness. It can lead, and often does lead, to a kind of gnosticism, elitist, anti-materialistic and marked by what A.D. Nock once called 'auto-intoxication'. Brueggemann warns of 'a self preoccupation that ends in self indulgence driving religion to narcissistic catering and consumerism, to limitless seeking after well being and pleasure, on one's own terms without regard to any other in the community.'[12] It has been claimed, with some justification, that 'spirituality blossoms as politics atrophies'.[13]

So it is encouraging to see a renewed concern for a spiritual life which is earthed, materialistic, rooted in the common life of prayer, service and hospitality. In recent years in cities there has been a marked growth in what we could call 'urban contemplatives',[14] groups and individuals for whom the urban cores are the context for prayer and attention to God. My early experience in the Franciscan house at 84 Cable Street was an experience of such a community. Its integration of prayer and service, contemplation and action, hospitality and commitment to justice, made an abiding impression on my whole spiritual, theological and pastoral praxis. More than any other place, this tumbledown slum house helped me to pray, to listen, to learn, and, only then, to try to minister within its troubled and turbulent, yet, in many respects, caring and loving neighbourhood.

It represented in a very powerful, yet humble and largely hidden, way the importance of prayerful contemplative presence along the lines developed by Charles de Foucauld and the Little Sisters and Brothers of Jesus. Without attempting directly to evangelise, the Franciscans, by their stability and consistent commitment over two decades, helped to make Christianity respected, and helped to prepare the way for other forms of Christian presence in the East End.

Working as a priest in the Soho district of London in the late 1960s, I found that a major area for which my theological training had not prepared me well was that of ascetical theology. We had, of course, received lectures on 'spiritualia', but there had been little attention to the need for a profound exploration of one's own inner depths if one was to be of any real use to people in distress and turbulence. Much of the stress in pastoral theology was on 'doing', on the nuts and bolts of the pastoral task. But in Soho, at the heart of the growing drug culture, surrounded by many people who had lost hope, by others who were homeless, suicidal, desperately lost, I found that the kind of resources which were needed were not so much skills or expertise as inner stability, exposure to brokenness, and ability to cope with darkness, and what Vanstone was later to call 'the stature of waiting'. So my theology had to become more passive, more receptive, in a sense less clear. I was beginning to understand something of the negative dimensions of theology, the way of ignorance.

I sense that a number of people in Britain and the USA, independently of each other and widely scattered, are feeling the need to create centres for contemplative prayer within the urban context. I have, in fact, felt this for a while and was writing about it in 1963.[15] But in recent years the practical manifestation of need for such places seems to have increased quite dramatically. It is, no doubt, one aspect of the quest for 'new ways of being church'.[16] I am a patron of the Elsie Briggs House of Prayer in Westbury-on-Trym in Bristol, a centre for contemplative prayer with a particular focus on peace and justice.[17] Around the same time, Emmett Jarrett and Anne Scheibner opened St Francis House in New London, Connecticut, as an Anglican house of hospitality on Catholic Worker lines, while in Tulsa, Oklahoma, Fr Pat Eastman convenes the Monos Community with a similar focus. And there are many other such centres.

There is also a concern, in Britain and the USA, to bring together in a loose network those who see themselves as in some sense urban contemplatives, intercessors or solitaries. This is all part of a recovery of the mystical dimension within the contours of the urban experience, itself leading to a kind of democratisation of the mystical as being a central feature of the common life of the body. The 'urban mystics' who are emerging are of the type identified by Grace Jantzen as 'mystics of integration'.[18]

What is an urban spirituality? I believe that it is, first and foremost, materialistic spirituality. It takes matter, the flesh, the physical, human, material needs, seriously, reverencing matter as the vehicle of the spirit, not its enemy. It is highly significant that hospitality, the breaking of bread, is at the heart of this great explosion of urban contemplation, for it is through the common meal that we come to know and love one another. The extraordinary is encountered in the midst of the ordinary, the holy within the common.

It is a spirituality of compassion, a word which means suffering together. Pope John Paul II has spoken of the importance of 'collective spirituality' and has called for 'a robust spirituality of compassion'.[19] At the heart of urban spirituality in the Christian sense is the cross, and our solidarity with the crucified Christ, Christ the victim. That Christ is found in, and identified with, our own engagement now with the victims we encounter. The Christology here is crudely materialistic and stark. 'Christ as criminal, Christ as madman, Christ as alcoholic vagrant: all this and more is implied in the unconditional identification of God with the victim'.[20]

Urban ministry and theological reflection will inevitably involve constant encounters with people who have suffered great pain, anguish, oppression and violence. Many never fully recover. But we will, in my experience, also meet people who, bruised and deeply wounded, have been able to move beyond the pain to some kind of resurrection experience. Take some words written by a woman who had been raped. She ends her poem with an address to the wounded Christ.

You were not ashamed of your wounds,
You showed them to Thomas
As marks of your ordeal and death.
I will no longer hide these wounds of mine,
I will bear them gracefully.
They tell a resurrection story.[21]

Compassion is not a sentimental condescension: it is a recognition that we are bound up together, and that the image of God in the human person is never extinguished. It is a spirituality which involves tears. 'We need to take the tears we shed for Jesus and use them to wash the bloodstained faces of the Good Friday people of our own day'.[22]

The urban context is marked by extremes of anger, and urban spirituality must also engage with questions of conflict, turbulence, anger, and rage. Charles Peguy claimed that a great philosophy is one which 'introduces uneasiness' and 'opens the door to commotion',[23] and restlessness is central to the Hebrew Scriptures, even to its understanding of God.[24] Certainly anger is an integral element in prophecy. Heschel's study of prophecy sees the fire of anger as 'the condition of the prophet's soul'.[25]

However, there is a deep ambiguity and unease within Christian history, spirituality, and moral discourse about the place of anger, and even about whether it has a place at all. Luther referred to 'angry love', while Stewart Headlam, commenting on the injunction 'Be angry and sin not', observed that it is much easier not to be angry at all than to be angry and not to sin.[26] But the general direction of Christian thought has been to see anger as an impediment to spirituality. In the sixth century, Dorotheos of Gaza said that anger was incompatible with wisdom, but went on to add that anger could be healed by tears. Both anger and tears are the fruit of passion. Only a passionate person can express either anger or weeping. This does suggest that anger is in some way necessary to being human, and yet is itself in need of transformation and direction. Poets and mystics have often related anger in some way to love. According to Denise Levertov, there is 'a time when the only anger is love'. Levertov realised that anger, anguish, rage and praise were all related, for they all depended upon passion and energy, without which the future lay only with annihilation.[27]

Feminist writers have argued that the handling of anger presents particular problems for women. Kathleen Fischer distinguishes the anger of hope from the anger of despair, while Beverly Harrison, in an important lecture on 'The Power of Anger in the Work of Love', sees anger as a mode of connection, a spur to action and to change. Audre Lorde calls for a 'symphony of anger', orchestrated anger rather than a cacophony.[28] Here is an urgent part of the agenda for urban spirituality.

Urban spirituality must also involve the sense of wonder, awe and amazement at 'this exhilaratingly sacred, wonderfully human and awful urban mess'.[29] A central part of the urban experience is the encounter with the strange, the alien, the other, the unpredictable, and this can only be approached with awe and amazement. And these are the conditions for celebration and festivity. The city, in spite of its injustice and oppression, is a place of carnival, and an urban spirituality is a spirituality of fun as well as of lament. In the Christian movement, it must be marked by 'Alleluia'.[30]

And yet it is also a spirituality of silence. One of the most serious dangers confronting those who minister in the city is that their lives come to be built on frenzy and compulsive busyness. This usually leads to a lack of focus, a tendency to accumulate more and more things, a collapse of reflection, and the cultivation of a personal culture of obligatory tiredness. This personal culture then becomes socially infectious so that one may communicate little to others other than one's own exhaustion – not a very kind gift to people who may already have enough problems of their own. The practice of silence and solitude, including the cultivation of inner stillness and inner peace, is a vital component of an urban spirituality.

Urban spirituality is a spirituality of hope and of liberation. The nourishing and sustaining of hope is one of the features which emerges most powerfully from the East End experience over the years. And hope involves cultivating a vision of an alternative future, and constant discerning of 'the signs of the times'.[31]

But perhaps the most important dimension of the urban experience is that it opens up for us, in a particularly powerful way, the experience of perplexity, darkness and 'unknowing' (*agnosia*). In the dissolution of the fixed structures of false clarity, we are led into a dark night, a *via negativa*, in which alone we begin to understand. The urban experience can only be fully experienced within the range of the mystical. This has recently been expressed in a remarkable article by Steve Latham, Baptist minister in Paddington and formerly in East London. Latham stresses the need for 'a contemplative attitude of attentive humility', and calls for a recovery of mysticism in the midst of action.

> Urbanology is a mystical exercise in which you intuit the spirit of place. It requires a feeling for the whole, a revelatory experience that unveils the hidden principalities and powers which overlay and underlie the visible urban structure. It requires an urban prophetics that sees behind the surfaces of urban experience.

There are references to the 'cloud of unknowing' and to a 'via negativa urbana', and a call for 'apophatic social studies' and for the 'recovery of an urban mysticism'. In all this, 'prayer is the first requirement of anyone who would understand the urban'.[32]

To all of which one can only reply: Amen.

II

Theology and politics revisited

Our 'charity' has meant far too exclusively what may be called
ambulance work for mankind – the picking up of the wounded
and the curing of their wounds. We have neglected to attack
the forces of wrong. We have been content with the ambulance
work when we ought to have been assaulting the strongholds
of evil.

Christianity and Industrial Problems (1919)[1]

To presume to care for other human beings without taking
into account the social and political causes of whatever it is
they may be experiencing is to confirm them in their distress
while pretending to offer healing.

PETER SELBY[2]

I have stressed throughout this book the importance of
learning from the context in which one is set, and the central place
of historical action in the work of theological reflection. In the
course of activity, in given historical situations, theological themes
are developed, deepened, clarified, often found wanting, shaped and
re-shaped. I want to reflect in this chapter on theology and politics
as illuminated by the East End experience.

The changing face of the political

It is necessary, first, to note that political life has changed
enormously. Indeed, all forms of collective action seem to be in
decline – churches, pubs, political parties, trade unions, most organisations which involve active participation. All have declined in the
last thirty years. Most people stay at home. All national organisations
have declined. Conventional politics has also declined, both in terms
of those who vote, and in the deeper sense that such politics is now

seen, not as the work of the people, but as a means of employment for the paid professionals. These individuals are often not viewed as representatives of the people, but as individuals pursuing a career. Not surprisingly, fewer and fewer people regard politicians as worthy of respect.

Nor is this only a British phenomenon. A comrade in a New York voting district noted that, out of a population of 15,000, in 1996 only twenty-seven people voted. A headline in the *New York Times* on 3 November 1998 read: 'Bored, Dispirited, Disgusted. Most won't vote'. In the local elections in Britain in May 1998, one ward in Liverpool showed a 9 per cent turn-out. But does this mean that politics is in decline, or that there has been a redefinition of what it is to be political? For example, more people belong to environmental groups, and much, probably most, political action occurs outside the party machines. Religious groups are increasingly involved with political issues. What seems to have occurred has been a shift in the centre of gravity of the political. It is therefore vital that churches in the future do not allow their approach to political action to be confined within dated conceptions.

The political Church in East London

There was a tradition of political activity in some parts of the Church in East London from the nineteenth century. Like all parts of the country, and the world, Christian testimony was not uniform. But East London was a key site of Christian social critique, reflection and action. Many priests and ministers in East London were key figures in the Christian social movement. Names such as Henry Scott Holland, Stewart Headlam, and, more recently, John Groser, Jack Boggis, Stanley Evans, and Bill Sargent are of abiding significance in the history of East London. Nor was this history exclusively clerical. There were people like George Lansbury, Mary Hughes, Ethel Upton, Edith Ramsey, and many others. Mary Hughes (1869–1941), a Christian socialist social worker, took over a disused pub in Whitechapel in 1926. As the Dewdrop Inn, it became a centre for work with homeless and needy people, and later was run by the Stepney Family Service Unit. There was the economist Denys Munby, a resident of Toynbee Hall in the 1940s and a key figure in the Stepney Reconstruction Group after 1945. Much of the activity around housing, unemployment, poverty and fascism in the 1930s involved church people.

There has, however, been a continuing debate among Christians in politics about the idea of a 'specifically Christian' position or role, and this too was reflected in the East End. One group, which was very influential in the Church of England for many years, was the Christendom Group which held strongly to the view of a distinctively Christian society and a Christian worldview. Denys Munby attacked this view. 'Specifically Christian' approaches, Munby argued, tended to be platitudes which were too vague and useless as guides to action, or the nostrums of the latest fashionable figure. Munby concluded that it was no longer possible to confuse Christian faith with 'any kind of social gospel' or to identify the Kingdom of God with a 'new social order'.[3] Munby was a close colleague of John Groser, certainly the best-known Christian minister of any tradition in East London from the 1920s to the 1960s, and probably the best-known Christian socialist priest in Britain.[4] As a model of political action, rooted in Christian incarnational and sacramental theology, Groser is worth some attention.

Groser was not respectable, he broke the rules, and he did not fear conflict with authority. He had no patience with those who wished to fight injustice from ten miles above the battle, at the same time preserving their reputations and prospects. In 1929, he was appointed Vicar of Christ Church, Watney Street; the hierarchy apparently felt that, because this parish was so run down, and in danger of closure, he could do no harm there! In the event he built up a lively and socially involved community, and many people in East London still remember the joyful festivals and processions, the hospitality, and the political struggles around Watney Street. It was during this period that the rent strikes occurred, and the Battle of Cable Street, described in Chapter 3, took place in October 1936. Groser played a key role both in the housing conflicts and in the resistance to fascism. In 1940 Christ Church was destroyed, and he and his congregation moved to St George's in the East where he remained until 1948. In 1948 he became Master of the Royal Foundation of St Katherine, a medieval community newly located at the Limehouse end of Cable Street, and it was here that he spent the last years of his active life. He made St Katherine's a centre for Christian discourse, and a powerhouse of debate and discussion about the future of East London. Here dockers and trade unionists, Christians and Jews, old people, and a wide range of social and political groups would meet, making the centre a kind of think tank and focus of commitment to the health and welfare of the East End. He saw that Christians in political life need to be organised, well informed, and rigorous in their analysis of events.

What struck one, first, about Groser was the sheer length of his time here. He arrived in 1922 and left in 1962. He saw the importance of the local community and of long-term commitment, in contrast to the situation today (and no doubt in his day too) when clergy and other pastoral workers tend to move on every few years and get 'promotion'. Such commitment is itself a political statement.

Second, Groser was concerned with 'the personal as political', a term which only became current some years after his death. His only book, published in 1949, was significantly called *Politics and Persons*. He is remembered in the East End today mostly for his pioneering pastoral and social work rather than for his 'thought' though the two were inseparable. He was deeply concerned with the welfare of elderly people and his work antedated that of groups such as Age Concern and pensioners' action groups. Stepney Old People's Welfare Association was formed in 1948, and Groser was a key figure in its emergence along with Ethel Upton, Dorothy Halsall and Olive Wagstaff. Old East Enders still speak of Groser as one who influenced their own lives, an inspiration and source of strength. He was one of the earliest critics of what later became known as 'sus', the arrest of individuals on suspicion of being likely to commit an offence. He wrote in the *Daily Herald* in 1935 about the abuse of police powers in relation to unemployed people in Stepney. His stress on human dignity and on the need to help people recover a sense of their own worth and value was at the heart of all his pastoral work and politics.

Third, while Groser was committed to local issues, he saw local issues, issues around housing and fascism, for example, in their national, international and global context. He saw the importance of making connections, but realised that effective connections could only be made in the course of actual concrete struggles. He was one of the first priests within the Anglican Catholic tradition to take issues of class struggle seriously. He was grappling with Marxism in the early 1930s and saw fascism as 'the greatest menace to the Christian religion in the world today'. However, Groser saw that political consciousness and action in the world had to begin with the very local and concrete.

Fourth, in contrast to much of the Christian left which was somewhat grim and intense, Groser's politics was rooted in worship and dramatic celebration. He was profoundly influenced by Conrad Noel and the Catholic Crusade, and the Stepney chapter of the Crusade was based at Watney Street. Like Noel, he saw the importance of festivity, of colour, music and dancing, in the creation of a Christian social consciousness. With Emma Goldman, he wanted no part in any revolution which did not include dancing. In some ways Groser's community at Watney Street was, with Holy Trinity, Sneyd, in the Midlands, a kind of urban representation of what Thaxted was struggling to manifest in the countryside. Here too was the sense of a democratic Christian community, with the liturgy as a sacramental prefiguring of a liberated world. Groser saw that politics was always a mingling of the utopian and visionary, and the pragmatic.

Christians in politics: seven models

All Christians are political, whether they recognise it or not, particularly when they do not recognise it. While the relationship between theology and politics is complex and constantly in flux, there are, I believe, seven models which I have termed reinforcement (and sometimes restoration), retreat, rescue, reform, radicalism, resistance and revolution. Of course no Christian, no church, no theological tradition fits any of these in a pure and simple form, and most of us move in and out of these models throughout our lives, but caricatures can be helpful in clarifying approaches. It is also worth remembering that one model may fit a historical phase better than others, though we need to be wary that particular models can be highly convenient and cosy, temptations to conformity rather than to commitment and challenge. Yet, in spite of enormous differences, there has been widespread agreement among most Christians that the redemption of the world does involve some 'interference' in its social and political affairs. Newman claimed that 'the church was framed for the express purpose of interfering, or (as irreligious men will say) meddling with the world'.[5]

1. The politics of reinforcement

From ancient times religion has been used as an instrument of legitimation for political structures. The ritual prophets of ancient Israel were cultic officials who acted as chaplains to power, uttering their liturgically prescribed message at allotted moments. Their contemporary equivalents are not hard to find. The 'reinforcement' model is often seen as 'non-political', but in fact is the commonest and most effective form of political action.

The politics of reinforcement is still very common, not least among Anglicans in England. It was the core of the 'Christendom' era. Recent research has provided a good example of the use of church leaders to reinforce secular government positions. Cyril Forster Garbett, Archbishop of York from 1942 to 1955, was clearly used, and allowed himself to be used, by the Foreign Office, to give religious support to a particular phase of the Cold War. One national newspaper called him the 'spokesman of the national conscience'.[6]

Central to this political model is the belief that Church and government are on the same side. Thus a recent Minister of Defence commented that he 'would not be happy if the Church of England were to adopt a policy entirely different from that of the government', while the Bishop of Birmingham has said that 'the state's interest in religion' is 'that it should help to keep the people quiet'.[7] However, it is wrong to conclude, as Hauerwas and Willimon seem to do, that all political theology is committed to the maintenance of Christendom.[8]

In the East End, the civic Churches, mainly products of the eighteenth century, were symbols of stability, privilege and the established order, and attracted those members of the rising working class who were seeking status and respectability. The Roman Church, as an enclave of the Irish working class, played no role in wider political life, though it tended to support those political causes which were in accord with Vatican politics, such as the regimes of Mussolini and Franco. Roman Catholics were also significantly over-represented in the membership of the British Union of Fascists. The political involvement was supported by a pietist theology.

2. *The politics of retreat*

The politics of retreat takes the position that politics is not the Church's concern. That concern is with personal salvation and with increasing the population of heaven. However, this also is a form of reinforcement by default, since to take no part in politics is to support the established order. Retreatist versions of Christianity are still very common, not least in the East End, but also elsewhere. A recent study showed that around 25 per cent of white American Christians were utterly individualistic, and that tools for social critique were 'subculturally unavailable' to them.[9]

3. *The politics of rescue*

This approach is associated with groups like the Salvation Army, where it is combined with considerable social service work. Yet from early times the Army took the view that nothing really mattered except the salvation of the soul. Thus *The War Cry* in 1881:

> Oh! how I see the emptiness and vanity of everything compared with the salvation of the soul. What does it matter if a man dies in the workhouse? If he dies on the doorstep covered with wounds like Lazarus – what does it matter if his soul is saved?[10]

Robert Beckford has pointed out how central has been the idea of rescue in the spirituality of the black Pentecostal tradition, and that this is not necessarily incompatible with a strong social and political commitment.[11] But for the most part it has been rescue and nothing else.

4. *The politics of reform*

The politics of reform is one which seeks to change elements within the system. It is associated with many churches working often through boards, divisions and working parties. Its key phrases are 'social concern', 'social responsibility' and 'influence'. Its work is usually very thorough and well researched. The Board for Social Responsibility of the Church of England has been called 'one of the two most effective ecclesiastical social action groups operating in the world today'.[12] Yet this model can never be more than one of 'service' to, and 'influence' on, the status quo. It is clear in the role of bishops in the House of Lords. Thus the Bishop of Southwark, responding to the possibility that the number of bishops there might be reduced, said that those who remained would 'still offer the same service'.[13]

The excellent report *Faith in the City* stood firmly within the reformist tradition. The authors began by telling us of the 'basic Christian principles of justice and compassion which we believe we share with the great majority of the people of Britain.' This in itself was a profoundly theological and sociological assumption, highly questionable, but clearly the basis of the report, as indeed it had been of much Anglican social thinking. Individualism had 'crept into both public and private life', as if, having crept in, it could just as easily creep out. It was unreasonable, the report argued, for Christians to offer more than a critique of the present system.[14]

5. The politics of radicalism

'Radicalism' and 'Christian radicalism' are among the most ambiguous and confused ideas in recent rhetoric. The notion of 'radical', of going to the roots, itself highlights the ambiguity. For one can go to the roots in order to uproot the original plant, to start all over again, or in order to return to the original source. The idea of radicalism has been used in both senses. However, there is one facet of this rhetoric which remains important. Christians need constantly to be going back to the source, to the fount, to the roots, constantly seeking to disentangle the original material from that which has accumulated around the stem, but which is at best peripheral and at worst damaging. Radical scrutiny is a necessary part of the theological and political task in every age, even though it can only take us part of the way.

Of course, from time to time the reformist tradition assumes a radical stance. Thus Resolution 74 of the Lambeth Conference Report of 1920 called for 'a fundamental change in the spirit and working of our economic life'. This followed the 1919 report on *Christianity and Industrial Problems*, the so-called Fifth Report. It has been rightly said that 'it is difficult to overstate the importance of the Fifth Report'.[15]

6. The politics of resistance

This model takes the normal theological and political stance of the Church to be one of resistance to the powers. There is little doubt that, within mainstream Christian social thinking, there is a place for resistance. Brueggemann has shown that the God of the Bible is 'endlessly restless with socio-economic power arrangements that the world takes as normal'.[16] But this model sees resistance not simply as one aspect of the Church's life but as the essential feature of its existence. It is by its nature a community of resistance. This model is associated particularly with the Anabaptist tradition, though it figures in other streams of Christianity.

One weakness of the resistance model is that it can easily focus more on the position of the Church than on the character of injustice itself. The Barmen Declaration, significant though it was in the emergence of the Confessing Church movement in Nazi Germany, was more concerned with the threat to the spiritual autonomy of the Church than with the oppression of the Jews as such and the issues it raised.[17]

7. The politics of revolution

Harvey Cox claimed in 1965 that a theology of revolution should be 'the first item on the theological agenda today'.[18] It hardly needs to be said that it has not been. Of course, revolutions of one kind or another occur throughout the world, and few would argue that revolutions should be supported under all circumstances. In another sense, however, the Christian is always a revolutionary, since s/he is always dissatisfied with the present structures and always seeking an alternative or better way. In this sense, all politics has a revolutionary component, but, in the more specific sense, a theology becomes revolutionary at the point that it recognises that change is no longer possible within the existing structures of society.

All these models have some value, even the retreatist one. (There is a time when retreat is the most effective, and the only workable, political option.) Each of them needs to be a component of the political resources of the Church, and if any are lost, the loss may be serious.

The need for prophecy

One of the constant dangers, however, is that the servant Church or the pragmatic Church replaces the prophetic Church. Established Churches are always happier with chaplaincy than with prophecy. However, the Christendom model effectively excludes prophecy. So churches become service providers, ambulance stations, sites of devotion, theatres of preaching, but they do not bring people to 'the shaking place', the point of scrutiny of their positions. At the point of prophetic discernment, they fail us.[19]

12

Who will sound the trumpet?
Kingdom, Jubilee and the
movement beyond Christendom

The call today is to return to what the New Testament calls 'the Gospel of the Kingdom' – the Kingdom of God, the cardinal doctrine of our preaching, regulative of our theology, and the touchstone by which all the activities of the Church are tested. This will involve a Reformation in comparison with which the Reformation of the Sixteenth Century will seem a small thing ... The Church ... must recognise that it is a means and not an end in itself. Its end is the Kingdom of God. So long as men [*sic*] serve the Church first and what it should promote second, they are not loyal to the Kingdom of God.

PERCY WIDDRINGTON, 1922[1]

Jubilee is, pre-eminently, a set of bodily actions – not only a seeing but a solid and particular doing that is incarnated in the bodily practices of blowing trumpets and proclaiming freedom, making and granting forgiveness, doing the work of mercy that serves justice, and preparing for a great feast with song, celebration and praise.

MARIA HARRIS, 1996[2]

The social doctrine of the church ... is rooted in the tradition of the Jubilee Year.

POPE JOHN PAUL II, 1994[3]

The Kingdom of God as regulative principle

In this final chapter I want to reflect on the pursuit of theology at a local level within the biblical framework of the Kingdom of God and the Year of Jubilee. To do this with any kind of adequacy will need a new book: the most I can offer here is some pointers towards what this theological task might involve. At the heart of my approach to contextual theology has been the symbol of the Kingdom of God. I say 'symbol' rather than 'concept' because the Kingdom of God in biblical tradition is not a concept which can be analysed and comprehended at the cerebral point, but rather a symbol which swallows us up, and within which we live our lives and seek to pursue our vision. The Kingdom of God is, in fact, a way of speaking about God's work within human time and history. It is the fruit of grace, and our task is to receive, and co-operate with, God's initiative. All Christian life, ministry and theology is Kingdom work. As such it is the governing theological idea for those Christians whose commitment is to the transformation of the world, not simply to the building up of the Church.

I remember vividly my old friend Gresham Kirkby, for many years parish priest of St Paul's, Bow Common in the East End, saying to me in 1961: 'Always remember that the Kingdom of God is the regulative principle of theology'. In saying this, he was quoting Percy Widdrington's memorable essay of 1922 on 'The return of the Kingdom of God', cited above, which led to the foundation of the Christendom Group.

The location of all our theological and pastoral work within the framework of the symbol of the Kingdom is of critical importance. It will determine the entire shape, direction and focus of our work. It is emphatically not 'simply a matter of stress' but one of fundamental theological direction. One of the commonest clichés that one hears, with wearisome repetition, is 'It's all a question of where you put the stress' – as if that solved something. In 1939 Conrad Noel perceptively pointed out that 'people who talk airily of its only being a question of where you lay the stress forget that the stress in Gothic architecture, if laid in the wrong place, will bring the cathedral down in ruins, or that the stress in music will so completely alter an air that it becomes unrecognisable.'[4] Increasingly I believe that how we view the Kingdom of God is the really critical question around which Christians are converging and dividing.

The Kingdom of God is the heart of the Christian gospel, the central social metaphor of salvation. Its centrality in the teaching of Jesus was unique. The term was used in apocalyptic and Jewish literature, and in the Dead Sea Scrolls, but only in the teaching of Jesus was it central. He used the term 'Kingdom of God' or 'Kingdom of Heaven' 121 times in the synoptic Gospels. In his use of the Kingdom as the central theme of his proclamation, Jesus filled it with a new content which was without parallel.

In 1977 Wolfhart Pannenberg referred to 'a steady erosion of the notion of the Kingdom of God', while ten years later Marcus Borg called the Kingdom a 'relatively unused notion within the church'.[5] However, I am not at all clear that they were correct. The rediscovery, among Christians of diverse traditions, of the centrality of the Kingdom of God, not only in the teaching of Jesus but in Christian discipleship, preaching and ministry today, has been quite striking, and was well under way at the time they were writing. It is worth identifying some of the key features of this rediscovery.

The centrality of the Kingdom in the teaching of Jesus has come to be accepted by New Testament scholars without exception. The recovery among evangelicals has been particularly significant. For some time George Eldon Ladd had been emphasising that the Kingdom was a kingdom within history, whose primary concern was not with the salvation of the individual soul but with the salvation of God's people. There was no purely spiritual salvation, Ladd stressed, and the Kingdom would come on earth – a renewed earth, but still this earth.[6] Jim Wallis was attacking the neglect of the Kingdom of God in current evangelical preaching, but his own writing, and the influence of *Sojourners,* which he founded, has been a key factor in changing this situation.[7] Walter Brueggemann has been emphasising the Kingdom as 'the core metaphor for a new social imagination'.[8] Meanwhile, Kingdom theology has been central to the liberation theologians of Latin America, and has been a central feature in Third World theological thinking as well as in feminist theology.[9] In all our local concerns, commitments and struggles, we need to be asking, constantly and consistently: what does this have to do with the coming of the Kingdom of God? It is the key theological link between the local and the global.

Doing theology in Whitechapel Road

In 1990 a group of us at St Botolph's, Aldgate, including the staff of what was then called the 'Crypt Centre' for homeless people, decided that it was important to employ a theologian, a member of the team whose primary activity was to pray, reflect and think – not on behalf of others or instead of them, but in co-operation with them, and to contribute to the work of theological reflection within the Christian community in this area. We felt that it was very easy for churches to avoid serious thinking, and simply to carry on doing what they have always done.

We were at that time a very active parish, seeking to respond to the variety of human needs within the East End. It seemed particularly dangerous for us to operate a crisis ministry, binding up the wounded and responding to one urgent need after another, but never to make the time to reflect on what it was all about, what it had to do with the gospel, what the wider social and political issues were, and what God was up to in the struggles and upheavals which confronted us. It was because of this need that I was employed as a community theologian.

There are still three aspects to my work: to develop, in co-operation with others, thinking and action in the fields of drug abuse, homelessness, and racial justice, building on work which I had been doing on these issues in the East End for many years; to help link the local with the global, connect the work at St Botolph's with wider networks of thought, with the Church beyond Aldgate, and with social and political issues nationally and internationally; and to pursue theological reflection from the context of inner East London, making links with the growing numbers of people in many different places who have chosen to do their theology mainly outside the academic world.

The context of my work is the East End of London, the district east of Aldgate, south of Shoreditch, north of the river and west of Canning Town, whose history I described in Part One. I have stressed the importance of context, of contextual theology, of local theology. On the other hand, I find myself inevitably drawn into involvement with similar and often closely parallel struggles and 'sites of significance' elsewhere – in Newham, further east, or in places further afield, such as Manchester, Liverpool, Chicago, Oklahoma, Nova

Scotia. The negotiation of this local/trans-local dialectic can be quite tricky. Very focused work often leads to connections of an unexpected kind which should be followed. The main focus of my work as a theologian, locally and more broadly, occurs within the framework of corporate activity and reflection. In 1997, for example, there were at least seventeen specific groups with which I was involved, most of them not exclusively Christian, though all of them part of the theological project.

My geographical location in Whitechapel is important. The building where I live and work, once the vicarage of St Mary's, Whitechapel, stands at the point where two main roads – Whitechapel Road and Commercial Road – move towards convergence. Aldgate East station is so close as to be in effect our neighbour. It would be difficult to imagine a site so convenient for gathering people from all parts of East London, and so it is hardly surprising that a former Mayor of Tower Hamlets was heard to comment that it was far more accessible than the Town Hall. Yet for many years the building was neglected and its pastoral significance ignored. Since 1978 the adjacent site of St Mary's Gardens, now always known as Altab Ali Park, has been revered as a shrine to the victims of racial violence, for it was here, in May 1978, that Altab Ali was murdered. So it is important to emphasise the strategic pastoral importance of this building.

Having said that, I do try to restrict my involvement with issues, including those which arise from local churches, to the geographical area identified above, only following trails which lead afar when they seem to be natural, and God-directed, developments of the work here. So my theological work is contextual in a geographical sense and its focal point is the couple of miles around Aldgate East station. The question 'What's in it for Whitechapel Road?' has always been central to my work.[10] At the same time, it is crucial to locate local work within the global and cosmic symbol of the Kingdom of God.

At the very outset of the work, having no funds, we approached the Christendom Trust, set up by the late Maurice Reckitt on 31 March 1971 for the promotion of Christian social thought. The earlier Christendom Group, of which Reckitt was the key figure, had grown out of the League of the Kingdom of God, launched in 1922 with the publication of the book *The Return of Christendom*. While I, and probably most of the Christendom Trustees, believe that we must now move beyond Christendom, the Trust has funded my work here longer than it has ever funded any other piece of work.[11]

A key element in local theological work, one with which we are still struggling, is that of mutual accountability and what is becoming known as 'gospel audit'. Theology is a co-operative task, and needs to be pursued in solidarity with, and subject to the scrutiny and critique of, a group of people to whom the individual theologian is accountable. Hence my Support Group is of central importance in keeping the work democratic and rooted in common life. (The Canadian criminal justice system refers to 'circles of support and accountability', and that would be a more accurate term in this case too. Each word is of equal importance: support *and* accountability.) However, while more churches and organisations are taking seriously the need for 'appraisal', 'assessment', 'supervision' and 'ministerial review', many of these programmes follow entirely secular models, derived from line management approaches. Rarely is accountability seen as a demand of radical discipleship. Two Jubilee Group members, Angela West and Una Kroll, are developing Gospel Audit as a way of helping to subject the work of individuals and groups to radical questions such as: where here is the following of Jesus? How does this shape up in the light of the demands of the gospel?

My work has been based at St Botolph's Church, Aldgate. While the church is in the City, it is not far from the East End. We chose to locate the work here because the staff were sympathetic, it was a place which had credibility, and it had been heavily involved in community issues in the East End. Today, as a result of demographic and structural shifts, and of changes in pastoral ministry, the church is more marginal to the East End, and few of the staff or congregation live in the area, or are involved in East End issues. The Sunday congregation is very eclectic and 'gathered', in contrast to the situation prior to the 1980s, though this could change again as more people come to live nearby. It has seemed best to keep my base here, while focusing on the East End work, and exploring ideas for other developments. One idea has been the creation of some sort of Community Theology Network which would affirm and strengthen the corporate character of theological work. The experience of other networks (such as the Community Research Networks around health care in Tower Hamlets and Newham) suggests that this could work well. The network would seek to be a facility for the Christian communities in the East End, and beyond, building on and developing the work begun here.

A people of the Jubilee

Much of my theological reflection, over the past twenty-six years, has been pursued and circulated through the discussion papers, newsletters and regular updates issued by the Jubilee Group, described as 'a loose network of socialist Christians, mainly within the Anglican Catholic tradition'. The group contains a range of types of socialist – Marxists (ranging from 'critical Marxists' to fairly orthodox Trotskyists), anarchists, socialist feminists, Labour Party members of varying shades, and many 'unattached socialists', often with passionate concerns for green, monetary justice, peace, and anti-racist issues. The co-ordination of this network takes up a lot of my time.

The beginnings of the Jubilee Group were in September 1974 when I was instituted as Rector of St Matthew's Church, Bethnal Green, and I wrote a letter to a number of friends about the current state of the 'Catholic movement' in the Church of England. We were particularly concerned about 'the renewal of the social conscience of Anglo-Catholicism'. I put these phrases in inverted commas because this was the language we used at the time. In fact, in those years some people were writing of the death of the Catholic movement altogether. As time went on, the idea that the movement was in crisis became widespread.[12]

Yet within a few weeks of our formation, we had moved beyond this concern. Since its foundation, a major part of the work of the Jubilee Group has been the circulation of discussion papers. Indeed, our first discussion paper was David Lake's 'Crisis of Democracy – which way for the churches', issued early in 1975, and it is fascinating, and at points depressing, to read it in the current climate. The idea of discussion papers grew from a sense that theology needed to engage with ideas in formation, half-baked, still in process of clarification. Discussion papers carry no authority other than that they reflect an author's current thinking, and they are produced for the purpose of response, further debate, and perhaps refutation. They have fallen into three main categories: commentaries on political structures and areas of concern; commentaries on theological issues, with a sub-section of commentaries on current ecclesiastical issues; and reflections on specific events, debates, publications, and so on. The arrival of the Internet has, of course, made the circulation of this material much easier, and much Jubilee discussion now takes place through the website *anglocatholicsocialism.org* and the 'Anglican Left' e-group.

We chose the name Jubilee because of its biblical roots, and because it played an important role in earlier Anglican social thinking. I even wrote an article in *The Times* on the meaning of the Jubilee idea![13] Few people had any notion what Jubilee meant, or that it had anything to do with the Bible. In the Bible, the fundamental idea of Jubilee is that of release. The Hebrew words which figure in the *shabbat* (Sabbath) and Jubilee traditions are not *tsedeq*, (justice) so much as *schmitah* and *dror* (release, liberation). Abandoning control of the earth is at the heart of Jubilee ethics, as is the need for a regular cancelling of debt and setting free of captives. The Year of Jubilee was not once for all. It was very pragmatic, a call for repeated acts of remission and restoration so that injustice and inequality would not accumulate to the point where nothing but violent revolution could change things. The vision of Jubilee, 'the acceptable year of the Lord', was central to both the law and the prophets, and it was the symbol which sparked the ministry of Jesus in his Nazareth manifesto.[14]

The Jubilee network is an anarchic, disorganised, shambolic phenomenon, more like an atmosphere than an organisation. Like all groups which are located at the 'edge of chaos', it is difficult to pin Jubilee down too precisely. That is its strength though it can also be a source of weakness and ineffectiveness. Nevertheless it does seem to fulfil different kinds of needs in different places and at different times, and to have played a number of important roles. We have, through Jubilee, been trying to do collective theology since its formation in 1974, and have done so from the perspective of a 'community'. We have tried to create a network of loving support and solidarity for the 'Catholic left', along the lines suggested by Alasdair MacIntyre in *After Virtue* (1981) when he referred to 'networks of small groups of friends', or by Cornel West and Bell Hooks in *Breaking Bread* (1991) when they spoke of the need for 'a community of comrades who are seeking to deepen our spiritual experience and our political solidarity'. West elsewhere emphasised the importance of affirming and enabling 'subcultures of criticism',[15] and we have tried also to take this seriously. Jubilee is not an organisation but a loose network, a word we were using long before Castells and others began to describe our age as a network society.[16] While Jubilee is perhaps primarily seen as a community of solidarity, it also tries to be a community of interpretation, one which seeks to read texts, documents, statements and liturgies in a mutually supportive way and with some kind of shared consciousness.

Through Jubilee too we have tried to develop a form of theological and political reasoning and reflection which is not academic, though it involves academics, and yet does seek to reconnect serious intellectual debate and analysis with commitment, action and struggle at local and national levels. Historically our antecedents are groups such as the Guild of St Matthew (1877), the Catholic Crusade (1916) and the League of the Kingdom of God (1922), but, while we look to tradition and the movements of the past for inspiration and nourishment, we seek to relate Catholic social theology to the issues of the twenty-first century. We have no membership, simply a mailing list and local groups, and all our literature is 'anti-copyright', that is, anyone is free to re-issue it without permission. Our organisation is minimal – an annual meeting and an executive – with the maximum amount of freedom and flexibility. There is an important anarchist tradition within the network which produces both a chaotic feel and an ability to act quickly. It also leads on occasions to exaggerated claims by others: thus a briefing to Margaret Thatcher on movements of subversion within the Churches in 1990 described us as 'the best known and probably the most influential of these groups'.

The way in which the symbol of the Year of Jubilee has re-entered Christian action and reflection over the last twenty years has been in marked contrast with the situation in 1974. Since then, both at the level of biblical studies and at the level of popular writing, the Jubilee symbol has become a central one. The publication of John Howard Yoder's *The Politics of Jesus* in 1973 was a turning-point. By 1976 the Jewish scholar Arthur Waskow was promoting a 'Jubilee Network' in the USA, complaining of 'the recent split between social and spiritual concerns' and suggesting that the Year of Jubilee was a symbolic way of transcending this split. He noted the interest in

Jubilee from a range of groups – Jewish, Mennonite, Methodist, Anglican, and so on.[17] By 1999, Frank Griswold, presiding Bishop of the Episcopal Church in the USA, was calling for Christians to become 'a people of Jubilee'.[18]

Of course, by far the biggest and most politically effective use of the symbol has been in the Jubilee 2000 movement, which began with Martin Dent at Keele University and Bill Peters of the United Society for the Propagation of the Gospel. Dent and Peters met in 1990 and launched what became Jubilee 2000. By 1999 it had supporters in over sixty countries. From 2001, two new bodies, Jubilee Plus and Drop the Debt, will take over its work. Little could we have known, when eight of us started the Jubilee Group in a kitchen in Bethnal Green in 1974, that the theme would become so central in the thinking and praxis of Christians and others. As a symbolic frame for theological work, it remains vital with its fourfold stress on setting free the oppressed, the cancelling of debts, the restoration of the land, and the pursuit of all this in a spirit of festivity, symbolised by the blowing of trumpets. It is possible that Jubilee 'may contain the spark that can ignite spiritual fires capable of bringing about the personal, ecclesial and social transformation that today's world so urgently needs'.[19]

As Christians enter the twenty-first century, they do so as exiles, strangers and pilgrims, aliens in a strange land. They will need to learn strategies of survival, and to sing the songs of Zion in the midst of Babylon. The era of Christendom is over, and we need to develop post-Christendom theologies of liberation. For, as Marcia Griffiths reminded us over twenty years ago, our call is not only one to survive in the midst of exile, but to take part in the process of deliverance from Babylon, for we are

> steppin' out of Babylon,
> one by one.[20]

Notes

The place of publication is London unless otherwise stated.

Introduction

1. Rowan Williams, address at the Lambeth Conference, 22 July 1998.
2. On the history of Aldgate see Malcolm Johnson, *Outside the Gate: St Botolph's and Aldgate 950-1994* (Stepney Books, 1994). For a theological reflection on 'outside the gate' see Orlando Costas, *Christ Outside the Gate: Mission beyond Christendom* (Orbis, 1988).
3. Mitchell Duneier, *Slim's Table: racism, respectability and masculinity* (University of Chicago Press, 1992).
4. I have reflected on my early years in Chicago in *Struggle in Babylon* (Sheldon Press, 1988), Chapter Nine, 'The urban church in retreat: some lessons from Chicago', pp. 151-64. For more material on Arthur Brazier see his *Black Self Determination* (Grand Rapids: Eerdmans, 1969), and Raoul V. Mowatt, 'Leading a spiritual movement', *Chicago Tribune*, 12 June 2000. For Claude Marie Barbour see Chapter 9 below.
5. On space and place see Hans Lefebvre, *The Production of Space* (ET, Blackwell, 1991); Michael Keith and Steve Pile (eds.), *Place and the Politics of Identity* (Routledge, 1993); and Doreen Massey, *Space, Place and Gender* (Cambridge: Polity Press, 1994). For the idea of 'death of distance' see Frances Cairncross, *The Death of Distance* (Orion Business Books, 1997).
6. Edward Said, Reith Lecture, in *The Independent*, 8 July 1993; Rosi Braidotti, *Nomadic Subjectivities: embodiment and sexual difference in contemporary feminist theory* (New York: Columbia University Press, 1994); Gloria Anzaldua, 'Speaking in tongues: a letter to Third World women writers' in Cherie Moraga and Gloria Anzaldua (eds.), *This Bridge Called My Back: writings by radical women of colour* (New York: Kitchen Table, 1981), pp. 165-75; Paul Gilroy, *Against Race* (Harvard University Press, 2000). (The British edition is entitled *Between Two Camps*, Allen Lane, 2000. I have referred to the USA edition.)

   Gilroy points out that Diaspora has been carefully distinguished from exile, 'particularly in the Jewish histories with which the term is most deeply intertwined'. However, 'Diaspora yearning and ambivalence are transformed into a simple unambiguous exile once the possibility of easy reconciliation with either the place of sojourn or the place of origin exists' (*Against Race*, p. 124).
7. Letter to Diognetus 5:1-10.

8. Richard Sennett, *The Conscience of the Eye: the design and social life of cities* (Faber, 1993), p. 6.
9. See Walter Brueggemann, *Theology of the Old Testament: Testimony, Dispute, Advocacy* (Minneapolis: Fortress Press, 1997), p. 77; and *Deep Memory, Exuberant Hope* (Minneapolis: Fortress Press, 2000), p. 77.
   On the theology of exile see Brueggemann, *Theology of the Old Testament*, p. 74; Vinay Samuel, 'Strangers and exiles in the Bible', *Transformation* 12:2 (April–June 1995), pp. 28-9; Daniel S. Smith, *The Religion of the Landless: the social context of the Babylonian exile* (Bloomington: Meyer-Stone, 1989); and John Howard Yoder, 'Exile and Exodus: two faces of liberation', *Cross Currents*, Fall 1973, pp. 297-309.
   On exile in historical perspective see William Leach, *Country of Exiles: the destruction of place in American life* (New York: Pantheon, 1999).
10. Anthony Dyson, *We Believe* (Church House Publishing, 1977), p. 124.
11. Alan Ecclestone, *The Night Sky of the Lord* (Darton, Longman and Todd, 1980), p. 37.

Chapter 1. The East End: an emerging community

1. *East London Magazine* 1:19 (1892), p. 256.
2. *The Survey of London* by John Stow, 1603 edn (Everyman, 1929), pp. 374-5.
3. The term is often used more loosely, but I have maintained the practice of using the term 'East End' to mean the London Borough of Tower Hamlets, and have used 'East London' when a wider area is intended.
4. See Malcolm Johnson, *Outside the Gate: St Botolph's and Aldgate 950-1994* (Stepney Books, 1994).
5. See Christopher Thomas *et al.*, *Excavations at the Priory and Hospital of St Mary Spital, London* (Museum of London Archaeology Services, 1997); Jonathan Andrews *et al.*, *The History of Bethlem* (Routledge, 1997).
6. On the East End in the Middle Ages see K.G.T. McDonnell, *Medieval Stepney* (1978); and M.J. Power, 'The origin and early use of the name "Tower Hamlets" ', *East London Papers* 8:2 (December 1965), pp. 67-80.
7. Cited in M. Dorothy George, *London Life in the Eighteenth Century* (Routledge and Kegan Paul, 1930), p. 66. On the growth of Shadwell see Michael Power, 'The development of a London suburban community in the seventeenth century', *London Journal* 4:1 (May 1978), pp. 29-46.
8. George, *London Life in the Eighteenth Century*, pp. 342-3; *A Tour Thro the Whole Island of Great Britain by a Gentleman* (1748), p. 105. On Spitalfields see the London County Council, *Survey of London*, Vol. 21, *Spitalfields and Mile End New Town*, 1957.
9. Nehemiah Curnock (ed.), *The Journals of the Revd John Wesley* (Epworth Press, 1938), Vol. 6, p. 136; John Hollingshead, *Ragged London in 1861* (Smith, Elder and Co., 1861), p. 67.
10. See Norman Brett-Jones, *The Growth of Stuart London* (1935), Chapter Three, 'Attempts by Crown to check London growth prior to 1625', pp. 67-104.
11. D.L. Munby, *Industry and Planning in Stepney* (Oxford University Press, 1951), p. 21.
12. John Stow, *The Survey of London*, 1603 edn (Everyman, 1929), pp. 374-6.

13. *Acts of the Privy Council* 28:427. On the seventeenth-century developments see M.J. Power, 'East London housing in the Seventeenth Century' in P. Clark and P. Slack (eds.), *Crisis and Order in English Towns 1500-1700* (Routledge and Kegan Paul, 1972), pp. 237-62.

14. Moritz, *Travels in England*, 1782 (1924 edn), p. 225.

15. Cited in George, *London Life in the Eighteenth Century*, p. 354.

16. The sources for these statements can be found in manuscripts in Tower Hamlets Central Library, Bancroft Road, London E1.

17. Roy Porter, introduction to Stephen Inwood, *A History of London* (Macmillan, 1998), p. xvii. Cf. Peter Ackroyd, introduction to Alan Palmer, *The East End* (John Murray, 2000), p. xiv: 'The history of London is the history of its immigrants'.

18. Stow, *Survey of London*, p. 113.

19. Ben Jonson, *The Alchemist*, Act 5, Scene 3. Cf. *The Devil Is An Ass*, Act 1, Scene 1.

20. For references see George, *London Life in the Eighteenth Century*, pp. 119ff.

21. *The Orthodox Churchman's Magazine* 2:30 (1802).

22. See note 16 above.

23. On the Huguenots see Bernard Cottret, *The Huguenots in England: immigration and settlement c. 1550-1700* (Cambridge University Press, 1991); A.V.B. Gibson, 'Huguenot weavers' houses in Spitalfields', *East London Papers* 1:1 (April, 1958), pp. 3-14; Robin Gwynn, *The Huguenots of London* (Brighton: Alpha Press, 1998); C.F.A. Marmoy, 'The Huguenots and their descendants in East London', *East London Papers* 13:2 (Winter, 1970), pp. 72-88; Irene Scoloudi, 'Alien immigration and alien communities in London 1558-1640', *Proceedings of the Huguenot Society of London* 16 (1937–41), pp. 27-49; Irene Scoloudi (ed.), *Huguenots in Britain and their French Background 1550-1800* (Macmillan, 1987); Peter Thornton and Natalie Rothstein, 'The importance of the Huguenots in the London silk industry', *Proceedings of the Huguenot Society of London* 20:1, pp. 60-88; and C.M. Weekley, 'The Spitalfields silk weavers', *ibid.*, 18 (1947-52), pp. 284-91.

24. See S.D. Chapman (ed.), *The History of Working Class Housing* (David and Charles, 1971).

25. Charles Booth, *Life and Labour of the People of London*, Vol. 3 (Williams and Norgate, 1892), pp. 64, 77. Cited henceforward as *Life and Labour*. On the growth of Poplar, Bow and the Isle of Dogs, see Francois Bedarida, 'Urban growth and social structure in Nineteenth Century Poplar', *London Journal* 1:2 (November 1975), pp. 159-88.

26. See W. Wilford, *The History of St John the Baptist Church and Schools, Hoxton, 1815-1918*, unpublished MS 1966, pp. 27ff.

27. R.H. Hadden, *An East End Chronicle: St George's in the East* (1880), p. 59; G. Burrington, *An Answer to Dr William Brackenridge's Letter* (1857), p. 37. For a recent study of the German population in the East End see Panikos Panayi, *German Immigrants in Britain during the Nineteenth Century 1815-1914* (Oxford: Berg, 1995).

28. These data are drawn from the *Report of the Medical Officer of Health to the Vestry of St George's in the East*, 1863, pp. 22-3; 1864, p. 22; 1865, pp. 20-1, and 1867, p. 28. William Farr of the Registrar-General's Office, in a report dated 1866, pointed out that the area of distribution of the cholera coincided with that covered by the

East London Water Company. Water supply was to remain a problem until the end of the nineteenth century and continues to this day.

29. Booth, *Life and Labour* (1892), Vol. 3, pp. 63, 65.
30. *ibid.*, p. 122.
31. *ibid.*, p. 100.
32. *ibid.*, p. 102; *East London Observer*, 30 March 1912.
33. Panayi, *German Immigrants in Britain*, pp. 23, 166-8.
34. Booth, *Life and Labour* (1896), Vol. 7, p. 364.
35. *Illustrated London News, Supplement*, 7 March 1868, p. 237.
36. Charles McNaught in *East London Observer*, 25 May 1912.
37. Joseph Salter, *The Asiatic in England* (1873), pp. 10, 20, 26, 70, 73, 199.
38. Joseph Salter, *The East in the West* (1896), pp. 20, 37.
39. Henry Mayhew, *London Labour and the London Poor* (1861), Vol. 4, pp. 228, 229, 425.
40. Commander P.K. Kemp, former Librarian of the Admiralty, personal communication.
41. Thomas Burke, *Nights in Town* (1917), p. 69.
42. Anna Davin, 'Aliens and little Britons', *Socialist History* 13 (1998), pp. 37-52.

Chapter 2. Between slum and ghetto: social conditions in the nineteenth century

1. S.A. Barnett and H. Barnett, *Practicable Socialism* (1894), p. 294.
2. John A. Steuart, *Wine on the Lees* (1899), p. 58.
3. Arthur Morrison, 'Whitechapel', *Palace Journal*, 24 April 1889. Morrison then wrote a story 'The Street' (1891) and *Tales of Mean Streets* (1894) before completing his most famous novel *A Child of the Jago* (1896). This is based in the Boundary Estate of Shoreditch and draws much of its material from the life of Rev. A.O. Jay, the parish priest of Holy Trinity, Shoreditch.
4. See *The Nineteenth Century* 24 (1888), p. 262: 'Invention about 1880 of the term "East End" . . .'
5. See Gareth Stedman Jones, *Outcast London* (Oxford: Clarendon Press, 1971), pp. 15-16.
6. Booth, *Life and Labour*, 1889, pp. 591-2.
7. Ken Worpole in *Rising East* 1:1 (1997), p. 142.
8. G. Davis in S.M. Gaskell (ed.), *Slums* (Leicester University Press, 1990), p. 144. See also Anthony S. Wohl, *The Eternal Slum: housing and social policy in Victorian London* (Edward Arnold, 1977); and R. Vladimir Steffel, 'The evolution of a slum control policy in the East End 1889-1907', *East London Papers* 13:1 (Summer, 1970), pp. 25-35.
9. See Judith Walkowitz, *City of Dreadful Delight: narratives of sexual danger in late Victorian London* (Virago, 1994).
10. Thomas Beamish, *The Rookeries of London, Past, Present and Prospective*, 2nd edn (1852), pp. 149-50.
11. M.P. Banton, *The Coloured Quarter* (Jonathan Cape, 1955), p. 28.
12. Thomas Thirlwall, *A Vindication of the Magistrates* (1817), pp. 6, 16, 69, 95.

13. Charles Booth, *Conditions and Occupations of the People of the Tower Hamlets* (1887), p. 42, note 3.

14. Jerry White, *Rothschild Buildings: life in an East End tenement block 1887–1920* (Routledge, 1980), p. 6; James Greenwood, *In Strange Company* (1883), p. 158.

15. White, *Rothschild Buildings*, p. 128.

16. *ibid.*, p. 7.

17. *Daily Telegraph*, 22 September 1888.

18. Peter Thompson, cited in R.G. Burnett, *These My Brethren* (1946), p. 53.

19. Rudolf Rocker, *The London Years* (1956), p. 81.

20. In fact the title 'Itchy Park' has also been used about St Mary's Gardens, the site of the old church of St Mary, Whitechapel, and now known as Altab Ali Park. Many people in the East End regard this as the original 'Itchy Park'.

21. Gavin, report to Health of Towns Association, 1848.

22. White, *Rothschild Buildings*, pp. 29-30.

23. John Ward, *Letters to 'Ivy' from the First Earl of Dudley* (Longmans, 1905), pp. 146-7.

24. Peter Thompson, cited in R.G. Burnett, *These My Brethren*, p. 52.

25. C. F. Lowder, *Twenty One Years in St George's Mission* (1877), p. 202.

26. Booth, *Life and Labour*, 1892, Vol. 1, p. 66; Vol. 2, p. 25.

27. J.H. Mackay, *The Anarchists* (Boston, 1891), p. 152.

28. John Wheale (ed.), *London Exhibited in 1851* (1851), p. 220.

29. Stedman Jones, *Outcast London*, pp. 109, 184-6.

30. See Colm Kerrigan, 'The coal heavers of East London', *East London Record* 1 (1978), pp. 2-12.

31. See J.L. Oliver, 'The East London furniture industry', *East London Papers* 4 (October, 1961), pp. 97ff.; Booth, *Life and Labour*, Vol. 3 (1892), p. 97, and Vol. 4 (1893), p. 209.

32. *ibid.*

33. See Andrew Mearns, *The Bitter Cry of Outcast London*, ed. Anthony S. Wohl (Leicester University Press, 1970 edn).

34. Gareth Stedman Jones, *Languages of Class* (Cambridge University Press, 1983), p. 247.

35. Stewart Headlam in *Church Reformer* (June 1888), p. 128: 'An Eton Mission to Hackney Wick, promoted by that eminent friend of humanity, Mr Arthur Balfour, strikes us as decidedly the most comic item in the news of the day. A mission to Eton from Hackney Wick, which with all its ugliness and misery is probably an infinitely more moral place than Eton, would be a great deal more reasonable. If the "classes" who get false views on life and education at Eton think they can spiritualise the "masses" by such kid-glove enterprises as that now set on foot, they are mistaken. They want spiritualising themselves, a vast deal more than the people of whose miseries they are in a very large degree the cause. If they want to do any missionising in the East End, let them take to heart the case of the rich young man in the gospel and divest themselves of their "great possessions" beforehand.'

36. On settlements see J.M. Knapp (ed.), *The Universities and the Social Problem: an account of the University Settlements in East London* (1895); S. Meacham, *Toynbee Hall and Social Reform 1880-1914* (Yale University Press); and Werner Picht, *Toynbee Hall and the English Settlement Movement* (1914). For the American develop-

ments, spearheaded by Jane Addams, see Jane Addams, *Twenty Years at Hull House* (New York: Signet, 1960 edn, originally 1910); Christopher Lasch (ed.), *The Social Thought of Jane Addams* (Indianapolis: Bobbs-Merrill Co., 1965); and *Opening New Worlds: Jane Addams's Hull House* (University of Illinois at Chicago, 1989).

For the interesting relationship between Edith Ramsey and Toynbee Hall see Bertha Sokoloff, *Edith and Stepney: the life of Edith Ramsey* (Stepney Books, 1987), especially Chapter Eight, 'Toynbee Hall', pp. 116-120.

37. William Hale, *A letter to Samuel Whitbread, Esq, MP, concerning observations on the distresses peculiar to the poor of Spitalfields arising from their local situation* (1806), p. 6.
38. *East End News*, 5 October 1888.
39. 'John Law', *In Darkest London: Captain Lobo, Salvation Army* (1989), pp. 189-90.

Chapter 3. The coming of the Irish and the Jews

1. *Poor Law Enquiry* (Ireland), 1835.
2. *Mr Giffen's Annual Report to the Board of Trade*, 1891.
3. Christopher Hill, *God's Englishman: Oliver Cromwell and the English revolution* (Weidenfeld and Nicolson, 1970), p. 113.
4. For a more detailed account, including the references for the above statements, see Liz Curtis, *Nothing But The Same Old Story: the roots of anti-Irish racism*, Information on Ireland, 1984.
5. See F.L. Wilson, 'The Irish in Great Britian during the first half of the nineteenth century', MA dissertation, Manchester University 1946.
6. Cited in M. Dorothy George, *London Life in the Eighteenth Century* (Routledge and Kegan Paul, 1930), p. 122.
7. On the background of the crop failure see Cormac O'Grada, *Black '47 and Beyond: the great Irish famine in history, economy and memory* (Princeton University Press, 2000).
8. Lynn Hollen Lees, *Exiles of Erin: Irish migrants in Victorian London* (Manchester University Press, 1979), p. 42.
9. Samuel Garratt, 'The Irish in London' in *Motives for Mission* (1853), p. 186.
10. On the Irish presence in London see R. Swift and S. Gilley (eds.), *The Irish in the Victorian City* (Croom Helm, 1985); and Steven Fielding, *Class and Ethnicity: Irish Catholics in England 1880-1939* (Open University Press, 1993).
11. Lees, *Exiles of Erin*, p. 58.
12. J.A. Jackson, 'The Irish in East London', *East London Papers* 6:2 (December 1963), pp. 105-19.
13. Cited in *ibid.*, p. 108.
14. Henry Mayhew, *London Labour and the London Poor* (1861), Vol. 2, pp. 109-17, etc.
15. *ibid.*, pp. 118-19.
16. *Report on the Handloom Weavers, Parliamentary Papers* 1840, Vol. 23, p. 112.
17. V.D. Lipman, *Social History of the Jews in England 1850-1950* (Watts, 1954), p. 34.
18. John Mills, *The British Jews* (1853), pp. 257-8.
19. For more detailed material on the Jewish trades see Mayhew, *London Labour*, and V.D. Lipman, *Social History of the Jews*.
20. *Jewish Chronicle*, 20 August and 1 October 1880.

21. C. Russell and H.S. Lewis, *The Jew in London* (1900), p. 24.
22. Lloyd P. Gartner, *The Jewish Immigrant in England 1870-1914* (1960), p. 145.
23. Lipman, *Social History of the Jews*, p. 94.

Chapter 4. The Whitechapel ghetto, Anglo-Jewry and antisemitism
1. George Lansbury, *Looking Forwards and Backwards* (1935), p. 15.
2. C. Russell and H.S. Lewis, *The Jew in London* (1900), pp. 2, 9.
3. Danny Abse, *Ash on a Young Man's Sleeve* (1954), p. 27.
4. Jewish Chronicle, 28 September 1888.
5. As late as 1965, when I was a curate in Hoxton, the dresses and rose petals for the outdoor Corpus Christi procession were made by a Jewish woman with help from her (Jewish) dressmaker friends from Wentworth Street.
6. James H. Robb, *Working Class Anti-Semite* (1954), p. 199.
7. Jerry White, *Rothschild Buildings: life in an East End tenement block* 1887-1920 (Routledge, 1980), p. 136.
8. W. Victor Sefton, *Growing Up Jewish in London*, Folklore Research Centre Studies No. 5 (Hebrew University of Jerusalem, 1976).
9. Booth, *Life and Labour*, 1892, Vol. 2, pp. 29, 30.
10. Walter Besant, *East London* (1901), pp. 193, 196.
11. Israel Zangwill, *Children of the Ghetto* (1895), pp. 1, 9.
12. Montague Crackenthorpe in Arnold White (ed.), *The Destitute Alien in Great Britain* (1892), pp. 5-56.
13. *Jewish Chronicle*, 26 February 1886.
14. For the quotation from Rothschild see Henry Walker, *East London* (1896), p. 23. For Joseph see W.J. Fishman, *East End Jewish Radicals 1875-1914* (Duckworth, 1975), p. 69. On the wider issues see Eugene C. Black, *The Social Politics of Anglo-Jewry 1880-1920* (Oxford: Blackwell, 1989), and David Cesarani, *The Jewish Chronicle and Anglo-Jewry 1841-1891* (Cambridge University Press, 1994).
15. See 'East London Jewish orphans', *East London Observer*, 3 January 1914.
16. *East London Observer*, 3 and 10 January 1914.
17. Frank R. Lewey, *Cockney Campaign*, undated, p. 76.
18. See Maurice Wohlgelernter, *Israel Zangwill* (1964), p. 24.
19. See *Jewish Chronicle*, 22 April 1887.
20. S.G. Reaney in Arnold White, *Destitute Alien in Great Britain*, pp. 79–88.
21. *Hansard*, 11 February 1893, col. 1205.
22. *The Clarion*, 28 August 1896, p. 268.
23. Evans-Gordon, *Hansard*, 2 May 1903, col. 717.
24. Henry Walker, *East London* (1896), p. 36.
25. W. Evans-Gordon, *The Alien Immigrant* (1903), p. 10.
26. *East London Observer*, 6 January 1906.
27. Russell and Lewis, *The Jew in London*, pp. xiii, 41.
28. *East London Advertiser*, 26 November 1898.
29. *Hansard*, 10 March 1887, col. 1724.
30. Louis Zangwill claimed that the abandonment of the bill was directly influenced by the publication of his brother's book (*Jewish Chronicle*, 25 May 1894). On the legislation see Michael Landa, 'The Aliens Act and its administration', *Jewish*

Chronicle, 11 October 1907; Christopher Vincenzi, 'The Aliens Act 1905', *New Community* 12:2 (Summer 1985), pp. 275-84.

31. *East London Observer*, 25 June 1892.
32. *Hansard*, 29 January 1902, col. 1279; John A. Garrard, *The English and Immigration 1880-1910* (Oxford University Press/Institute of Race Relations, 1971), p. 85.
33. Cited in *Jewish Chronicle*, 17 December 1897.
34. *Hansard*, 22 May 1905, col. 740.
35. Howard Vincent, MP, *Hansard*, 2 February 1904, col. 157; J.A. Dixon, 'On Emigrants', *Labour Leader*, 9 June 1894.
36. Arnold White, cited in *Jewish Chronicle*, 8 April 1887.
37. For anti-aliens material see Arnold White (ed.), *The Destitute Alien in Great Britain* (Swan, Sonnenschein and Co., 1892).
38. *East London Observer*, 6 January 1906.
39. S. Cohen, 'Antisemitism, immigration control and the welfare state', *Critical Social Policy* 13 (1985), p. 86.
40. W.J. Fishman in Aubrey Newman (ed.), *The Jewish East End* (Jewish Historical Society of England, 1981), p. 237.
41. Rudolf Rocker, *The London Years* (1956), p. 136.
42. Joe Jacobs, *Out of the Ghetto* (Janet Simon, 1978), p. 28.
43. Thomas P. Linehan, *East London for Mosley: the British Union of Fascists in East London and South West Essex 1933-40* (Frank Cass, 1996), p. 43.
44. Lord Trenchard to the Under Secretary of State, Home Office, 28 September 1934, in Trenchard Papers, RAF Museum, Hendon.
45. *Hansard*, 10 July 1936, col. 1575.
46. Joe Jacobs, 'The police and the fascists: East London 1932-6', *Race Today* (December 1973), pp. 341-2.
47. R.J. Benewick, 'The British Fascist Movement 1932-40', doctoral dissertation (1963), p. 283; Colin Cross, *The Fascists in Britain* (1961), p. 154. Benewick's thesis appeared as *Political Violence and Public Order* (1969). My references are to the original dissertation.
48. Benewick, 'The British Fascist Movement 1932-40', p. 303.
49. John Groser, *Politics and Persons* (SCM Press, 1949), pp. 54-5.
50. Joyce Goodman in 'The Battle of Cable Street revisited', *Contemporary Record* 8:1 (Summer 1994).
51. Public Record Office, MEPO 2/3043, November 1936.
52. Lord Trenchard, memorandum, 2 July 1934, Cabinet Papers 24/250.
53. Linehan, *East London for Mosley*, pp. 242, 247.
54. Robb, *Working Class Anti-Semite*, p. 93.
55. See Oswald Mosley, *My Life*, Chapter 18, pp. 336-57.
56. Piratin, op cit. pp. 15, 20; Rev. E.C.A. Graham-Hamilton, letter to *The Times*, 31 October 1969.
57. *Action*, 24 July 1937; Mick Clarke at BUF meeting, 23 June 1937, PRO/MEPO 2/3115.
58. Robert Skidelsky, *Oswald Mosley* (Macmillan, 1975), pp. 327, 393, 396.
59. *ibid.*, p. 130; Jacobs in *Race Today*.

Chapter 5: From Cable Street to Brick Lane: racial minorities in the East End 1920–71

1. Arnold Wesker, *Chicken Soup with Barley*, Act 1, Scene 1.

2. Stephen Watts. This poem is part of a collection of poems about Brick Lane, in English, Bengali and Somali, gathered by the Multicultural Arts Consortium. It is hoped that, if funds can be found, this collection will be published soon. The MAC is based at Toynbee Hall, 28 Commercial Street, London E1.

3. H. Llewellyn Smith (ed.), *The New Survey of London Life and Labour*, 9 Volumes (1930-35). See especially Vol. 3, pp. 7-8, 87, 127, 263.

4. *Report on the Health and Sanitary Conditions of the Metropolitan Borough of Shoreditch* (1931), p. 105. I was curate in the parish here from 1964 to 1967. For an account of the neighbourhood at that time see my *The Eye of the Storm: spiritual resources for the pursuit of justice* (Darton, Longman and Todd, 1992), pp. 149-53.

5. 'Changing scene in East London', *The Times*, 23 March 1953.

6. *East London Advertiser*, 25 March 1948 and 14 March 1949.

7. Sir Walter Besant, *East London* (1901), pp. 176-7; Smith, *New Survey*, p. 353.

8. *The Times*, 23 March 1953.

9. Roi Ottley, *No Green Pastures* (1952), pp. 29-30.

10. Ashley Smith, *The East Enders* (1961), p. 75.

11. Lionel Crane, 'Hell's Gate, London E1', *Sunday Pictorial*, 30 July 1961.

12. George Foulser, 'Cablestrasse', *The Observer*, 28 August 1960.

13. Vivien Batchelor, *John Bull*, 6 December 1947; *Daily Mail*, 31 October 1947; Mabel Elliott, *News Chronicle*, 28 December 1947.

14. *The Economist*, 30 July 1955.

15. Patrick O' Donovan, 'The challenge of Cable Street', *The Listener*, 16 February 1950, pp. 287-8.

16. Phyllis Young, *Report on Investigation into the Conditions of the Coloured Population in a Stepney Area*, 1944.

17. I was closely involved with the last ten years of the Cable Street cafe quarter and with the pastoral ministry offered by the Franciscans. Unfortunately the history of the Franciscans in the Church of England by Peta Dunstan, *This Poor Sort* (Darton, Longman and Todd, 1997) is disappointing in its treatment of the Cable Street house and inaccurate in the little it does say. See my review in *Heythrop Journal* 41:4 (October, 2000), pp. 497-8. A proper study of this phase in Christian ministry is needed, and I have said a little more about it in Chapter 10.

18. Edith Ramsey's papers are in Tower Hamlets Central Library, Bancroft Road, London E1.

19. M.P. Banton, *The Coloured Quarter* (Jonathan Cape, 1955), pp. 13, 86, 115.

20. Anna Craven, *West Africans in London* (1968), p. 3.

21. The undated work by Kathleen Hunter, *History of Pakistanis in Britain* is extremely unreliable. She describes streets as 'practically monopolised by them', including Commercial Road and Cable Street.

22. Letter from A.G. Fraser, Edith Ramsey and St John B. Groser, *The Times*, 3 February 1949.

23. 'Portsoken improvement', *City Press*, 27 March 1920.

24. Catherine Carswell in *News Chronicle*, 6 February 1934.

25. Andrew Sharf in *Toynbee Outlook*, June 1939; 'The great rent question', *City and East London Observer*, 3 June 1939; 'Spitalfields tenants demand reductions', *East London Observer*, 14 January and 25 February 1939.

26. Cited in Elizabeth Burney, *Housing on Trial* (Oxford University Press, 1967), p. 88.

27. *East London Advertiser*, 26 August 1960.

28. London County Council, Town Planning (Development Plan) Sub-Committee, Joint Report, 26 June 1961, by Architect and Valuer, West Cable Street Area, Stepney: Revised Proposals for Zoning and Programming, TP 636.

29. *Daily Mail*, 17 May 1961.

30. *Hackney Gazette*, 17 July 1964; *Evening Standard*, 13 July 1964; *Stratford Express*, 6 July 1962.

31. Henry Brooke to Joseph Williamson, 3 October 1960.

32. 'Hell is my parish', *Today*, 1 October 1960.

33. On Williamson see Kenneth Leech, 'The end of the Dolling era? Fr Joe Williamson in Stepney' in Kenneth Leech, *The Anglo-Catholic Social Conscience: two critical essays* (Croydon: Jubilee Group, 1991), pp. 13-23. The Duke of Edinburgh's statement, during a visit to the East End in July 1962, that he 'had no idea that so little progress was being made in improving the area' was undoubtedly provoked by Williamson. As far as I could ascertain from discussions with him, he asked Prince Philip whether he had realised how little progress was being made, and received the answer 'No.' He then issued a press statement saying that the Duke had said that he 'had no idea . . .' It was absolutely typical of Williamson's style of campaigning.

34. *East London Advertiser*, 2 December; Edith Ramsey, 'Let's have housing justice', *ibid.*, 25 November 1960.

35. *Hansard*, 2 February 1962, col. 1451.

36. *The Guardian*, 13 November 1963; Sir Keith Joseph, *Hansard*, 31 July 1962, col. 327. Ironically, on the very same day that he spoke in the Commons, Sir Keith wrote to Fr Williamson about Spitalfields, pointing out that most of it was outside any clearance programmes, and that much of it was not zoned for clearance until 1972–2005, and some of it after 2005!

37. Cited Burney, *Housing on Trial*, p. 101.

38. *The Times*, 7, 8, 9 May 1963.

39. David M. Downes, *The Delinquent Solution* (Routledge, 1965), pp. 140-8.

40. C.H. Rolph, *Women of the Streets* (1955), pp. 12, 51.

41. *ibid.*, p. 245.

42. Harold Macmillan to Joseph Williamson, 24 March 1961; Peter McCowen, *The Mental Health of East London* (1966), p. 10.

43. On Cable Street and its myths see Kenneth Leech, 'Cable Street: the making of a myth', *Jewish Socialist* 11 (Autumn 1987), pp. 23-4.

44. Cited in Nicholas Deakin, 'The Immigration Issue in British Politics 1958-1964', D.Phil. dissertation, University of Sussex, 1972.

45. Beverley Nicholls, *Sunday Dispatch*, 5 March 1961.

46. On Brick Lane see Kenneth Leech, *Brick Lane 1978: the events and their significance* (Stepney Books, 1994 edn); and 'A tale of two streets: Cable Street, Brick Lane,

and organised racism' in Deborah Duncan Honore (ed.), *Trevor Huddleston: essays on his life and work* (Oxford University Press, 1988), pp. 53–77.

Chapter 6. *Urbanism and its discontents*

1. Cited in *New Society*, 15 February 1979.
2. Harley Sherlock, *Cities Are Good for Us* (HarperCollins, 1991).
3. For some recent work, see David Harvey, *Social Justice and the City* (Baltimore: Johns Hopkins University Press, 1973); and Manuel Castells, *The Urban Question* (Cambridge, MA: MIT Press, 1977).
4. Leonard Woolley, *Excavations at Ur* (New York: Barnes and Noble, 1955); Lewis Mumford, *The City in History* (New York: Harcourt Brace, 1961), pp. 62, 218-220; Daniel Sperber, *The City in Roman Palestine* (Oxford University Press, 1998).
5. Lester K. Little, *Religious Poverty and the Profit Economy in Western Europe* (1978), p. 22; Christopher Dyer, 'How urban was medieval England?', *History Today* (January 1997), pp. 37-43.
6. Ruth Glass, *Clichés of Urban Doom* (Oxford: Blackwell, 1989), pp. 125-8. See also Peter Wilsher and Rosemary Righter, *The Exploding Cities* (Deutsch, 1975); and 'How the cities are exploding', *Sunday Times*, 22 June 1975. As long ago as 1962 the urban theologian Gibson Winter in *The Suburban Captivity of the Churches* (Garden City: Doubleday, 1962), p. 15, noted that the notion of an exploding city was misleading. Yet the language was still evident at the Istanbul Conference in 1996.
7. On some of these problems see *Urbanising World* (United Nations Centre for Human Settlements, 1996). On edge cities see Joel Garreau, *Edge City: life on the new frontier* (New York: Doubleday, 1991). For work on cities in general see Susan S. Fainstein, Ian Gordon, and Michael Harloe (eds.), *Divided Cities: New York and London in the contemporary world* (Oxford: Blackwell, 1992).
8. Peter Hall, 'The south-east: Britain's tarnished golden corner', *New Society*, 29 July 1976, pp. 228-31.
9. See Tony Champion and Anne Green, 'Local prosperity and the north-south divide', Paper to the Institute of British Geographers, Loughborough University, 6 January 1988, p. 4; Anne Green, 'The north-south divide in Great Britain: an examination of the evidence', *Transactions of the Institute of British Geographers* (NS) 13 (1988); and *Regional Economic Prospects*, Cambridge Econometrics and Northern Ireland Economic Research Centre 1989.
10. See Michael Bregeney *et al.*, *The People: where will they work?* (Town and Country Planning Association, 1999).
11. Peter Ackroyd, introduction to Alan Palmer, *The East End* (John Murray, 2000), p. xiv.
12. John Saville, *Rural Depopulation in England and Wales 1851–1911* (1957).
13. *New York Times*, 17 April 1991; Mike Davis, *Magical Urbanism: Latinos Reinvent the US Big City* (Verso, 2000).
14. *Wall Street Journal*, 13 March 1999.
15. Martin J. Wiener, *English Culture and the Decline of the Industrial Spirit 1850–1980* (Cambridge University Press, 1981), p. ix. Eric Hobsbawm, *Industry and Empire: an economic history of Britain since 1705* (1968), p. 142. On the anti-urban tradition see

Ruth Glass, 'Urban sociology: a trend report' (1955), reprinted in her *Clichés of Urban Doom*, pp. 27-50. The classic of urbanism is Louis Wirth, 'Urbanism as a way of life' in Paul K. Hatt and Albert J. Reiss (eds.), *Reader in Urban Sociology* (New York: Free Press, 1951), pp. 32-49.

16. Richard Sennett, 'Cities without care or connection' in *New Statesman*, 5 June 2000, pp. 25-7.

17. Richard Skeates, 'The Infinite city', *City* 8 (December 1997), pp. 6-20. On the 'New Jerusalem' idea see J. Stevenson, 'The new Jerusalem' in L.M. Smith (ed.), *The Making of Britain: echoes of greatness* (Macmillan, 1988), pp. 53-70.

18. Glass, *Clichés of Urban Doom*; Andy Merrifield and Eric Swyngedouw (eds.), *The Urbanisation of Injustice* (Lawrence and Wishart, 1996); Robert A. Beauregard, *Voices of Decline: the postwar fate of US cities* (Oxford: Blackwell 1993); and Fainstein *et al.*, *Divided Cities*.

19. Jerry Herron, *After Culture: Detroit and the Humiliation of History* (Detroit: Wayne State University Press, 1993).

20. Ruth Glass and John Westergaard, *London's Housing Needs* (Centre for Urban Studies, 1965), p. x.

21. Barry Bluestone and Bennett Harrison, *The Deindustrialisation of America* (New York: Basic Books, 1982).

22. Andrew Davey, 'London as a theological problem', *Theology*, May–June 1998, pp. 188-96.

23. Glass and Westergaard, *London's Housing Needs*, pp. 4-5.

24. Ruth Glass in David Donnison and David Eversley (eds.), *London: urban patterns, problems and policies* (Heinemann, 1973), p. 426.

25. *Policy for the Inner Cities*, Department of the Environment, Cmnd 6845, 1977.

26. See Graham Russell, 'City Challenge offers lessons for the future', *Urban Environment Today*, 9 March 2000, p. 13.

27. Joan Higgins *et al.*, *Government and Urban Poverty* (Oxford: Blackwell 1983). For recent work see *Involving Communities in Urban and Rural Regeneration*, DETR 1997; Michael Keith and Alisdair Rogers (eds.), *Hollow Promises? Rhetoric and Reality in the Inner City* (Mansell, 1991), p. 6; Anne Power and Katharine Mumford, *The Slow Death of Great Cities? Urban Abandonment or Urban Renaissance* (Joseph Rowntree Foundation, 1999); *Towards an Urban Renaissance*, Final Report of the Urban Taskforce, 1999.

28. *Final Report of the Expert Committee on Compensation and Betterment*, HMSO 1942.

29. Darrel Crilley, 'Heat and dust from crumbling Olympia', *Times Higher Educational Supplement*, 12 June 1992.

30. Sue Brownill, *Developing London's Docklands: another great planning disaster?* (Paul Chapman, 1990); Rogers, cited in *The Independent*, 6 March 1995.

31. Janet Foster, *Docklands: Cultures in Conflict, Worlds in Collision* (UCL Press, 1999), pp. 336, 2, 139, 248.

32. Nigel Spearing MP, cited in *New Statesman*, 26 April 1999.

33. Vanessa Houlder, 'Docklands gets that sinking feeling', *Financial Times*, 8 May 1991. See also her later article 'Tower of trouble on the waterfront', *ibid.*, 16-17 May 1992. On Docklands see Janet Foster, *Docklands: Cultures in Conflict, Worlds*

in Collision (UCL Press, 1999). On the historical background of the Isle of Dogs see Thomas J. Cole, 'Life and Labour in the Isle of Dogs: the origins and evolution of an East London working class community 1800–1980', Ph.D. dissertation, University of Oklahoma, 1984.

34. Roger Burrows' study for the Joseph Rowntree Foundation, cited in *Sunday Times*, 11 October 1998.

35. Doreen Massey, *Space, Place and Gender* (Cambridge: Polity Press, 1994), p. 163.

36. Darrel Crilley *et al.*, *New Migrants in London's Docklands* (Queen Mary Westfield College, 1991).

37. On Spitalfields see Jane M. Jacobs, *Edge of Empire; postcolonialism and the city* (New York: Doubleday 1996), Chapter Four, 'Eastern trading: diaspora, dwelling and place', pp. 70-102.

38. Will Hutton, *The State We're In* (Jonathan Cape, 1996), p. 213.

39. Richard G. Wilkinson, *Unhealthy Societies: the afflictions of inequality* (Routledge, 1996). On health and inner cities see also *Deprivation and Ill Health* (British Medical Association, 1987); *Interdepartmental Inquiry into Inequalities in Health* (Acheso Report), (HMSO, 1998); *Report on Inequalities in Health related to Social Class* (Black Report), Department of Health and Social Security, August 1980, re-issued by Penguin Books as *Inequalities in Health* (1992); *The Widening Gap*, Townsend Centre for International Poverty Research, University of Bristol, 1999.

40. See DETR data, September 2000; Sophie Hyndman, 'Housing dampness and respiratory illness in parts of East London', Ph.D. dissertation, Queen Mary Westfield College, London, 1989; John Eversley, 'Planning for health in East London', *Rising East* 2:3 (1999), pp. 47-68.

41. Alasdair MacIntyre, *Whose Justice? Which Rationality?* (Duckworth, 1988); Leon Trotsky, *Their Morals and Ours* (New York: Pathfinder Press, 1973 edn).

42. Ruth Glass, 'Uneasy partnership: the application of sociological knowledge to regional and town planning', Paper to the International Sociological Congress 1959, reprinted in *Clichés of Urban Doom*, pp. 9-26.

43. Michael Pacione, 'Church, state and deprivation in the modern city', Paper at Religion and the Resurgence of Capitalism Conference, Lancaster University, 14–17 July 1991, MS 1991.

44. See Andy Merrifield and Eric Swyngedouw (eds.), *The Urbanisation of Injustice* (Lawrence and Wishart, 1996).

45. Cf. Andrew Sils *et al.*, *The Politics of the Urban Crisis* (Hutchinson, 1988), p. 16: 'the parallels are so striking that it is questionable why so little appears to have been learnt in each country by the mistakes in the other.'

46. See, for example, 'Can churches save America?', *US News and World Report*, 9 September 1996; Joe Klein, 'Should Washington let the churches take over the inner cities?', *The New Yorker*, 16 June 1997; Arthur E. Farnsley III, 'Can churches save the city? A look at resources', *Christian Century*, 9 December 1998, pp. 1182-4.

47. Michael Young and Gerard Lemos, *The Communities We Have Lost and Can Regain* (Lemos and Crane, 1997); Michael Simmonds (ed.), *Street Credo: churches in the community* (Lemos and Crane, 2000); Derek L. Phillips, *Looking Backward: a critical appraisal of communitarian thought* (Princeton University Press, 1993).

48. See *Toxic Wastes and Race in the United States* (New York: United Church of Christ Commission for Racial Justice, April 1987).

49. Howard Clinebell, 'Greening pastoral care to reciprocally heal persons and the earth', *Contact* 133 (2000), pp. 3-12. See Jean Roelofs, *Greening Cities: building just and sustainable communities* (New York: Bootstraps Press, 1996).

50. See John Eversley, 'Planning for health in East London', *Rising East* 2:3 (1999), pp. 47-68.

51. See Geoff Wykurz, 'I'm still not sure how housing affects people's teeth', *Community Health Action* 32 (1994), pp. 16-19; and Geoff Wykurz and Diana Kelly, 'Working in partnership with the community: a community oriented approach to medical education', MS 1996.

52. Walter Brueggemann, *The Land* (SPCK, 1977), pp. 4, 187.

53. See Brevard Childs, *Myth and Ritual in the Old Testament* (SCM Press, 1968), pp. 92-3.

54. Alan Ecclestone, *The Night Sky of the Lord* (Darton, Longman and Todd, 1980), p. 42.

55. Denys Turner in *Voices from the Urban Wilderness* (Bristol Jubilee Group, 1984), p. 2.

Chapter 7. The captivity and liberation of theology

1. J.B. Metz, *Faith in History and Society* (Burns and Oates, 1980), p. 58.

2. Cited in Timothy Gorringe, *Alan Ecclestone: Priest as Revolutionary* (Sheffield: Cairns, 1994), p. 65. Barth made his comment as Hitler annexed Austria and moved towards Czechoslovakia.

3. See E.R. Hardy (ed.), *Christology of the Later Fathers* (Philadelphia: Westminster Press, 1984), p. 136; and Steven Peter Tsichlis, 'The nature of theology in the Theological Orations of St Gregory Nazianzen', *Diakonia* 16:3 (1981), pp. 238-46.

4. For the view that theology is in a state of decay see E.L. Mascall, *Theology and the Future* (Darton, Longman and Todd, 1968), p. 20; Carl E. Braaten, *Principles of Lutheran Theology* (Philadelphia: Fortress 1983), p. ix, etc. Edward Farley, *Theologia: the fragmentation and unity of theological education* (Philadelphia: Fortress Press, 1983), p. ix, speaks of the 'decline and eventual eclipse of theology'.

5. On the idea of paradigm shifts see Thomas S. Kuhn, *The Structure of Scientific Revolutions* (1962), and Barry Barnes, *T.S. Kuhn and Social Science* (New York: Columbia University Press, 1982). On paradigm shifts in theology see Hans Kung and David Tracy (eds.), *Paradigm Change in Theology* (New York: Crossroad, 1989). P.C. Hodgson, *Winds of the Spirit: a constructive Christian theology* (SCM Press, 1994), p. 53, speaks of 'a new paradigm in theology'. Of course, the very term 'do theology' is quite new and its use raises some questions.

6. See Charles Carpenter, *Theology as the Road to Holiness in St Bonaventure* (New York: Paulist Press, 1999).

7. Karl Barth, *Church Dogmatics* I/1, 1975 edn, p. 423. See William Stacy Johnson, *The Mystery of God: Karl Barth and the postmodern foundations of theology* (Louisville, Westminster: John Knox Press, 1997).

8. Letty M. Russell in Colin Podmore (ed.), *Community – Unity – Communion: Essays in Honour of Mary Tanner* (Church House Publishing, 1998), p. 66.

9. On the idea of 'one culture' see Bernard Lonergan, *Method in theology* (Darton, Longman and Todd, 1972), pp. 326-7.

10. Walter Rauschenbusch, *Christianity and the Social Crisis* (New York: Macmillan, 1907), p. 46.

11. The image of the web has been important. See Bridget Walker, 'Weaving the web: liberation theologies from a feminist perspective', *Third World Book Review* 1:4-5 (1985), pp. 51-5. Kathryn Tanner, *Theories of Culture: a new agenda for theology* (Minneapolis: Fortress Press, 1997) argued that theology is not simply for educated elites.

12. See Martin Marty, 'Two kinds of civil religion' in Russell Richey and Donald Jones (eds.), *American Civil Religion* (New York: Harper and Row, 1994), pp. 139-57; John Atherton, *Public Theology for Changing Times* (2000).

13. Irving Greenberg, cited in *Manna*, Summer 1994; Donald Nicholl, 'Is there a locus classicus for theology?' in his *The Beatitude of Truth* (Darton, Longman and Todd, 1997), pp. 52-64.

14. See Laurie Green, *Power to the Powerless* (Marshall Pickering, 1987), Chapter One, 'To make theology democratic', pp. 1-12; Ian Fraser, *Recovering Theology as the People's Work* (USPG, undated).

15. The use of theology as a synonym for 'irrelevance' is a mainly recent development, though as early as the fourteenth century Richard Rolle spoke of the 'theologian with his useless studying' (*The Fire of Love*, tr. Clifton Wolters, Penguin, 1972, p. 61). Lenin referred to 'the old prejudices of theology' (*Marxism and Revisionism*, 1908, in *V.I. Lenin on Petty Bourgeois Revisionism*, Moscow, Novosti Press Agency, 1986, p. 11). In recent years the term has been used to mean either irrelevant, doctrinaire (usually equated with rigid, narrow) or archaic. Thus *The Guardian* editorial on incomes policy 'In place of theology' (22 May 1972) stated, 'There is no point in being too theological'. Cf. Giles Radice MP: 'Labour's lack of a modern statement is not a theological irrelevancy which the "realists" in the party can ignore' (*The Guardian*, 15 February 1988). J.K. Galbraith, in a lecture at the House of Commons on 24 November 1992, warned that 'there can be no escape from thought into theology' (*The Guardian*, 25 November 1992). *The Economist* on 3 July 1993 referred to the 'theology of European union'. Ian Taylor described the free market as a 'theological belief' (*New Statesman and Society*, 8 October 1993, p. 18). The late John Smith saw the debates about Clause Four as 'a theological distraction' (Peter Kellner, *Sunday Times*, 6 February 1994).

16. For example, Daphne Hampson (ed.), *Swallowing a Fishbone?: feminist theologians debate Christianity* (SPCK, 1996), p. ix, says that her contributors 'had had theological training at an advanced level'. Cf. Gareth Jones, 'After Kant: the Liverpool Statement', *Reviews in Religion and Theology*, August 1998, pp. 85-91: 'the vast majority of British theologians now work in secular academic institutions'.
    Sometimes academic theologians write as if they are somewhat contemptuous of those involved in 'practical' work. Cf. for example, Stephen Pattison's complaint that 'there is a frustrating lack of publications from actual practitioners, reflecting at a high level of intellectual competence on everyday experiences'. Pattison also notes that there are many more pastoral theologians in the USA than in Britain,

but this seems to mean more academics (*A Critique of Pastoral Care*, 3rd edn, SCM Press, 2000, pp. ix, 2).

17. Elaine Graham, *Transforming Practice: Pastoral Theology in an Age of Uncertainty* (Mowbray, 1996), p. 24.

18. One South London priest, Michael Armitage, noted that his time at the theological college at Cuddesdon had been 'a waste of time . . . I was equipped in no way at all for the job I have been doing in the last eleven years in Brixton' (Submission to the Archbishops' Commission on Urban Priority Areas, undated).

19. James W. McClendon, *Systematic Theology: Ethics* (Abingdon Press, 1988), p. 33. McClendon's work is called Systematic Theology, but this too has come under question. Perhaps the whole idea of a 'systematic theology' is at an end. This is suggested, for example, by Nicholas Lash, *Theology on the Way to Emmaus* (SCM Press, 1986), p. x, and Elizabeth A. Johnson, *She Who Is: the mystery of God in feminist theological discourse* (New York: Crossroad, 1992), p. 10. Robert McAfee Brown claimed in 1976 that 'for a while at least the writing of theology needs to be done in loose-leaf notebooks' (Introduction to Sergio Torres and John Eagleson, eds., *Theology in the Americas*, Orbis, 1976, p. xi). See also Gavin D' Costa. The end of "theology" and "religious studies" ', *Theology*, September–October 1996, pp. 338-51.

20. Harvey Cox, 'The place and purpose of theology', *Christian Century*, 5 January 1966, p. 7.

21. Elisabeth Schussler Fiorenza, *Jesus, Miriam's Child, Sophia's Prophet* (SCM Press, 1995), p. 10.

22. David J. Adams, *Cross Cultural Theology* (Atlanta: John Knox Press 1987), Chapter 1, 'The theologian as a caring person', pp. 6-16.

23. See Ellen T. Cherry, *By the Renewing of Your Minds: the pastoral function of Christian doctrine* (New York: Oxford University Press, 1997); R. John Elford, *The Pastoral Nature of Theology* (Cassell, 1999); and Robert Boak Slocum (ed.), *A New Conversation: essays on the future of theology in the Episcopal Church* (New York: Church Publishing Inc., 1999).

24. Oh Jae Shik and John England (eds.), *Theology in Action: a Workshop Report*, Manila, East Asian Christian Conference, 1–12 September 1972.

25. Graham Ward, *Theology and Contemporary Critical Theory* (New York: St Martin's Press, 1996), p. 1.

26. Colin Morris, *The Discovery of the Individual 1050-1200* (SPCK, 1972).

27. Bishop Steve Charleston in *The Witness*, April 1999, p. 26.

28. Robert J. Schreiter, *Constructing Local Theologies* (Orbis, 1993 edn), p. 16; Marcella Althaus-Reid, 'Both indecent and ex-centre: teaching feminist theology for articulation or for exoticism?', *Liberating the Vision*, LSU Summer School, Southampton 1996, pp. 71-7.

29. St John Climacus, *The Ladder of Divine Ascent* (ET Faber, 1959), p. 264; Vladimir Lossky, *The Mystical Theology of the Eastern Church* (James Clarke, 1957).

30. See Joseph Pieper, *The Silence of St Thomas* (1957), p. 45.

31. See Martin Thornton, *The Function of Theology* (Hodder and Stoughton, 1968).

32. Edward Farley, *Theologia: the fragmentation and unity of theological education*

(Philadelphia: Fortress Press, 1983); Mark A. Mcintosh, *Mystical Theology: the integrity of spirituality and theology* (Oxford: Blackwell, 1998).

33. See, for example, Robert P. Imbelli's plea for a 'kneeling theology' in *Commonweal*, 7 April 1995, pp. 24-52.

34. Gavin D'Costa, 'On cultivating the disciplined habits of a love affair, Or On how to do theology on your knees', *New Blackfriars* (March 1998), pp. 116-36, especially pp. 118, 120; Rowan Williams, *On Christian Theology* (Oxford: Blackwell, 2000), p. 13.

35. See Samuel Amirtham and John Pabee (eds.), *Theology by the People: reflections on doing theology in the community* (Geneva: World Council of Churches, 1986); David J. Hesselgrau and Edward Rommen, *Contextualisation: methods, meanings and models* (Apollos, 1989); J.W. de Gruchy and Charles Villa-Vicencio (eds.), *Doing Theology in Context: South African Reflections* (Orbis, 1994); Jean-Pierre Jossua and Joannes Metz (eds.), *Doing Theology in New Places, Concilium* 115 (1979).

36. Douglas John Hall, *Thinking the Faith* (Minneapolis: Fortress Press, 1991); Mcintosh, *Mystical Theology*, p. 22.

37. John Vincent claims that 'every theology is determined by its context'. This is probably a loose use of language, but if it is taken literally, it is clearly nonsense. Theology is influenced, shaped, affected, and may be for a time determined, by its context until an impetus for rethinking occurs. But if every theology were determined by its context, the possibilities for change and renewal would not exist, and theologians would be of all people the most miserable. See J.J. Vincent, 'Liberation theology and the practice of ministry' in *Southwell and Oxford Papers in Contemporary Society* (Oxford Institute for Church and Society, 1992), p. 5. For a recent assessment of context see Ian K. Duffield, 'The challenge and responsibilities of contextual theology', *Reviews in Religion and Theology* (February 1997), pp. 7-13.

38. James Cone, *God of the Oppressed* (New York: Seabury, 1975).

39. Amos Funkelstein, *Theology and the Scientific Imagination* (Princeton University Press, 1986).

40. *Octogesima Adveniens* is in *AAS* 63 (1971), pp. 401-44. See Mary Elsbernd OSF, 'Whatever happened to Octogesima Adveniens?', *Theological Studies* 56:1 (March 1995), pp. 39-60. On the influence of Paul VI see Peter Hebblethwaite, 'The Popes and politics: shifting patterns in "Catholic social doctrine" ', *Daedalus* 3:1 (Winter 1982), pp. 85-99; and Kenneth Leech, 'Some recent trends in Catholic social theology', *Theology* 88 (1985), pp. 365-73. Pope John Paul II has cited Paul VI's letter, but with the opposite sense to the one the earlier Pope intended. For the Jesuit document see Society of Jesus, 32nd General Congregation 1975, no. 44.

41. Joe Holland and Peter Henriot, *Social Analysis: Linking Faith and Justice* (Orbis, 1983 edn).

42. Christine Allen, Notes on Christendom Trust Consultation, 22 June 1993.

43. Robert J. Schreiter, *The New Catholicity* (Orbis, 1997), p. ix. See also his earlier work *Constructing Local Theologies* (Orbis, 1985, 1993), especially Chapter One, 'Who is a local theologian?', pp. 16-20.

44. Allen, Notes on Christendom Trust Consultation.

45. Schreiter, *The New Catholicity*.

46. John Reader, *Local Theology* (SPCK, 1994).
47. Rowan Williams, 'Making moral decisions', Address at the Lambeth Conference, 22 July 1998.
48. Elaine Graham, *Transforming Practice: Pastoral Theology in an Age of Uncertainty* (Mowbray, 1996).
49. Laurie Green, *The Challenge of the Estates* (Urban Bishops Panel, 1998), p. 1.
50. William C. Placher, 'Why bother with theology?', *Christian Century*, 2–9 February 1994, pp. 104-8.
51. On the Canadian experience see Chris Lind and Joe Mihevc (eds.), *Coalitions for Justice: the story of Canada's interchurch coalitions* (Ottawa: Novalis, 1994).
52. See *Poverty Network*, Summer 1991, especially Craig Russell, 'Theological imagination and facing the realities of Hulme and Moss Side, pp. 15-20.
53. Michael Northcott (ed.), *Urban Theology: a Reader* (Cassell, 1998), pp. 3, xi.
54. E.R. Wickham, *Church and People in an Industrial City* (Lutterworth, 1957). Robin Gill has said that it is 'wrong in almost every point' (*The Myth of the Empty Church*, SPCK, 1993).
55. On Vincent see the numerous publications of the Urban Theology Unit, especially Ian K. Duffield (ed.), *Urban Christ: responses to John Vincent* (Sheffield: Urban Theology Unit, 1997).
56. See *Towards an International Urban Programme for the Anglican Communion*, Urban Bishops' Panel 2000.
57. Duffield, *Urban Christ*, p. 17.
58. *ibid.*
59. See, for example, William Johnston, *The Inner Eye of Love* (HarperCollins, 1990), pp. 195-6.
60. Ernst Kasemann, 'The problem of New Testament theology', *New Testament Studies* 19 (1973), p. 236; Chris Rowland, *Open Thy Mouth for the Dumb: a task for the exegete of scripture*, Inaugural Lecture as Dean Ireland Professor, Oxford University, 11 May 1992, *Biblical Interpretation* 1:2 (1993), pp. 228-45.
61. See Don S. Browning, *A Fundamental Practical Theology* (Minneapolis: Fortress Press, 1991); and Lewis S. Mudge and James N. Poling (eds.), *Formation and Reflection: the promise of practical theology* (Philadelphia: Fortress Press, 1987).
62. See John Milbank, *Theology and Social Theory* (Oxford: Blackwell, 1991); and John Milbank *et al.*, *Radical Orthodoxy* (Routledge, 1999). For critical comments see Douglas Hedley, 'Should divinity overcome metaphysics? Reflections on John Milbank's theology beyond secular reason and confessions of a Cambridge Platonist', *Journal of Religion* 80:2 (April 2000), pp. 271-98; and Steven Shakespeare, 'The new romantics: a critique of Radical Orthodoxy', *Theology* (May–June 2000), pp. 163-77.
63. Philippa Berry and Andrew Werrnick (eds.), *Shadow of Spirit: postmodernism and religion* (Routledge, 1992), p. 4.
64. Catherine Pickstock, *After Writing* (Blackwell, 1998), p. xiii.
65. *Reviews in Religion and Theology* (May 1998), pp. 11-13.
66. Alasdair MacIntyre and Paul Ricoeur, *The Religious Significance of Atheism* (New York: Columbia University Press, 1967), p. 24.

Chapter 8. Theology, race and plurality

1. Kobi Nazrul is one of the main Bengali poets.
2. Johnson's hymn has become the 'national anthem' of black Christians in the USA.
3. On the Bengali cultural background see Tazeen M. Murshid, *The Sacred and the Secular: Bengali Muslim discourses 1871-1977* (Calcutta: Oxford University Press, 1995). On the Bengali community in Britain see John Eade, *The Politics of Community: the Bangladesh community in East London* (Aldershot: Avebury, 1989); Katy Gardner and Abdus Shukur, 'I'm Bengali, I'm Asian, and I'm living here: the changing identity of British Bengalis' in Roger Ballard (ed.), *Desh Pardesh: the South Asian presence in Britain* (Hurst, 1994), pp. 142-64; and *Bangladeshis in Britain*, Government Reply to the Home Affairs Committee (HMSO, July 1987).
4. The general view has been that workers were never religious, a view held by Engels and many others. For recent work see Hugh McLeod, 'Working class religion in late Victorian London: Booth's "religious influences" revisited', MS 1989, for Booth Conference at the Open University, and his 'The deChristianisation of the working class in western Europe', *Social Compass* 27:2-3 (1980), pp. 191-214.
5. Charles Booth, *Life and Labour, Religious Influences*, Vol. 2, p. 118.
6. *ibid.*, pp. 12-13.
7. Bryan King, *Sacrilege and its Encouragement, being an account of the St George's Riots and of their Successes . . .* (Joseph Masters, 1860), p. 7.
8. John M. Harwood, 'Vanished churches vanished streets: the parish of St Saviour's, Hoxton', *East London Record* 9 (1986), pp. 9-19.
9. For the claim that the Oxford Movement was radical from the start see John R. Griffin, 'The radical phase of the Oxford Movement', *Journal of Ecclesiastical History* 27:1 (January 1976), pp. 47-56. On Lowder see Lida E. Ellsworth, *Charles Lowder and the Ritualist Movement* (Darton, Longman and Todd, 1982), though she says little about the social context in which he worked. On the slum priests see J.E.B. Munson, 'The Oxford Movement at the end of the Nineteenth Century', *Church History* 44:3 (September 1975), pp. 382-95.
10. A commentator on the ministry of the late David Diamond in Deptford, which, although it is in South London, has many similarities with the East End, said that the liturgy was marked by 'pageantry, glamour, even vulgarity, a high camp that shared something with music hall' (Rodney Bomford and Harry Potter, eds., *Father Diamond of Deptford*, Burgess Hill, Ditchling Press, 1994, p. 46).
11. Austin Smith, *Passion for the Inner City* (Sheed and Ward, 1983); *The Easter People: a message from the Roman Catholic Bishops of England and Wales* (St Paul's Publications, 1980), para. 123; *From Charity to Empowerment*, Community Relations Committee of the Catholic Bishops Conference, 1992.
12. Michael Hornsby Smith and Raymond M. Lee, *Roman Catholic Opinion: a study of Roman Catholics in England and Wales in the 1970s*, Department of Sociology, University of Surrey, 1979, p. 31. Cf. also Michael Hornsby Smith, 'Loss and gain', *The Tablet*, 19 May 1990, pp. 618-19.
13. Cited in J.L. Segundo, *The Sacraments Today* (Orbis, 1974), p. 57.
14. Michael P. Hornsby Smith (ed.), *Catholics in England 1950-2000: historical and theological perspectives* (Continuum, 1999).
15. R. Gilbert, *The Evolution of National Insurance in Great Britain* (1966), p. 28.

16. *Methodist Times*, 12 March 1885; *Methodist Recorder*, 15 November 1888. On Methodism see J.W.A. Roberts, 'Wesleyan Methodism and the Working Classes in Stepney 1885-1910', MS 1976 (in Tower Hamlets Central Library).

17. Booth, *Life and Labour*, Third Series, Vol. 2, pp. 23-4.

18. Henry Walker, *East London* (1896), p. 179.

19. Greg Smith, 'The Christ of the Barking Road', MS October 1999. Most of Greg Smith's research material is available on *www.astoncharities.org.uk/research*.

20. On the Caribbean background to black Pentecostalism see Diane J. Austin-Broos, *Jamaica Genesis: religion and the politics of moral orders* (University of Chicago Press, 1997). On the background of racism in the 'mainstream' churches see John Wilkinson, Renate Wilkinson, and James H. Evans, *Inheritors Together: black people in the Church of England, Theology and Racism 2*, Board for Social Responsibility 1985; John Wilkinson, *Black Anglicans in Birmingham: the response of the Diocese of Birmingham to the arrival of Anglicans from the West Indies 1950-1980* (Windsor: St George's House, 1984); and John Wilkinson, *Church in Black and White* (St Andrew Press, 1998), p. 3.

21. Robert Beckford, *Dread and Pentecostal: a political theology for the black church in Britain* (SPCK, 2000).

22. John K. Oliver, 'Christian Lay Learning in an East London Community', MA dissertation, Brunel University, 1992.

23. Laurie Green, *The Challenge of the Estates* (Urban Bishops' Panel, 1998).

24. Marc Ellis, *Unholy Alliance: religion and atrocity in our time* (SCM Press, 1997).

25. Richard Gutteridge, *Open Thy Mouth for the Dumb: the German Evangelical Church and the Jews 1879-1950* (Oxford: Blackwell, 1976).

26. On the resurgence of antisemitism see *A Very Light Sleeper: the persistence and dangers of antisemitism* (Runnymede Trust, 1993).

27. Alan Ecclestone, *The Night Sky of the Lord* (Darton, Longman and Todd, 1980), p. 51.

28. See Deborah E. Lipstadt, *Denying the Holocaust: the growing assault on truth and memory* (New York: Free Press, 1993); and Gill Seidel, *The Holocaust Denial* (Leeds: Beyond the Pale Collective, 1986).

29. See Ceri Peach and Gunther Glebe, 'Muslim minorities in western Europe', *Ethnic and Racial Studies* 18:1 (January 1995), pp. 26-43; Mohammed Anwar, *Muslims in Britain: 1991 Census and other statistical sources* (Birmingham: Centre for Study of Islam and Christianity, 1993); and Philip Lewis, *Islamic Britain* (I. B.Taurus, 1995). On Islam in East London see Jessica Jacobson, *Islam in Transition* (Routledge, 1998); John Eade, 'Nationalism, community and the Islamisation of space in London' in B. Metcalf (ed.), *Making Space for Islam: Muslims in Europe and North America* (University of California Press, 1995); and 'The political articulation of community and the Islamisation of space in London' in R. Barot (ed.), *Religion and Ethnicity* (Kampen, The Netherlands, Kok Pharos).

30. See *The Westophobia Report*, London Bible College Centre for Islamic Studies and Muslim-Christian Relations, 1999.

31. Bernard Lewis in *Atlantic Monthly* (September 1990); *The Economist*, 11 March 1995, p. 137; Mark Juerhensmeyer, *The New Cold War* (Berkeley: University of California Press, 1993).

32. Nicholas Boyle, *Who Are We Now? Christian Humanism and the Global Market from Hegel to Heaney* (T. and T. Clark, 1999), p. 53.

33. Lewis, *Islamic Britain*, p. 189.

34. Chris Searle, *None But Our Words: critical literacy in classroom and community* (Buckingham: Open University Press, 1998), p. 6.

35. *ibid.*, p. 39.

36. Robert J. Schreiter, *Constructing Local Theologies* (Orbis, 1993 edn), p. 17.

37. Stanley G. Evans, *The Church in the Back Streets* (Mowbrays, 1962), p. 28.

38. On 'Success for All' see Robert E. Slavin *et al.*, *Success for All: a relentless approach to prevention and early intervention in elementary schools* (Arlington, VA: Educational Resource Service, 1992); Robert E. Slavin *et al.*, 'Whenever and wherever we choose: the replications of Success for All', *Phi Delta Kappa* (April 1994), pp. 639-47; Nancy A. Madden *et al.*, 'Success for All: longitudinal effects of a restructuring program for inner city elementary schools', *American Educational Research Journal* 30 (1993), pp. 123-48. See also Ruth Miskin, *Superphonics* (Hodder and Stoughton, 2000), 5 Vols.

39. Mukunda Rama Kavikankan Chand, cited in Abdul Karim, *Social History of the Muslims in Bengal* (Dhaka, 1959), pp. 160-2.

40. See Muhammad Yunus, 'The Grameen Bank', *Scientific American* (November 1999), pp. 114-19.

41. See Dale E. Eickelman and James Piscatori (eds.), *Muslim Travellers: pilgrimage, migration and the religious imagination* (Routledge, 1991); Akbar Ahmed, *Discovering Islam: making sense of Muslim history and identity* (1988), p. 11.

42. On gay Muslims see Raza Griffiths in *Gay Times* (May 2000).

43. See Shabbir Akhtar, *The Final Imperative: an Islamic theology of liberation* (Bellew Publishing, 1991).

44. See Dilip Hiro, *Islamic Fundamentalism* (Paladin, 1989); John Esposito, *The Islamic Threat: myth or reality?* (Oxford University Press, 1993); Gilles Kepel, *The Revenge of God; the resurgence of Islam, Christianity and Judaism in the modern world* (Pennsylvania State University Press, 1994); Gita Sahgal and Nira Yuval-Davis (eds.), *Refusing Holy Orders: women and fundamentalism in Britain* (Virago, 1992).

45. On female genital mutilation see Aman, *The Story of a Somali Girl* (Bloomsbury Press, 1994); Julie Flint, 'The first cut', *The Guardian*, 25 April 1994.

46. See Ian Davies and Dave Wiles, *Community Organising in the UK* (Bristol: Children's Society, 1987); Richard Farnell *et al.*, *Broad Based Organising: a study for the Church Urban Fund* (Sheffield Hallam University: Centre for Regional Economic and Social Research, 1994); Robert Furbey *et al.*, 'Breaking with tradition? The Church of England and community organising', *Community Development Journal* 32:2 (April 1997), pp. 141-50; Jay Macleod, *Community Organising: a practical and theological appraisal* (Christian Action, 1993).

47. Roger Hooker and Christopher Lamb, *Love the Stranger: ministry in multi-faith areas* (SPCK, 1986), p. 11.

48. Much inter-faith work was anticipated and encouraged in the work of the British Council of Churches in the early 1980s. See Kenneth Cracknell and Christopher Lamb, *Theology on Full Alert* (British Council of Churches, 1984). For recent

material see Gavin D'Costa (ed.), *Christian Uniqueness Reconsidered: the myth of a pluralistic theology of religions* (New York: Orbis, 1990).

49. David Tracy, *Plurality and Ambiguity* (New York: Harper and Row, 1987), p. 19.

50. See Philip Cohen and Harwant S. Bains (eds.), *Multi-Racist Britain* (Macmillan, 1988), p. 12; Susan J. Smith, *The Politics of Race and Residence* (Polity Press, 1989). For church responses see Beverley Prevatt Goldstein, *Unequal Access: the housing experience of black people* (Catholic Housing Aid Society and Catholic Association for Racial Justice, 1993).

51. Paul Barker, *The Times*, 18 September 1993.

52. *The Observer*, 19 September 1993; Shekhar Bhatia, *Evening Standard*, 17 September 1993.

53. See Nicholas Holtam and Sue Mayo, *Learning from the Conflict*, Jubilee Group 1998 (obtainable from the Jubilee Group, 48 Northampton Road, Croydon CR0 7HT). The following paragraphs draw heavily on this pamphlet, and all the quotations come from the pamphlet. I am grateful to the authors for their work in bringing together these important reflections on the struggle against the BNP.

54. A. Sivanandan, introduction to Gunter Wallraff, 'Lowest of the low: the Turkish worker in West Germany', *Race and Class* 28:2 (1986), pp. 45-57.

55. David Cesarani, 'Between a dock and a hard place', *The Guardian*, 21 September 1993. Further on the episode see *Political Speech and Race Relations in a Liberal democracy, Report of Inquiry*, December 1993.

56. *Teaching Christian Ethics* (SCM Press, 1974), p. 104.

57. *Learning from diversity: a challenge for Catholic education* (Catholic Media Office, July 1984), p. 55.

58. Diocese of Westminster, *East London Area Report to Area Pastoral Assembly*, 22 February 1981, p. 5.

59. Amrit Wilson, 'Therapy for racism', *New Statesman*, 13 July 1984.

60. The phrase comes from a talk by Sivanandan in Newham in September 1983.

61. Jeremy Hawthorn and Judy Robinson, 'Watchpoints for Combating Racism in the 80s', cited in Kenneth Leech, *The Fields of Charity and Sin: reflections on combating racism in the Church of England*, Board for Social Responsibility 1986.

62. Leonardo Boff, *Church, Charism and Power: liberation theology and the institutional church* (SCM Press, 1985), p. 54.

Chapter 9. God on the edge: theology and 'social inclusion'

1. Kenneth Arnold, 'Structures of sin', *Cross Currents* 50:3 (Fall 2000), p. 291.

2. Cited in Peter Keating (ed.), *Into Unknown England 1866-1913* (Fontana, 1976), p. 91.

3. Harvey Cox, 'Religion in the Secular City', *Christian* (Summer 1986), p. 6.

4. For the development of this idea theologically see Jung Young Lee, *Marginality: the key to multicultural theology* (Minneapolis: Fortress Press, 1995).

5. Ruth Behar, *The Vulnerable Observer: anthropology that breaks your heart* (Boston: Beacon Press, 1996).

6. Homily 20 on 1 Corinthians (PG 61:540).

7. Cited by Stephen Timms MP in *The Tablet*, 15 July 2000, pp. 948-9.

8. R.A. Soloway, *Prelates and People: ecclesiastical social thought in England 1783-1832* (Routledge and Kegan Paul, 1969), p. 260.

9. F.D. Maurice, *The Prayer Book* (James Clarke, 1966 edn), p. 200.

10. William Temple, cited in Alan Wilkinson, *Christian Socialism from Scott Holland to Tony Blair* (SCM Press), p. 126.

11. John Willman and Chris Tighe, 'Rebels against their own locality', *Financial Times*, 14–15 September 1991.

12. See Howard M. Bahr, *Skid Row* (Oxford University Press, 1973). Bahr refers to 'the disaffiliated'. See John Marriott, 'Social inquiry and the discovery of the residuum', *Rising East* 3:1 (1999), pp. 33-47.

13. There is now a massive literature on the use of the term 'underclass'. I listed much of the material in *The Sky Is Red* (Darton, Longman and Todd, 1997), pp. 261-2. Some more recent material is discussed in Ruth Lister (ed.), *Charles Murray and the Underclass* (Institute of Economic Affairs, 1997).

14. Report from the Institute for Public Policy Research, 16 March 2000.

15. Office of National Statistics, July 2000.

16. Paul Boateng, *Any Questions*, BBC Radio 4, 9 April 1999.

17. Will Hutton in G. Kelly *et al.*, *Stakeholder Capitalism* (Macmillan, 1997), p. 3, my italics.

18. Richard G. Wilkinson, *Unhealthy Societies: the afflictions of inequality* (Routledge, 1996), p. 171.

19. Laurie Green, *The Challenge of the Estates* (Urban Bishops Panel, 1998).

20. See *Another Country: appropriate services for asylum seekers and refugees*, Audit Commission (June 2000).

21. Manuel Castells in *City* 7 (May 1997), pp. 6-16. See also his *The End of the Millennium* (Blackwell, 1997).

22. On homelessness in the 1960s see John Greve, *Homelessness in London* (Scottish Academic Press, 1971).

23. *No Way Home* (Centrepoint, 1988).

24. Hilary Klee, paper at National Homeless Alliance Conference on 'Accommodating Drugs', 21 March 2000.

25. See *People Not Paupers: Who Cares When Someone Dies Homeless?* (UNLEASH, 1998).

26. See *Coming In From The Cold: the government's strategy on rough sleeping*, Social Exclusion Unit 1999. On the work at St Botolph's Project see its own regular newsletters and reports, obtainable from St Botolph's Project, 2 Whitechurch Lane, London E1 7QR. For the role in establishing medical care for homeless people see Kevin Fisher and John Collins (eds.), *Homelessness, Health Care and Welfare Provision* (Routledge, 1993).

27. Tony Blair, foreword to *Coming In From The Cold*, p. 1, my italics.

28. Bernard Ingham, cited in *The Guardian*, 18 October 1991. The American novelist John Grisham describes the removal of homeless people before the recent Olympics in Atlanta. 'They damned sure didn't take them to shelters because they don't have any. They simply moved them around; dumped them in other parts of the city like manure' (John Grisham, *The Street Lawyer*, Arrow Books, 1998, p. 164).

29. See Hartley Dean (ed.), *Begging Questions: street level economic activity and social policy* (Policy Press, 1999).

30. See Jean Lewis, 'Primary health care for homeless people in A and E', *Professional Nurse* (October 1996), pp. 213-71; A.G. Davison *et al.*, 'Use and misuse of an accident and emergency department in the East End of London', *Journal of the Royal Society of Medicine* 76 (1983), pp. 37-40.

31. David Brandon, 'Homelessness and vagrancy in London', Paper given at St Anne's House, Soho, 23 February 1971.

32. *Homeless Single Persons*, National Assistance Board 1966. This was one of the better reports of these years. Very different was the Reading Report, *Residential Provision for Homeless Discharged Offenders* (HMSO, 1966), described by David Brandon as 'the worst government report of the Twentieth Century' (David Brandon, *Women Without Homes*, Christian Action, undated).

33. *Town Planning Review*, January 1970.

34. The term seems also to have been used by the Sri Lankan Jesuit Aloysius Pieris. For the work of Shalom see Claude Marie Barbour, 'Seeking justice and Shalom in the city', *International Review of Mission* 73 (July 1984), pp. 305-6, 'Shalom ministries: an urban base community comes of age', *Chicago Theological Seminary Register* 81 (Winter 1991), pp. 42-9; and 'Jesus, Shalom and rites of passage: a journey towards global mission and spirituality', *Missiology* 40:3 (July 1987), pp. 299-313. For a recent series of essays inspired by, and dedicated to, Claude Marie Barbour see Stephen Bevans *et al.*, *The Healing Circle: essays in cross-cultural mission presented to the Revd Dr Claude Marie Barbour* (Chicago: Chicago Centre for Global Ministries, 2000).

35. On the Church of the Advocate see *Citizen Times Asheville*, 9 November 1998.

36. For an immensely valuable study of the Bible in relation to homelessness, arising largely out of the work of the Open Door Community, see Stanley P. Saunders and Charles L. Campbell, *The Word on the Street: performing the Scriptures in the urban context* (Eerdmans, 2000).

37. Dr Cindy Fazey, at the Release Heroin Conference, London, 14 July 1999.

38. Ann Wright, *Faith Communities in the London Borough of Croydon and Drug-Related Issues*, Croydon Urban Industrial Mission Consultation Group, September 1996, p. 18.

39. J.M. Winter and D.M. Joslin (eds.), *R.H. Tawney's Commonplace Book, Economic History Review Supplement 5* (Cambridge University Press, 1972), p. 13.

40. John Paul Szura OSA and Depaul Genska OFM, 'Ministry with persons in female prostitution: its role in ministry education', *New Theology Review* 4:2 (May 1991), pp. 105-7.

41. See Mathew Southwell, 'Shape up or pay up', *Druglink* (January-February 1995).

42. Stephen Pattison, *Pastoral Care and Liberation Theology* (Cambridge University Press, 1994), p. 205.

43. Nigel Copsey, *Keeping Faith: the provision of community mental health services within a multi-faith context* (Sainsbury Centre for Mental Health, 1997).

44. David Randall, talk at St Anne's, Soho, 10 April 1995.

45. I quoted this and a related passage in my book *The Eye of the Storm* (Darton, Longman and Todd, 1992), pp. 61-2.

46. *The Sky Is Red* (Darton, Longman and Todd, 1997), p. 178.

47. On the Swaziland situation see *Children and HIV/AIDS: Assessment of the Situation of the HIV/AIDS epidemic in Swaziland* (Geneva: UNICEF, 1999).

48. Beryl Ingram-Ward in Letty M. Russell (ed.), *The Church with AIDS* (Louisville: Westminster/John Knox Press, 1990), p. 78.

49. Cited in *ibid.*, p. 26.

50. See Robert Doran sj, 'AIDS ministry as a praxis of hope' in William P. Loewe and Vernon G. Gregson (eds.), *Jesus Crucified and Risen: Essays in spirituality and theology in honour of Sebastian Moore* (Collegeville Liturgical Press/Michael Glazier, 1998), pp. 177-93.

51. Cited in John Carey, *The Intellectuals and the Masses*, p. 40.

52. Norman Ingram Smith, cited in London County Council report, *Crude Spirit Drinkers*, 1964.

53. John Pairman Brown, *The Liberated Zone: a guide to Christian resistance* (SCM Press, 1970), pp. 71, 76.

54. Kenneth Leech, *Drugs and Pastoral Care* (Darton, Longman and Todd, 1998).

55. See Ivan Illich *et al.*, *Disabling Professions* (Marion Boyars, 1977).

56. Stephen Pattison, *The Faith of the Managers* (Cassell, 1997).

57. Alison Gilchrist, 'The well-connected community: networking to the "edge of chaos" ', MS 2000, p. 8. See also her 'Connections and catalysts', *SCCD Newsletter* (Winter 1998), pp. 18-20; and 'Serendipity and the snowflakes', *SCCD Newsletter* (May 1999).

58. There was much writing about chaos in Christian circles in the 1940s. See, for example, Percy Dearmer (ed.), *Christianity and the Crisis* (Gollancz, 1933) with an introduction entitled 'Christ or Chaos?' and Part One entitled 'The Present Chaos'. One person who rejected the 'Christ versus Chaos' ideas in this period was Gilbert Shaw. See his 'Letter to a priest', 8 January 1951, cited in Sister Barbara June SLG, 'A wealthy place', *Fairacres Chronicle* 19:2 (Summer 1986), pp. 22-5. For a recent study see Melissa Raphael, *Theology and Embodiment* (Sheffield: Academic Press, 1996), Chapter Six, 'Theology from the edge of chaos', pp. 220-61.

59. Sandra M. Schneiders, 'Congregational leadership and spirituality in the postmodern era', *Review for Religious* 57:1 (January-February 1998), pp. 6-33.

60. See *Convocation of Canterbury Report of Joint Commission on Organisations to Reach the Classes Now Outside Religious Ministrations* (1889).

61. Abbé Michonneau, *Revolution in a City Parish*, (ET Blackfriars, 1949), p. 15. Cf. Joost de Blank, *The Parish in Action* (1954).

62. Arthur E. Farnsley III, 'Can churches save the city? A look at resources', *Christian Century*, 9 December 1998, pp. 1192-4.

63. St John Ervine, *God's Soldier: General William Booth* (Heinemann, 1934), p. 38.

64. Stanley G. Evans, *The Church in the Back Streets* (Mowbrays, 1962), p. 3.

65. Martin Thornton, *Pastoral Theology: a reorientation* (SPCK, 1956).

66. On Catholicity see R.J. Schreiter, 'The theological meaning of a truly catholic church', *New Theology Review* 7:4 (November 1994), pp. 5-17; Miroslav Volf *Exclusion and Embrace* (Nashville: Abingdon Press, 1996).

67. Dietrich Bonhoeffer, *Life Together* (SCM, 1954), p. 67; L.S. Thornton, *The Incarnate Lord*, p. 276.

68. Letter to me from Professor Richard H. Roberts, 6 December 1995. See also Richard H. Roberts, 'Religion and the Enterprise Culture: the British experience in the Thatcher era', MS, Paper given at the Religion and the Resurgence of Capitalism Conference, Lancaster University, July 1991; and 'Towards an executive church: should we welcome the Turnbull Report?' in Lawrence Osborn and Andrew Walker (eds.), *Harmful Religion* (SPCK, 1997), pp. 163-76.

69. Stephen Pattison, *A Critique of Pastoral Care*, 3rd edn (SCM Press, 2000), p. xi.

70. *Working As One Body* (Church House Publishing, 1995), p. xi. It is extraordinary and deeply depressing that the whole idea went through with a minimum of critical scrutiny. For one of the few episcopal warnings see Eric Kemp, 'Following the example of Mammon', *Church Times*, 17 November 1995.

71. The article is reprinted in Simon Barrow (ed.), *Expanding Horizons: learning to be the church in the world* (Diocese of Southwark Board for Church in Society, 1995), pp. 17-35. The passage cited is on p. 19.

72. See Illich, *Disabling Professions*.

73. Carter Heyward, 'Fighting boundary fundamentalism', *The Witness* (May 1995), pp. 25-6.

74. See Celia Davies, 'Cloaked in a battered illusion', *Nursing Times*, 6 November 1996, pp. 44-6.

75. Elaine L. Graham, *Transforming Practice: pastoral theology in an age of uncertainty* (Mowbray, 1996), p. 47.

76. Rev. Malcolm Johnson, letter 9 September 2000.

77. Douglas John Hall, *Confessing the Faith* (Minneapolis, Fortress Press, 1996), pp. 195-6.

78. The writings of Walter Brueggemann on prophecy are crucial in this respect.

79. Stanley Evans in *Junction* (October-December 1959).

80. Kip Tiernan, 'The moral crisis of social service', *Plumbline* (March, 1992), pp. 21-5.

81. Some writing uses the word 'servant' so vaguely that it loses any meaning. See, for example, Don May and Margaret Simey, *The Servant Church in Granby* (University of Liverpool: Centre for Urban Studies 1985), where, in spite of the title, the idea of servant is ignored entirely, and the word 'serve' occurs once.

82. Richard Chartres in Eric Blakebrough (ed.), *Church for the City* (Darton, Longman and Todd, 1995), p. 30. Yet it is important that we take the servant idea with theological seriousness. It is an attitude of the soul, one which is about the integration of compassion into the entire life of the Church. See Bennet J. Sims, *Servanthood: leadership for the Third Millennium* (Boston: Cowley Press, 1997), p. 29.

83. Urban T. Holmes, *The Priest in Community* (New York: Seabury Press, 1978), p. 26; L. William Countryman, *Living on the Border of the Holy: renewing the priesthood of all* (Harrisburg: Morehouse, 1999), pp. 81-110, 141.

84. A.M. van den Blink, 'Some thoughts on ordination, Anglican and Presbyterian', MS August 1992.

85. Richard Holloway, *Let God Arise* (Mowbray, 1972) p. 21; Ann Morisy, *Beyond the Good Samaritan: community ministry and mission* (Mowbrays, 1997).

86. Michael Lapsley, cited in *The Tablet*, 23 October 1999, p. 1429.

87. R.C. Moberly, *Ministerial Priesthood* (John Murray, 1910).

88. Kay Redfield Jamison, *An Unquiet Mind* (New York: Alfred A. Knopf, 1995), p. 119.
89. Edward Norman, 'AIDS: a task for the churches', *The Times*, 13 October 1986.

Chapter 10. Agenda for an urban spirituality

1. A Carthusian, *The Way of Silent Love* (ET Darton, Longman and Todd, 1993), p. 11.
2. Gregory the Great, *Homilies on the Prophet Ezekiel*, 1.11.6.
3. *The Poetical Works of John and Charles Wesley* (Wesleyan Methodist Conference Office, 1868), Vol. 1m, p. xxii.
4. Sheila Rowbotham, Lynne Segal and Hilary Wainwright, *Beyond the Fragments: feminism and the making of socialism* (Merlin Press, 1979), pp. 68-9.
5. Denise Levertov, *Light Up the Cave* (New York: New Directions, 1981), p. 96.
6. Alasdair MacIntyre, *Dependent Rational Animals* (Duckworth, 1999).
7. Martin Thornton, *Spiritual Direction* (SPCK, 1984), p. 1.
8. See David Lowes Watson, *Accountable Discipleship* (Nashville: Discipleship Renewal, 1985).
9. The word 'spirituality', in the sense in which it is currently used, is relatively new. It did not appear, for instance, in the *Oxford English Dictionary* until as late as 1971. Moreover, it is interesting that in other languages than English, its sense is much wider, to include intellectual work and the activity of the mind. (Hegel's *Phenomenologie des Geistes* is translated *Phenomenology of Spirit* in German, French and Italian – *geist, esprit, spirto* – but as *Phenomenology of Mind* in English.) See Owen C. Thomas, 'Some problems in contemporary spirituality', *Anglican Theological Review* 82:2 (Spring 2000), pp. 267-81.
10. E.L. Mascall, *Grace and Glory* (Faith Press, 1961), p. 15.
11. This distinction is common in some contemporary Roman Catholic writers. See, for example, Diarmuid O' Murchu, *Reclaiming Spirituality* (New York: Crossroads, 1999), specially Chapter Six, 'The shift from spirituality to religion', pp. 69-84. O' Murchu argues that this is a 'centrally important distinction' (p. vii). Yet he seems to equate 'religion' with 'formal religion' (pp. 1, 34) or 'the religious system' (pp. 33, 34). Bernadette Flanagan, in a gentler and less central way, tends also to make the distinction. See her *The Spirit of the City* (Dublin: Veritas, 1999), p. 7. My view is that, while spirituality and religion are not the same, the distinction between them has been overplayed.
12. Walter Brueggemann in *Theology Today* (October 1995), p. 317. On modern gnosticism see Harold Bloom, *The American religion: the emergence of a post-Christian nation* (New York: Simon and Schuster, 1992); Philip J. Lee, *Against the Protestant Gnostics* (Oxford University Press, 1987); A.D. Nock, 'Gnosticism', *Harvard Theological Review* 57 (1964), pp. 261-78.
13. Haddon Willmer, in Alistair Mason (ed.), *Religion in Leeds* (Shroud: Alan Sutton 1994), p. 183.
14. It has been claimed that 'monks hate cities'. These are the opening words of Thomas Renna's article, 'The idea of the city in Bernard of Clairvaux and Thomas Merton', *Michigan Academician* 15:2 (1983), pp. 241-52 – though Renna modifies them later. But it is clear that the monastic life and the life of religious community have revived in the urban context. Over twenty-five years ago Harvey Cox stressed

the need for a 'rebirth of the monastic movement' in the midst of cities (*The Seduction of the Spirit*, Wildwood House, 1974, p. 86).

15. Kenneth Leech, 'The church and the social outcast', *Prism* (January 1964), pp. 9-14.

16. See Stuart Murray and Anne Wilkinson-Hayes, *Hope from the Margins: new ways of being church*, Grove Evangelism Series No. 49 (Cambridge: Grove Books, 2000).

17. For information on Elsie Briggs House, write to Hebe Welbourn, Elsie Briggs House, 38 Church Road, Westbury on Trym, Bristol BS9 3EQ.

18. Grace Jantzen, *Power, Gender and Christian Mysticism* (Cambridge University Press, 1995).

19. Pope John Paul II, 'A robust spirituality of compassion', talk given on 14 February 1995, published in *Being One* 4:2 (1995), pp. 1-2. Earlier Karl Rahner had stressed that 'the spirituality of the future' would be 'communally lived spirituality' ('The spirituality of the future' in K. Lehmann and A. Raffelt, eds., *The Practice of Faith: a handbook of contemporary spirituality*, SCM Press, 1985, p. 24). See also Philip Sheldrake, *Images of Holiness* (Darton, Longman and Todd, 1987), pp. 5, 8, 16.

20. Rowan Williams, *Resurrection* (Darton, Longman and Todd, 1982), pp. 10, 18.

21. Cited in Ruth Page, *The Incarnation of Freedom and Love* (SCM Press, 1991), p. 164.

22. Sheila Cassidy, *Good Friday People* (Darton, Longman and Todd, 1991), p. 96.

23. Charles Peguy, *Basic Verities* (ET Chicago: Henry Regnery Co., 1965), p. 47.

24. See Walter Brueggemann, *Theology of the Old Testament: testimony, dispute, advocacy* (Minneapolis: Fortress Press, 1997).

25. Abraham Heschel, *The Prophets* (New York: Harper and Row, 1962), p. 117.

26. Cited in M.B. Reckitt, *Politics and the Faith* (Church Literature Association, undated), p. 69.

27. Denise Levertov, *To Stay Alive* (New York: New Directions, 1972), p. 81; and *New and Selected Essays* (New York: New Directions, 1992), p. 144.

28. Kathleen Fischer, *Women at the Well: feminist perspectives on spiritual direction* (SPCK, 1989), Chapter Nine, 'The problem of anger', pp. 175-94; Beverly Wildung Harrison, 'The power of anger in the work of love' in *Union Seminary Quarterly Review* 36 (Supplement) (1986), pp. 41-57, and also reprinted in Carol S. Robb (ed.), *Making the Connections: essays in feminist social ethics* (Boston: Beacon, 1985), Audre Lorde, 'The uses of anger: women responding to racism' in *Sister Outsider* (New York: Crossings Press, 1984), pp. 124-33; Carol Travis, *Anger: The Misunderstood Emotion* (New York: Simon and Schuster, 1982). More generally on anger see Alastair V. Campbell, 'The anger of a loving God', *Modern Churchman* 25:3 (1983), pp. 2-11.

29. Austin Smith, *Passion for the Inner City* (Sheed and Ward, 1983), prologue.

30. 'Alleluia' is entirely missing from the Book of Common Prayer of 1662 (and earlier) and from Anglican hymnody until 1708. See Nicholas Alldrit, 'The song of an Easter people', *Theology* (March-April 2000).

31. It was Pope John XXIII who put 'discerning the signs' on the agenda for Catholic theology. In his letter of 24 May 1963 he referred to the need to discern the signs, seize the opportunity and expand the view. See Sub-Committee of Vatican 2 *De signis temporum*.

32. Steve Latham, 'Urban semiotics: signs of the city', *Crucible* (April-June, 2000), pp. 91-102.

Chapter 11. *Theology and politics revisited*

1. *Christianity and Industrial Problems*, Report of the Archbishops' Fifth Committee of Inquiry (SPCK, 1919), p. 1.
2. Peter Selby, *Liberating God* (SPCK, 1983), p. 76.
3. Denys Munby, *God and the Rich Society* (Oxford University Press, 1961), p. 3. The term crops up constantly in Christian writing. Charles Gore argued for a 'Christian order', and claimed that the Church should aim for the 'sanctification of each new social order' (preface to *Lux Mundi*, 1890, p. ix). John A.T. Robinson called the Church 'the specifically Christian clue to the renewal of society' (*On Being the Church in the World*, SCM Press, 1964 edn, p. 70). The leaders of the 'Social Gospel' movement in the USA spoke of 'Christianising the social order'. See Walter Rauschenbusch, *Christianising the Social Order* (1912). In 1985 the *Daily Telegraph* asked of *Faith in the City* whether 'such documents owe anything whatsoever to a specifically Christian understanding' (*Daily Telegraph*, 24 December 1985).
4. Hannan Swaffer said that Groser was the best-known priest in the East End of London, *Daily Herald*, 19 October 1936.
5. J.H. Newman, *The Arians of the Fourth Century* (Basil Montague Pickering, 1876), p. 258.
6. *The Sketch*, 27 January 1964. On Garbett see Dianne Kirby, 'The Archbishop of York and Anglo-American relations during the Second World War and early Cold War 1941-1955', *Journal of Religious History* 23:3 (October 1999), pp. 327-45.
7. Peter Blaker MP, *The Sun*, 7 August 1982; Mark Santer in Donald Reeves (ed.), *The Church and the State* (Hodder and Stoughton, 1984), p. 113.
8. See Stanley Hauerwas and William Willimon, *Resident Aliens* (Nashville: Abingdon Press, 1990), p. 38.
9. Michael O. Emerson *et al.*, 'Equal in Christ but not in the world: white conservative Protestants and examinations of black-white inequality', *Social Problems* 46:3 (August 1999), pp. 398-417.
10. *The War Cry*, 7 July 1881.
11. See Robert Beckford, *Dread and Pentecostal: a political theology for the black church in Britain* (SPCK, 2000).
12. Henry Clark, *The Church Under Thatcher* (SPCK, 1993), p. 1.
13. Tom Butler, Bishop of Southwark, *Sunday*, Radio 4, 16 January 2000.
14. *Faith in the City* (Church House Publishing, 1985), p. 55.
15. Bruce Walsenburg, *Christian Social Thought in Great Britain Between the Wars* (University Press of America, 1996), p. 7.
16. Walter Brueggemann, *Deep Memory, Exuberant Hope* (Minneapolis: Fortress Press, 2000), p. 2.
17. Richard Gutteridge, *Open Thy Mouth for the Dumb: the German Evangelical Church and the Jews 1879-1950* (Oxford: Blackwell, 1976), pp. 41, 268.
18. Harvey Cox, *The Secular City* (1965), p. 107.
19. Haddon Willmer, 'Weariness with politics', *Theology* (June 1975), pp. 310-18.

Chapter 12. Who will sound the trumpet? Kingdom, Jubilee and the movement beyond Christendom

1. P.E.T. Widdrington in *The Return of Christendom* (Allen and Unwin, 1922), pp. 108, 110.
2. Maria Harris, *Proclaim Jubilee!* (Louisville: Westminster John Knox Press, 1996), p. 14.
3. Pope John Paul II, *Tertio Millennio Adveniente* (1994), para. 13.
4. Conrad Noel, *Jesus the Heretic* (Religious Book Club, 1939), p. 120.
5. W. Pannenberg, *Theology and the Kingdom of God* (Philadelphia: Westminster Press, 1977), p. 51; Marcus Borg, 'Jesus and the Kingdom of God, *Christian Century,* 22 April 1987, pp. 378-80.
6. G.E. Ladd, *The Gospel of the Kingdom* (Eerdmans, 1977 edn), p. 39.
7. Jim Wallis, *The Call to Conversion* (Tring: Lion Publishing, 1982).
8. Walter Brueggemann, *Hope Within History* (Atlanta: John Knox Press, 1987), p. 22.
9. I have discussed the relevance of these traditions for our situation in *The Eye of the Storm* (Darton, Longman and Todd, 1993).
10. See my *Care and Conflict: leaves from a pastoral notebook* (Darton, Longman and Todd, 1989), Chapter Five, 'What's in it for Whitechapel Road?', pp. 103-48.
11. It was only after the Christendom Trust had withdrawn that I realised that the establishment of the Trust in 1971 was linked with the publication of the last work edited by Maurice Reckitt, and the first work to which I had contributed – *For Christ and the People* (1968) – a pleasant and perhaps symbolic discovery! See Martin Jarrett-Kerr CR, 'History of Twenty Years of the Christendom Trust', MS 1990; Maurice B. Reckitt (ed.), *For Christ and the People* (SPCK, 1968).
12. Cf Alan Wilkinson, 'Requiem for Anglican Catholicism', *Theology* (January 1978), pp. 40-5. For a later view see Francis Penhale, *Catholics in Crisis* (Mowbray, 1986).
13. Kenneth Leech, 'The Jubilee theme and hope for a new covenant', *The Times*, 4 June 1977. On the nineteenth-century concern with Jubilee see Thomas Hancock, *The Pulpit and the Press* (S.C. Brown, Lasagna and Co., 1904); and Frederick Verinder, *My Neighbour's Landmark* (Henry George Foundation, 1940 edn).
14. For material on the theology of the Year of Jubilee see Mortimer Aries, 'The Jubilee: a paradigm for mission today', *International Review of Mission* (January 1984), pp. 33-48; Donald Blosser, 'Jesus and Jubilee: Luke 4:16-30 and the Year of Jubilee and its significance in Luke', Ph.D. dissertation, St Andrew's University, 1979; Brian Davies *et al.*, *The Millennium Jubilee* (CAFOD, 1996); Eryl W. Davies, *Prophecy and Ethics, Journal of the Society for Old Testament Studies* (Sheffield: JSOT Press, 1981), Ch. 3 'The acquisition of land', pp. 65-89; Jacob Elias, The Beginning of Jesus' Ministry in the Gospel of Luke, Th.D. dissertation, Toronto School of Theology, 1978; Jeffrey Fager, *Land Tenure and the Biblical Jubilee*, Journal for Study of the Old Testament, Supplementary Series 155 (Sheffield Academic Press, 1993); Laurie Green, *Jesus and the Jubilee* (Jubilee, 2000); Maria Harris, *Proclaim Jubilee! A Spirituality for the 21st Century* (Westminster: John Knox Press, 1996); Michael Northcott, *Life After Debt: Christianity and global justice* (SPCK, 1999); Robert B. Sloan Jr, *The Favourable Year of the Lord: a study of Jubilary theology in the Gospel of Luke* (Austin: Scholars Press, 1977); William M. Swarthey, 'An exegetical analysis of Yoder's *The politics of Jesus* with further probings of the Jubilee

interpretation of Jesus', MS 1978; Hans Ucko (ed.), *The Jubilee Challenge, Utopia or Possibility: Jewish and Christian insights* (Geneva: World Council of Churches, 1997); Michael Taylor, *Not Angels But Agencies: the ecumenical response to poverty* (SCM Press/World Council of Churches, 1995), Chapter 1 'The Year of the Lord's Favour', pp. 1-20, and Chapter 6, 'An Agenda for Jubilee', pp. 137-70; and John Howard Yoder, *The Politics of Jesus* (Grand Rapids: Eerdmans, 1972), especially Chapter Three, 'The implications of the Jubilee', pp. 64-77.

15. Cornel West, *Keeping Faith* (Routledge, 1993), p. 27.

16. See Manuel Castells, *The Information Age*, Vol. 1, *The Rise of the Network Society* (Blackwell, 1996-8), 3 Vols.

17. See Arthur Waskow, '1976: An American Jubilee Year', *Fellowship* (January-February 1976), pp. 18-19; Arthur Waskow and Randy Barber, *Project on an American Equivalent of the Biblical Jubilee* (Washington, DC: Jubilee Network 1976).

18. Frank Griswold, 'A reflection on becoming a people of Jubilee', Address, May 1999.

19. Ross Kinsler and Gloria Kinsler, *The Biblical Jubilee and the Struggle for Life* (Orbis, 1999), p. xv.

20. Marcia Griffiths, 'Steppin' out of Babylon' was top of the Jamaican charts around 1982.

Short Bibliography

Unless otherwise stated, the place of publication is London.

On East London

Adams, Caroline. *Across Seven Seas and Thirteen Rivers: life stories of pioneer Sylheti settlers in Britain,* Tower Hamlets Arts Project, 1987.

Alderman, Geoffrey, and Holmes, Colin (eds.). *Outsiders and Outcasts: essays in honour of William J. Fishman,* Duckworth, 1993.

Brownill, Sue. *Developing London's Docklands: another great planning disaster?* Paul Chapman, 1990.

Carey, Sean, and Shukur, Abdus. 'A profile of the Bangladeshi community in East London', *New Community* 12:2 (Winter 1985–6), pp. 405-17.

Eade, John. 'Nationalism and the quest for authenticity: the Bangladeshis in Tower Hamlets', *New Community* 16:4 (July 1990), pp. 493-503.

Fawzi El-Solh, Camilla. 'Somalis in London's East End: a community striving for recognition', *New Community* 17:4 (July 1991), pp. 539-52.

Fishman, William J. *East End Jewish Radicals,* London, Duckworth, 1973.

East End 1888, London, Duckworth, 1988.

Forman, Charlie. *Spitalfields: a battle for land,* Hilary Shipman, 1989.

Foster, Janet. *Docklands: Cultures in Conflict, Worlds in Collision,* UCL Press, 1999.

Garrard, John A. *The English and Immigration 1880–1910,* Oxford University Press/ Institute of Race Relations, 1971.

Husbands, Christopher T. 'East End racism 1900–1980: geographical continuities in vigilantist and extreme right-wing political behaviour', *London Journal* 8:1 (1982), pp. 3-26.

Jacobs, Jane M. *Edge of Empire: postcolonialism and the city,* Routledge, 1996, Chapter Four, 'Eastern trading: diaspora, dwelling and place' on Spitalfields, pp. 70-102.

Knowles, Caroline. 'Labour and antisemitism: an account of the political discourse surrounding the Labour Party's involvement with antisemitism in East London 1934-6' in Robert Miles and Annie Phizaklea (eds.), *Racism and Political Action in Britain,* Routledge and Kegan Paul, 1979, pp. 50-71.

Kushner, Tony, and Valman, Nadia (eds.). *Remembering Cable Street: fascism and antifascism in British society,* Vallentine Mitchell, 2000.

Lipman, V.D. *Social History of Jews in England 1850–1950,* Watts and Company 1954.

McCowen, Peter. *The Mental Health of East London,* Psychiatric Rehabilitation Association, 1966.

O'Neill, Gilda. *My East End,* Penguin, 2000.

Palmer, Alan. *The East End*, John Murray, 1989.

Phillips, Deborah A. 'Race and housing in London's East End: continuity and change', *New Community* 14:3 (1988), pp. 356-69.

Robinson, A.J., and Chesshyre, D.H.B. *The Green: a history of the heart of Bethnal Green and the legend of the Blind Beggar*, London Borough of Tower Hamlets, 1986.

Rocker, Fermin. *The East End Years: A Stepney Childhood*, Freedom Press, 1998.

Rose, Millicent. *The East End of London*, Cresset Press, 1951.

Sokoloff, Bertha. *Edith and Stepney: the life of Edith Ramsey*, Steoney Books, 1987.

Taylor, William. *This Bright Field: a travel book in one place*, Methuen, 2000.

White, Jerry. *Rothschild Buildings: life in an East End tenement block 1887–1920*, Routledge, 1980.

Young, Michael, and Willmott, Peter. *Family and Kinship in East London*, Penguin, 1962 edn.

On theology in the urban context

Beasley, Mary. *Mission on the Margins*, Lutterworth, 1997.

Blakebrough, Eric (ed.). *Church for the City*, Darton, Longman and Todd, 1995.

Duffield, Ian K. (ed.). *Urban Christ: responses to John Vincent*, Sheffield, Urban Theology Unit, 1997.

Flanagan, Bernadette. *The Spirit of the City*, Dublin, Veritas, 1999.

Green, Laurie. *Let's Do Theology*, Mowbray, 1990.

Leech, Kenneth. *Care and Conflict: leaves from a pastoral notebook*, Darton, Longman and Todd, 1990
  The Eye of the Storm, Darton, Longman and Todd, 1993.
  The Sky Is Red: discerning the signs of the times, Darton, Longman and Todd, 1997.
  Spirituality and Pastoral Care, Cambridge MA, Cowley Press, 1989.
  Subversive Orthodoxy, Toronto, Anglican Book Centre, 1992.

Linthicum, Robert C. *City of God, City of Satan*, Grand Rapids, Zondervan, 1992.

Meyers, Eleanor Scott (ed.). *Envisioning the New City*, Louisville, Westminster John Knox Press, 1992.

Morisy, Ann. *Beyond the Good Samaritan: community ministry and mission*, Mowbrays, 1997.

Northcott, Michael (ed.). *Urban Theology: A Reader*, Cassell, 1998.

Pasquariello, Ronald D., *et al. Redeeming the City: theology, politics and urban policy*, New York, Pilgrim Press, 1982.

Reader, John. *Local Theology*, SPCK, 1994.

Rowland, Chris, and Vincent, John (eds.). *Gospel from the City*, Sheffield, Urban Theology Unit, 1997.

Saunders, Stanley P., and Campbell, Charles L. *The Word on the Street: performing the Scriptures in the urban context*, Eerdmans, 2000.

Schreiter, Robert J. *Constructing Local Theologies*, Maryknoll, Orbis, 1993.

Sedgwick, Peter (ed). *God in the City*, Mowbray, 1995.

Tabb, William K. (ed.). *Churches in Struggle*, New York, Monthly Review Press, 1986.

The Cities: a Methodist Report, Methodist Church, 1997.

To Hear and To Heed: The Episcopal Church listens to and acts in the City, Cincinnati, Forward Movement and Urban Bishops' Coalition, 1978.

Villafane, Eldin. *Seek the Peace of the City: reflections on urban ministry*, Grand Rapids, Eerdmans, 1996.

Vincent, John. *Hope from the City*, Epworth Press, 2000.

Wilkinson, John. *Church in Black and White*, Edinburgh, St Andrew Press, 1993.

Index